# Science, Philosophy and Sustainability

For science to remain a legitimate and trustworthy source of knowledge, society will have to engage in collective processes of knowledge co-production, which not only include science, but also other types of knowledge. This process of change has to include a new commitment to knowledge creation and transmission and its role in a plural society.

This book proposes to consider new ways in which science can be used to sustain our planet and enrich our lives. It helps to release and reactivate social responsibility within contemporary science and technology. It reviews critically relevant cases of contemporary scientific practice within the Cartesian paradigm, relabelled as 'innovation research', promoted as essential for the progress and well-being of humanity, and characterised by high capital investment, centralised control of funding and quality, exclusive expertise, and a reductionism that is philosophical as well as methodological.

This is an accessible and relevant book for scholars in science and technology studies, history and philosophy of science, and science, engineering and technology ethics. Providing an array of concrete examples, it supports scientists, engineers and technical experts, as well as policy-makers and other non-technical professionals working with science and technology to redirect their approach to global problems, in a more integrative, self-reflective and humble direction.

**Ângela Guimarães Pereira** is a scientific officer of the Joint Research Centre, European Commission, Ispra, Italy.

**Silvio Funtowicz** is Professor at the Centre for the Study of the Sciences and the Humanities of the University of Bergen, Norway.

# Routledge Explorations in Sustainability and Governance

**Resource Accounting for Sustainability Assessment**
The nexus between energy, food, water and land use
*Mario Giampietro, Richard J. Aspinall, Jesus Ramos-Martin and Sandra G.F. Bukkens*

**Science, Philosophy and Sustainability**
The end of the Cartesian dream
*Ângela Guimarães Pereira and Silvio Funtowicz*

# Science, Philosophy and Sustainability

The end of the Cartesian dream

**Edited by Ângela Guimarães Pereira
and Silvio Funtowicz**

**Routledge**
Taylor & Francis Group

LONDON AND NEW YORK

First published 2015
by Routledge

2 Park Square, Milton Park, Abingdon, Oxfordshire OX14 4RN
52 Vanderbilt Avenue, New York, NY 10017

*Routledge is an imprint of the Taylor & Francis Group, an informa business*

First issued in paperback 2020

*British Library Cataloguing-in-Publication Data*
A catalogue record for this book is available from the British Library

*Library of Congress Cataloging-in-Publication Data*
A catalog record has been requested for this book

ISBN: 978-1-138-79640-9 (hbk)
ISBN: 978-0-367-66894-5 (pbk)

Typeset in Times New Roman
by HWA Text and Data Management, London

# Contents

# Contributors

**Alice Benessia** is a visual artist and research fellow on epistemology of sustainability at the University of Aosta Valley and the Interdisciplinary Research Institute on Sustainability (IRIS) based at the University of Turin. She is a founding member of the Italian Association for Sustainability Science. Her interdisciplinary research deals with epistemological issues arising in the framework of art, science and sustainability, with special interest in visual language. In her photography, she focuses on the relationship between human beings and socio-ecological systems.

**Paula Curvelo** is a Ph.D. candidate in environmental philosophy at the University of Lisbon, Portugal. She holds a degree in Geography (University of Lisbon, UL), a postgraduate diploma in Urban Sociology (Instituto Universitário de Lisboa, ISCTE-IUL), and a master's degree in Geographic Information Systems and Science (New University of Lisbon – ISEGI-NOVA). Her current research interests include the ethical, legal and social aspects of geoengineering, the governance of emerging technologies, the politics of risk and uncertainty, and the philosophy of technology.

**Ragnar Fjelland** is trained as a physicist and philosopher, and his current topics of interest include the significance of technology for the acquisition of scientific knowledge, philosophical implications of chaos theory and fractal geometry, complexity and uncertainty, ethical problems of modern science and technology, and the challenge of environmental problems to science. He is Professor Emeritus at Centre for the Study of the Sciences and the Humanities, University of Bergen, Norway.

**Silvio Funtowicz** taught mathematics and research methodology in Buenos Aires, Argentina. During the 1980s he was a Research Fellow at the University of Leeds, England. Until his retirement in 2011, he was a scientific officer at the Institute for the Protection and Security of the Citizen (IPSC), European Commission – Joint Research Centre (EC – JRC). Since February 2012 he is Professor II at the University of Bergen, Norway, based at the Centre for the Study of the Sciences and the Humanities (SVT). He is the author of *Uncertainty and Quality in Science for Policy* (1990, Kluwer, Dordrecht, Chinese version 2010) in collaboration with Jerry Ravetz, and numerous papers in the field of environmental and technological risks and policy-related research. He has lectured extensively and he is a member of the editorial board of several publications and the scientific committee of many projects and international conferences.

**Ângela Guimarães Pereira** works at the Joint Research Centre of the European Commission, holding a Ph.D. in Environmental Systems and their Tensions. In 1996 she started working at the JRC on European projects focusing on environmental and societal issues, future oriented activities and integration of information technologies with public engagement. Her work has been inspired by the post-normal science ideas developed by Funtowicz and Ravetz in the 1990s. She currently works on knowledge assessment and ethics of ICT, critically investigating their governance and correspondence with current innovation narratives. She is co-editor of *Interfaces between Science and Society* with Greenleaf in 2006 and *Science for Policy: Challenges and Opportunities* with Oxford University Press in 2009. Her current interests lie in science history and ways of knowing; her favourite story is H. C. Andersen's 'the emperor's new clothes'.

**Jerome Ravetz** is a leading authority on the social and methodological problems of contemporary science. With Silvio Funtowicz he created the NUSAP notational system for assessing the uncertainty and quality of scientific information, and also the concept of Post-Normal Science, relevant when 'facts are uncertain, values in dispute, stakes high and decisions urgent' (see http://www.nature.com/news/policy-the-art-of-science-advice-to-government-1.14838). His earlier seminal work *Scientific Knowledge and its Social Problems* (Oxford University Press 1971, Transaction 1996) now has a smaller sequel, *The No-Nonsense Guide to Science* (New Internationalist 2006). His other publications include a collection of essays, *The Merger of Knowledge with Power* (Mansell 1990). He is currently an Associate Fellow at the Institute for Science, Innovation and Society at Oxford University.

**Andrea Saltelli** has worked on physical chemistry, environmental sciences and applied statistics, publishing over 80 peer-reviewed papers and three books. His main disciplinary focus is on sensitivity analysis of model output, a discipline where statistical tools are used to interpret the output from mathematical or computational models, and on sensitivity auditing, an extension of sensitivity analysis to the entire evidence-generating process in a policy context. A second focus is the construction of composite indicators or indices. Presently he leads the Econometric and Applied Statistics Unit of the European Commission at the Joint Research Centre in Ispra (I). The unit, with a staff of 30, develops econometric and statistical applications, mostly in support of the services of the European Commission, in fields such as lifelong learning, inequality, employment, competitiveness and innovation. He participates in the training of European Commission staff on impact assessment.

**Daniel Sarewitz** is Professor of Science and Society, and co-director and co-founder of the Consortium for Science, Policy, and Outcomes (CSPO), at Arizona State University (http://www.cspo.org). His work focuses on revealing and improving the connections between science policy decisions, scientific research and social outcomes. His most recent book is *The Techno-Human Condition* (co-authored with Braden Allenby; MIT Press 2011). He is editor of the magazine *Issues in Science and Technology* (www.issues.org) and is also a regular columnist on science policy affairs for the journal *Nature*.

**Edvin Schei** (b. 1957) is a general practitioner and professor of general practice. He has published several books and is the founder of Filosofisk Poliklinikk, a public forum for dialogue and debate on issues concerning the interfaces between medicine and 'everything else' – ethics, philosophy of science, health politics, technology, medical education and professionalism, art, culture, the media. One of his favourite topics is the ancient concept of phronesis, and the related need to develop medical education in ways that will train clinicians to deal with uncertainty by improvising patient-centred, helpful strategies in complex situations where no control is available and technology does not provide ready-made solutions. Schei currently leads the programme for medical professionalism at the Faculty of Medicine, University of Bergen.

**Roger Strand** (b. 1968 in Norway), originally trained as a natural scientist (dr. scient., biochemistry, 1998), developed research interests in the philosophy of science and has worked on issues of scientific uncertainty and complexity. This has gradually led his research into broader strands of social research, philosophy and broader issues of policy, decision-making and governance at the science–society interface. Strand has coordinated two EU FP7 projects (TECHNOLIFE and EPINET) that addressed the need for a more dynamic governance of science in society. He is currently (2014) Chairman of the European Commission Expert Group on Indicators for Responsible Research and Innovation (RRI).

**Mariachiara Tallacchini** is Professor of Philosophy of Law at the Università Cattolica of Piacenza (Italy), and teaches Bioethics at the Faculty of Biotechnology of the University of Milan (Italy). After graduating in law, she earned a Ph.D. in Legal Philosophy (University of Padua), and was a postdoctoral fellow in the STS programme at the Kennedy School of Government (Harvard University). She is a member of several scientific and ethics committees in the fields of research ethics, genetics, xenotransplantation, animal and environmental protection. Between 2013 and 2015 she worked at the Joint Research Centre (JRC) of the European Commission. Her interests concern the legal regulation of science and technology, and the relations between science and democracy, especially in the life sciences and at the interfaces with ICT.

**David Waltner-Toews** is Professor Emeritus at University of Guelph, and was founding president of Veterinarians without Borders/Vétérinaires sans Frontières – Canada (www.vwb-vsf.ca) and of the Network for Ecosystem

Sustainability and Health (www.nesh.ca). He was the recipient of the inaugural award for Outstanding Contributions to the field of Ecohealth from the IAEH. David is the author or coauthor of more than 100 peer-reviewed papers as well as 19 books, including scholarly texts on ecosystem sustainability and health, and works of poetry, fiction and popular non-fiction. His most recent publications were a murder mystery (*Fear of Landing*, Poisoned Pen Press, 2008) and a book of popular science, *The Origin of Feces: What Excrement Tells Us about Evolution, Ecology, and a Sustainable Society* (ECW Press, May 2013). He is currently writing full time. For more on his various books and writing projects, visit his website (www.davidwaltnertoews.com).

**Fern Wickson** (BA (Hons), B.Sc., Ph.D.) is a cross-disciplinary scholar with a doctoral degree across biological sciences and science and technology studies on the environmental regulation of biotechnology. Upon completing her doctorate, Fern extended her interdisciplinary research into the development and governance of nanoscale sciences and technologies. She now works on a range of European and Norwegian projects related to the responsible governance of new and emerging life technosciences (including biotechnology, nanotechnology and synthetic biology). Fern is a member of the Norwegian Biotechnology Advisory Board and President of the international Society for the Study of Nanoscience and Emerging Technologies (S.Net). She also serves on the board of the European Network of Scientists for Social and Environmental Responsibility (ENSSER) and was recently appointed as an international expert for the Intergovernmental Panel on Biodiversity and Ecosystem Services (IPBES). Her current research focuses on the conservation of agrobiodiversity and the cultivation of resilient socio-ecological futures.

# Foreword

*Mario Giampietro, Series Editor*

We live in a world in which the majority of people in command seem to believe that all our problems have solutions. All we need to do is throw enough money at a problem so as to provide an adequate amount of research and economic incentives. According to the accepted *mantra*, more know-how (human ingenuity) and effective institutions (invisible hands) will sooner or later fix everything. Given the large variety of problems modern society is facing, the basis and ubiquity of this conviction are difficult to explain. In fact, in addition to the historic (but yet unresolved) set of problems – war, hunger, inequity, shortage of capital, fragility of social fabric – we now also face new problems typical of the modern era, such as environmental damage, shortage of resources, terrorism, migration and progressive ageing in post-industrial society. The accelerated rate of change in activities expressed by human society represents nowadays a constant source of stress on cultural identity, religions and institutions. In this situation, even if science (human ingenuity) and institutions (invisible hands) are able to solve some problems at the local scale, it is evident that the rate at which some solutions are found cannot match the rate at which new problems emerge or old problems exacerbate. To make things more difficult, the solutions of specific problems addressed at the local scale tend to generate new problems because of the emergence of unexpected side effects not considered in the original framing of the problem to be solved. In fact a problem is a discrepancy between an expected and a perceived state of affairs. This means that an increase in both our expectations and our knowledge about the external world unavoidably results in the generation of a larger number of new problems.

Yet, in spite of a long series of failures – nuclear energy generating electricity 'too cheap to meter'; genetically modified organisms 'eradicating hunger from this planet', biofuels generating 'an abundant, cheap and environmental friendly alternative to fossil fuels', the global scheme of tradable permits 'reducing $CO_2$ emissions', countries of the European Union 'innovating their way off of the crisis', big data generating good jobs aplenty and 'wider social and economic benefits' in the order of billions of euro – the ideological belief in the problem-solving power of science is unabated.

A quote may help in explaining the persistence of this intoxication. During the Second World War Kenneth Arrow served as a weather officer in the US Army Air Corps in a team producing month-ahead weather forecasts.

As Arrow and his team reviewed these predictions, they confirmed statistically that Corps' weather forecasts were no more useful than random rolls of a die. Understandably, the forecasters asked to be relieved of this seemingly futile duty. Arrow's recollection of his superiors' response was priceless: 'The commanding general is well aware that the forecasts are no good. However, he needs them for planning purposes.'[1]

The belief in the absolute power of both predictions and innovations has no rational basis. It is an illusion; a dream about power and control. It serves to escape the stress of decision-making created by uncertainty. The more important the decisions are, the stronger is the need to believe that we can know 'what is the best thing to do'. After the scientific revolution dissolved the universe of certainties established by religion, Western society had to adopt a new faith to legitimise the choices made by the establishment. A legitimate power structure had to claim to be able to individuate optimal solutions and strategies. According to this faith, in modern society, the established power makes decisions not just because of particular interests of lobbies or for the common good, but also because the chosen policies have been marked out as 'the best thing to do' according to the truth indicated by science, be it that this selection can be more ritual than factual.

This book, the second of the series Routledge Explorations in Sustainability and Governance, provides an informed reflection on these themes. The contributors represent a team of outstanding scholars who have spent a lifetime reflecting, from different angles, on the implications of the Cartesian dream in relation to the production and use of science for governance. While the first monograph of this series presented an innovative approach to quantitative assessment, this book provides a critical appraisal of the quality of the narratives used in science for governance. It does not provide *solutions* to the issue of science for governance in face of uncertainty, but it offers the fruits of reflexivity, and reflexivity is the essential ingredient to appreciate what is good and what is bad in dreams.

## Note

1  R.W. Fisher, 'An Economic Overview: What's Next. Remembering Carol Reed, Aesop's Fable, Kenneth Arrow and Thomas Dewey', Remarks before the Rotary Club of Dallas, 13 July 2011(http://www.dallasfed.org/news/speeches/fisher/2011/fs110713.cfm) accessed Aug. 2014.

# Preface

## Descartes and the rediscovery of ignorance

*Jerome Ravetz*

Reviewing this rich collection of insights on the working out of the dream of René Descartes, we are struck by the variety of fields in which we are his intellectual children, and where we now feel the need to grow up. Descartes was a universal genius, making revolutionary contributions to mathematics, mechanics, physics and philosophy. Although he was ahead of his time, by the later seventeenth century the educated common-sense of north-western Europe was inhabiting the world that he created. Both the humanised universe of Aristotle and the magical cosmos of the alchemists were fading. The voices of divine authority and inner illumination were being stilled, in science as in society. Knowledge was to be modelled on the disenchanted mathematics of geometry, allied with disciplined sense-experience. All this harmonised with the growth of the new *possessive individualist* society, more clearly expressed by Hobbes than by Descartes. This synthesis provided mutually supportive rationales, along with opportunities for the eventual fruitful applications of the sciences (natural and social), that stemmed from Descartes's teaching.

The intervening centuries saw the growth and maturity of the modern worldview, in the theory and in the practice of both science and society. There were many complications and setbacks, and many unfinished struggles in all spheres. By the time of the age we call *Victorian*, the dream of Descartes seemed triumphant: science and progress ruled all. But it is now just a century since it began visibly to fall apart, in the collapse into the Great War. And in Cartesian science, the subversion of Descartes's dream from within has proceeded apace, first in Einstein's relativistic physics and Gödel's anti-foundational meta-mathematics, and then in the ever deepening paradoxes of quantum theory. The essays in this volume show clearly how Descartes's vision has been deeply compromised, in one area after another.

In this prologue, we should consider the question, is there some core element of the Cartesian dream that we should identify, the better to come to terms with it and move on? For this, we can go back to the beginning of his endeavour. According to his autobiography in the *Discourse on Method*, he did not initially set out confidently to recast the world of knowledge. Rather, he was seized by doubt and disillusion, and was desperate to find a way out. This doubt was not the *methodological doubt* of his meditations that have formed the fodder of philosophical investigations ever since. It was a much more common and urgent sort of doubt: distrust of everything that his teachers had taught him at his enlightened Jesuit school. His autobiographical account starts with this declaration:

> From my childhood, I have been familiar with letters; and as I was given to believe that by their help a clear and certain knowledge of all that is useful in life might be acquired, I was ardently desirous of instruction. But as soon as I had finished the entire course of study, at the close of which it is customary to be admitted into the order of the learned, I completely changed my opinion.

Immediately he describes his moment of *endarkenment*:

> For I found myself involved in so many doubts and errors, that I was convinced I had advanced no farther in all my attempts at learning, than the discovery at every turn of my own ignorance.

This is amplified and explained, when he goes through the admirable humanist curriculum at his school, and proceeds to assassinate it, showing that each subject, however attractive it seems, contains within it the seeds of its own refutation. This culminates in a passage that more than any other single text, expresses the transformation of culture from the Renaissance to the modern age.

> I was especially delighted with the mathematics, on account of the certitude and evidence of their reasonings; but I had not as yet a precise knowledge of their true use; and thinking that they contributed to the advancement of the mechanical arts, I was astonished that foundations, so strong and solid, should have had no loftier superstructure reared on them. On the other hand, I compared the disquisitions of the ancient moralists to very towering and magnificent palaces with no better foundation than sand and mud: they laud the virtues very highly, and exhibit them as estimable far above anything on Earth; but they give us no adequate criterion of virtue, and frequently that which they designate with so fine a name is but apathy, or pride, or despair, or parricide.

The last accusation is thought to refer to the justification of Brutus, who killed his *father* Caesar for the sake of Rome. We all know that Descartes then resolved to use geometry as the model for true and certain knowledge, setting the conceptual paradigm for the next four centuries of European thought.

In one crucial respect, I need to correct a common misconception about Descartes. The focus of scholarly inquiry on his philosophy has left the impression that his project was a rather abstracted one, starting with philosophy and extending through mathematics to physics and beyond. But Descartes was also a prophet of modern technology, sharing the magicians' desire for power over Nature but believing that in his disenchanted world it would not be too dangerous. Indeed, in a superbly optimistic passage at the end of the *Discourse* he states a vision.

For by them I perceived it to be possible to arrive at knowledge highly useful in life; and in place of the speculative philosophy usually taught in the schools, to discover a practical [knowledge], by means of which, knowing the force and action of fire, water, air the stars, the heavens, and all the other bodies that surround us, as distinctly as we know the various crafts of our artisans, we might also apply them in the same way to all the uses to which they are adapted, and thus render ourselves the masters and possessors of Nature.

Here indeed, we have the modern scientific-technical, or should I say, technocratic paradigm, stated clearly for all to see.

That is where Descartes got to, as his own vision unfolded. But if we want to find the core of his message, we need to go back to the origins. Let us look at the statement of the discovery of his ignorance. To us, that might seem quite a natural reaction; many of us have had a similar experience at some point in our education. But there are resonances there for Descartes's readers. Raised on the same humanistic learning as himself, they would have known that the discovery of one's ignorance is not an occasion for despair, but according to Socrates, the aim of all learning! But with his characteristic stylistic genius, Descartes did not waste words on his transformation of philosophy. For him, wisdom and self-knowledge were discredited goals; what he needed, and all of us ever since, is certain truth and absolute power. These were promised on the example of geometry, and although success was not immediate in coming, we are now living with the realisation of Descartes's positive dream.

The essays in this volume are all about how the dream has turned into something else, in all sorts of ways. Doubt and complexity are now an inescapable part of our discussions of science and its applications. In Descartes's own paradigm natural science, physics, the simple certainties have given way to paradox and confusion. Ignorance now sits in the middle of the equations of fundamental physics, with the names *dark matter* and *dark energy*. It is quite possible that this ignorance, like so many sorts before it, will be conquered by the advance of science. But for now and the foreseeable future, we haven't a clue.

Similarly, error and miscalculation have come to haunt the science that we are applying in the pursuit of absolute power. The misapplication of mathematics to finance nearly undid the whole monetary system, coming close to an unintended experiment of how long civilisation could survive after the cash-machines emptied. The triumphs of applied chemistry have created supergerms and super weeds that become ever more threatening. Far from being 'masters and possessors of Nature', we are coming to see ourselves as disruptors, perhaps as 'Sorcerer's Apprentices', unable to turn off this wonderful machine of invention that now threatens to destabilise or even destroy us.

It could be argued that behind all these negative outcomes lies an assumption, or paradigm, or mindset deriving from Descartes: that science can produce certain truths and absolute power, both of them secure and safe. Students go through their most formative years learning by experience that every problem has just one solution, precise to several digits. If a scientific argument has numerical data and mathematical techniques, what could possibly be wrong? Ignorance is irrelevant, and awareness of ignorance is a bore. Uncertainty gets only limited attention from professional philosophers, and quality hardly any at all. This is not surprising. Both are quite difficult topics, involving complexity at several levels. How much easier it is to hope to tame uncertainty with mathematics, and to believe that the misuses and abuses of scientific power could be controlled just by better regulation. But our modern predicament is not to be resolved by comforting formulas. If Descartes's rejection of awareness of ignorance is an important element of our problem, then the rediscovery of ignorance, in practice and in education, is essential to its solution.

Of course, one might expect me to be making this argument. After all, Silvio and I have been concerned with uncertainty and quality, and with the social problems of scientific knowledge, for a long time now. By putting our own work in the context of the Cartesian dream, we are showing that it is not merely practical, but is also genuinely philosophical. Participating in a dialogue that goes back to Descartes and Socrates, we belong to an important tradition.

It would be unjust to Descartes for me to omit one important reservation that he made about the applications of science. In discussing the possibility of getting external support for his work, he gave a characteristically concise formula: that he could not work on projects that 'cannot be useful to some without being hurtful to others' (*Discourse*, last paragraph of Part 6). Thus, Descartes himself was not a simple Cartesian – something on which we could well reflect.

# Acknowledgements

The editors are thankful to all authors that have found time and inspiration to contribute to this endeavour and adventure.

The contributions to this book are peer-reviewed thanks to a number of selected reviewers. The editors of this book are especially grateful to the external reviewers of the contributions to this book, namely Bruna de Marchi, Gregory Hill, Greet Janssens-Maenhout, Rob van Kranenburg, Jerome Ravetz and Kjetil Rommeteveit.

# Abbreviations

| | |
|---|---|
| AR4 | Fourth Assessment Report |
| AR5 | Fifth Assessment Report |
| BECCS | bioenergy with carbon capture and storage |
| CDR | carbon dioxide removal |
| DSGE | dynamic stochastic general equilibrium (models) |
| EGE | European Group of Ethics |
| EIDs | emerging infectious diseases |
| ELSA | ethical, legal and social aspects |
| EPA | Environment Protection Agency (of the USA) |
| ESSC | Earth System Science Committee |
| ESSP | Earth System Science Partnership |
| HAZMAT | hazardous materials |
| GAEIB | Group of Advisers on the Ethical Implications of Biotechnology |
| GIGO | garbage in garbage out |
| GMO | genetically modified organism |
| GP | general practitioner |
| ICT | information and communication technology |
| IHDP | International Human Dimensions Programme |
| IGBP | International Geosphere-Biosphere Programme |
| IoT | Internet of Things |
| IPCC | Intergovernmental Panel on Climate Change |
| MUS | medically unexplained symptoms |
| NAS | National Academy of Sciences |
| NASA | National Aeronautics and Space Administration |
| NUSAP | numeral unit spread assessment pedigree |
| NGO | non-governmental organisation |
| OTA | Office of Technology Assessment |
| RCP | Representative Concentration Pathway |
| RRI | responsible research and innovation |
| SARS | severe acute respiratory syndrome |
| SRM | solar radiation management |

| STS | science and technology studies |
| UNCED | United Nations Conference on Environment and Development |
| WCRP | World Climate Research Programme |
| WGI, WGII, WGIII | Working Groups I, II and III respectively of the IPCC. |
| WHO | World Health Organization |

# Cartesian dreams

*Silvio Funtowicz and Ângela Guimarães Pereira*

## 'Meditations'

> This is, after all, just how I have always thought ideas are produced in me
> when I am dreaming.
>
> (Descartes, *Meditations*)

René Descartes had dreams, and the arguments in them have been thoroughly discussed by scholars since then; but those dreams are not the dream in the title of this volume. Here we discuss instead a metaphorical dream, expressing the aspirations and expectations of his time, which Stephen Toulmin described in his Cosmopolis as 'the hidden agenda of Modernity' (Toulmin 1990).

Descartes's optimistic vision about the role of mathematics, science and technology was shared and developed by other influential philosophers of the time, such as Galileo Galilei and Thomas Hobbes, but we decided to dedicate the volume to Descartes because he describes so vividly the hopes and expectations of the age of rationality, following many years of conflict and despair. Jerry Ravetz, in his epilogue to this book, quotes Descartes's famous 'masters and possessors of Nature' paragraph in the *Discourse*, saying that 'we have the modern scientific-technical, or should I say, technocratic paradigm, stated clearly for all to see'. Ravetz also remarks, quoting from the same text, that Descartes could not work on projects that 'cannot be useful to some without being hurtful to others'. His conclusion is that Descartes showed reflexivity, and in this sense he 'was not a simple Cartesian', a judgement we could easily extend to many other protagonists of the time.

The dream that the emergent rational method and the deployment of science and science-based technology would deliver the truth (expressed in quantitative terms) and empower humanity to fulfil its destiny as masters and possessors of Nature, was a fundamental tenet of Modernity. Francis Bacon argued that 'human knowledge and human power come to the same thing, for where the cause is not known the effect cannot be produced' (Bacon 1620, aphorism III), and in an utopian prophecy, he lists the wonders to be expected, such as

> the prolongation of life, the retardation of age, the alleviation of pain, the
> repairing of natural defects, the deceiving of the senses; ... of transmuting

substances, of strengthening and multiplying motions at will, of making impressions and alterations in the air, of bringing down and procuring celestial influences; arts of divining things future, and bringing things distant near, and revealing things secret; and many more.

(Bacon 1627)

Mathematics was a fundamental component of this vision because it was considered essential in order to know and act in a mechanical world. According to Galileo, the book of the universe 'is written in the language of mathematics, and its characters are triangles, circles, and other geometric figures without which it is humanly impossible to understand a single word of it; without these, one wanders about in a dark labyrinth' (Galilei 1630/1970).[1] Gottfried Leibniz not only agreed about the centrality of mathematics but also imagined a prophetical intelligence that could see the future as in a present mirror (Bishop 2003; Leibniz 1695/1924).

This quantitative understanding, enabling prediction and control, was considered an instrument of power and the means for the perfection of human faculties without limit. Transcending the natural world, it was also applicable to the social and political realms. Condorcet, for instance, stating that 'if man can predict, almost with certainty, those appearances of which he understands the laws; if, even when the laws are unknown to him, experience or the past enables him to foresee, with considerable probability, future appearances; why should we suppose it a chimerical undertaking to delineate, with some degree of truth, the picture of the future destiny of mankind from the results of its history?' (Condorcet 1795). Years later, and following Leibniz's imagined entity, Pierre-Simon, marquis de Laplace, envisaged an intelligence, known as the *Laplace demon,* which could predict the future, precisely and without uncertainty because 'nothing would be uncertain and the future, as the past, would be present to its eyes' (Laplace 1814/1951).

At the beginning of the twentieth century, emerging notions of indeterminacy and complexity in mathematics and physics started to destabilise beliefs in the achievement of certainty and complete prediction and control. Those foundational principles of Modernity became questioned, and eventually scholars could proclaim the loss of certainty in mathematics and natural science (Kline 1980). The epistemological and methodological costs of the war against uncertainty were becoming clear and some of their reductionist premises were contested. Among these, the strict demarcation between object of study and the human observer or the power of formal deduction to demonstrate truth in all cases.

If it is no longer universally possible to separate ourselves (Hume's passions or Galileo's secondary qualities) from a perfect, mechanical universe, how can we banish uncertainty or clearly distinguish between facts and values? Already in the early 1950s, some scholars were arguing that scientists, working as scientists, used value judgements, as in the case of statistical tests of hypotheses (Rudner 1954). Something that was socially and institutionally recognised in the realm of the learned arts (for instance, engineering, medicine and architecture) was still opposed when related to science. For some, it even constitutes a demarcation criterion between the scientific practice and other forms of human activity; scientific knowledge had to continue to be value-free and objective in order to preserve its privileged role in adjudicating legitimate action for the common good.

Francis Bacon, Galileo Galilei, René Descartes, Gottfried Leibniz, the marquis de Condorcet and Pierre-Simon marquis de Laplace are some of the actors in a standard account of the power of science and rationality, lending credibility to contemporary narratives of science-based innovation. Unfortunately, these latest narratives lack the originality and the intellectual capacity of the former. In 1954, for example, the *New York Times* reported of a speech given a day before by Lewis Strauss, then chairman of the US Atomic Energy Commission, to the National Association of Science Writers. Strauss's message evoked Bacon's wonders of the New Atlantis: 'Our children will enjoy in their homes electrical energy too cheap to meter … will travel effortlessly over the seas and under them and through the air with a minimum of danger and at great speeds, and will experience a lifespan far longer than ours, as disease yields and man comes to understand what causes him to age' (17 September 1954).

The pathologies of progress, the limits of growth, value conflicts and the pervasiveness of relevant uncertainty and indeterminacy provided an intellectual and political context in which ideas of extended participation, sustainable lifestyles and precautionary action could flourish. But the loss of certainty did not undermine dogmatic forms of rationality, such as 'sound science', institutionalised through national and international constitutional, legal and administrative arrangements. Cost benefit and risk analysis were becoming the contemporary versions of Laplace's demon in order to provide legitimacy to questioned ideals of progress and unlimited growth. Utilitarian computations, now enshrined in mainstream economics and decision theories and underpinned by the growing power of algorithms and computer models and simulations, transformed democratic challenges of what to sustain and for whom into technocratic *silver-bullets* of what is to be substituted.

It was not only the scientific technocratic worldview that was challenged but also the role of humankind in the universe. Many did not identify themselves as 'masters and possessors of Nature'; rather they proposed more equitable relations with other beings and our planet as a whole. The struggle for recognition (cultural, legal and institutional) of these perspectives became a new stage in a long list of human battles for the extension of rights, previously reserved to privileged minorities. Ironically the 'masters and possessors of Nature' destiny, with its implicit violence, conflicted with ethical standpoints originating in the humanistic tradition of Modernity, exemplified, for instance, by Michel de Montaigne.

Nuclear energy was not alone in promising everything at the cost of nothing ('electrical energy too cheap to meter'); a host of new and emerging technologies become promoted, funded and justified in similar fashion. For example, sustainability in the public discourse adopted the meaning of quantitative substitution, like in 'ecosystems functions and services'. Why engage in messy political processes if technology resolves the problem cleanly and with pinpoint accuracy? Powerful science-based innovation would secure continuous growth, create jobs and would conquer hunger, poverty, inequality and even death. Big data and synthetic biology are just the latest of a succession of reductionist technologies attempting to rekindle the dreams of control.

An anticipatory criticism of the perverse effects of the industrialisation of science and the politics of expertise came from an unlikely source, former US President Dwight Eisenhower in his Farewell Address to the Nation. The speech is still remembered for the explicit reference to the military-industrial complex; here, instead, we want to recall another relevant passage in which Eisenhower warns that 'we must also be alert to the ... danger that public policy could itself become the captive of a scientific-technological elite' (Eisenhower 1961).

**The chapters in this book**

The Cartesian dream pervades disciplines, small and mega-projects, normativities and policies, indeed nearly all action in the Western world. The contributions to this book constitute just a sample of the crisis of worldviews and practices sustained by that dream. This book covers salient issues that feed into these narratives we live by: sustainability, individual and public health, connectivity, growth, security, etc. Each contribution challenges the Cartesian dream with a relevant case that has been promoted as essential for the well-being of humanity. These claims have become objects of debate in an ever-growing economy of promises: from more traditional fields like physics (Fjelland), medicine (Schei and Strand; Waltner-Toews) to the emerging techno-sciences such as life techno-sciences (Wickson; Tallacchini), and mega-projects such as geo-engineering (Curvelo), internet of everything (Benessia and Guimarães Pereira) as well as supporting modes of enquiry such as modelling (Saltelli and Funtowicz) and numbers (Sarewitz).

Fjelland starts with Feynman's investigation of the Challenger disaster in 1986 to illustrate and make the case that in physics and other sciences, such as biology, the naïve 'reductionism' central to the Cartesian dream needs to be combined with an 'antireductionist approach'. Through Fjelland's historical account, the reader can understand how great physicists in time have been rebelling against the Cartesian vision driving the development of physics. In other words, the reader can appreciate that physical sciences cannot be considered 'fundamental' as they cannot be reduced to a single fundamental 'Theory of Everything' (Anderson, Laughlin, Pines); neither can they be considered exhaustive as they are not complete and do not operate in a closed system since there are boundary conditions (Polanyi). Furthermore, the *objectivity* traditionally attributed to physical sciences cannot hold as the reality described through physics is not 'reality as it is' regardless of an observer (Heisenberg, Bohr). One could argue that there are other substantial notions that prevail in physics and are inherent to the Cartesian thought that would need substantial interrogation, such as certainty and determinism following the advent of quantum mechanics.

In a delightful conversation about food, freedom and friends, Waltner-Toews takes us on a journey through prevalent Cartesian responses to disease and epidemics control, where the roots of our current predicament are precisely attributable to the underlying framings and reductionisms. Surely, the fast genomic sequencing of viruses and bacteria that has created public health havoc has its function, but in the author's experience it is the process from which health and disease emerge (the conversation between the *conversants*: bacteria, hosts, environments) that matters most. The reductionist view in this area expresses itself also as transference; for example, of food production practice across geographies and cultures, or as panacean hymns that create, unsurprisingly, the damage that subsequently requires further panacean remedies. Reductionism is fundamentally present in narratives of cure proposed by world organisations that persistently focus on the diseases instead of on the processes through which they emerge; until changes in the social contract of many countries are pursued, matters will not be solved and more vaccines and antibiotics (control strategies) won't help. The global burden of disease, he argues, reflects more than ever the success of the Cartesian science (paradoxically?) with massive increases of food production sustained by insufficiently discussed health, social and economic narratives.

Schei and Strand offer another critical journey of the Cartesian dream through the evolution of the science of medicine and conceptions of human health. They note that René Descartes, the *practitioner*, recognised this and had great hopes for his method to tame the 'diseases of body and of mind, and perhaps even from the infirmity of old age' (Descartes 1637/2007). As Curvelo writes of Geoengineering (also in this volume), they too describe today's version of biomedicine as a Cartesian project. Biomedicine, the authors argue, privileges *disease* instead of the *patient* person; after all, the universe of disease is more orderly and therefore more tractable, as in principle it is predictable and curable. This is certainly reductionism of the first order. In fact, the authors see in the Cartesian dream of medicine much more than a hope for good health. They argue that this dream has led to a comprehensive programme of discredit and exclusion of all other paradigms of knowledge production about health (understanding and practice), in favour of the orthodox views of the biomedical establishment. Another Cartesian idea discussed by the authors is the mind–body dichotomy[2] and dialectics that Descartes believed to exist, even locating it in the *pineal gland*. Their discussion is mapped onto the persistence of the idea that a patient's *subjective* experience is substituted by the *objective* reductionism of molecular and cellular chemical and physical processes. The authors support the view that both humanistic and scientific medicine need to enter in a dialectic of opposition, learning and synergy, a dialectic that the authors say, remarkably, is embedded in Descartes's original epistemic proposition, i.e. a need for *hybrid* ways of knowing in medicine.

This divide, which extends to so many other areas, discouraging much needed sciences–humanities dialectics, is one of the key messages of this edited book: the need for a project going beyond the Cartesian dream of intentional rational separations, exclusions and substitutions.

Wickson offers an ontological objection that potentially sets plausible and legitimate grounds to challenge emerging life techno-sciences. The objection starts with a rejection of the mechanistic Cartesian view of Nature and the dualisms it assumes: humans and Nature, body and mind, reason and passion. She proposes a relational ontology where entities dynamically co-construct each other. In order to examine those, she proposes an ethics based on relations of care and on cultivation of virtue. This proposal *per se* cannot coexist with Cartesian ideals of rational representations and control of life. Reviewing deep ecology thought and the ethics of care and virtue, Wickson develops an ontological objection that favours the scrutiny of intentions, assumptions and norms behind techno-science development. Her framework allows a shift from asking what is wrong and bad about a technology to instead questioning as to the available options for approaching a particular (grand) challenge, thus avoiding deontological and consequentialist assessment frameworks, such as those based on risk. The advantage of this approach, she argues, is precisely in the possibility of asking questions and not incurring what Mumford (1934/2010, 390) described as the 'aimless expansion of production' based on nothing else but 'custom and accidental desire'.

Benessia and Guimarães Pereira consider the Internet of Things the climax and failure of the Cartesian dream, offered to us as a desirable and inescapable dream, a dream of connectivity, automation and mediated experience among existing (known) and new ontologies, embedding, enacting and co-creating undiscussed values and norms. But new ontologies cannot be treated with the ethics we know (see also Wickson, and Schei and Strand in this volume). Throughout their journey across the visual discourses of innovation of growth associated with the IoT scenario, within private and public institutions, the authors identify the Cartesian idea(l)s of control, prediction and reductionism which are deeply embedded in the transformations of received notions of human agency that IoT implies. The promises of IoT are immense, but the costs of the scenario are correspondingly high: the norms enacted challenge received notions of humanity and culture; the price of the loss of agency and other ethical issues is too high to ignore. Like Wickson, the authors propose that one must find the space to ask other kinds of questions, beyond consequentialist and other existing ethics frameworks. We need to be able to enquire about alternatives to, and the inevitability of, the (IoT) dream.

Tallacchini discusses yet another expression of the Cartesian dream: the normalisation of our lives through the normalisation of technology; in particular she discusses how the biological and digital domains have been mutually redefining each other. Using the example of the development of biobanks, she illustrates how, in turn, the digital culture is challenging this state of affairs through the active participation of citizens in the definition and function of biobanks. As in Wickson's piece, Tallacchini challenges the consequentialist approach to looking at technologies, inviting the reader on a journey that scrutinises which knowledges, values and norms get enacted in and through technology, an exercise that lessens the responsibility of ethics assessments currently relegated to professional groups. Tallacchini maintains that opening up choices available to citizens and extending the experimentation of normativity to all will avoid more of what she describes as technologies embedding 'normative fixes played as technical fixes', yet another form of reductionism.

Through the proposal of geo-engineering as a means to tame the changing Earth climate, Curvelo questions both the Cartesian views and dream of *human* control over Nature embedded in such proposals, as well as the paradoxical Cartesian *nightmare* that she describes as the imperative to study this proposal through framings that cannot be described within Cartesian inspired methods, vocabulary and tools used for centuries.

As Sarewitz explains, numbers are accepted as the preferred representations of knowledge, often presented as aspiring to correspond to real world descriptions. Numbers are the ultimate expression of the search for objectivity in the Cartesian dream – and Galileo's dream too, as we have noted earlier. Through a review of a series of cases in health, environment and energy, Sarewitz reflects on the quality and purpose of numbers that are often used to send signals, inform, underpin policies, structure behaviours and expectations and other choices encountered in our individual and collective lives; *numbers* that often represent reductionist views of the issues they try to describe. Moreover, Sarewitz argues, numbers that claim to derive from 'the scientific method' often cannot be classified as more than 'quantified beliefs' originating from a trans-science activity – i.e. they are answers to questions that cannot be fully addressed by science; in this case numbers become best described as rituals whose value is protected and ensured by scientific norms. As in the post-normal science argument, numbers have a value and a fitness for purpose that needs to be explicated, otherwise as for mathematical modelling (Saltelli and Funtowicz in this volume), the result of purposeless numbers is an 'increasing sense of incoherence, contradiction, and dismay' and the advent of 'Big Data' is just adding to the 'chaos', continuing the dream of reductionism. As in other contributions, Sarewitz urges an extension of the questions to encompass more imaginative and deeper interests and views of human purpose.

Mathematical models, one could claim, are the symbolic and material expressions of the Cartesian dream and Galileo's call for a world coded in mathematics; they are reductionist by design, representing a chosen view of the universe they model, dealing with issues coded in mathematic formulations. But they fall short of comprising a complete metaphor for this dream, as models encode the ethics, values and passions of those who develop them in the form of assumptions, the choice of questions asked, the choice and treatment of uncertainty, and the choice of reasoning and model inputs to deal with the issue they are handling. Saltelli and Funtowicz discuss the recurrent pitfalls of mathematical modelling used to back up policy-making; pitfalls that risk making the whole of the mathematical modelling enterprise sound flawed. More than that, they argue, current modelling practices, through their development and use, constitute a significant threat to the legitimacy and utility of science in contested policy settings. They suggest that forms of organised quality control are needed and provide a set of rules aiming at ensuring transparent and balanced use of models, which they have called sensitivity auditing. In a post-normal context where 'facts are uncertain, values in dispute, stakes high and decisions urgent' sensitivity analysis of models is not enough; in a nutshell their rules investigate the quality (fitness for purpose) of the model, by interrogating the questions asked, assumptions made and uncertainties considered.

By looking at techno-science developments of our time, all the authors of this book are actually scrutinising the narratives by which we live. Many of us working at the interface between science and policy now see how entrenched the Cartesian dream is in the rhetoric of our policy institutions as expressed in the narratives we live by, including those of growth, 'evidence-based' everything (including policy), innovation everything, responsible research, and innovation. Schei and Strand note that the term *evidence-based* first emerged in the medical realm with A. Cochrane, i.e. 'a rational attempt to understand what worked in medicine', but this programme is having far more ramifications, as evidence-based has become the view by which we have both to do things (policies, etc.) and to investigate their goodness.

Fjelland observes that the urgent questions we face today need a different culture, a culture that makes space for different gazes of the challenges we face. Across all of the contributions, 'conversation' appears as a foundational element needed to escape the entrenched and tempting strategies of reductionism, prediction and control in and through science and technology development (Waltner-Toews; Wickson; Benessia and Guimarães Pereira; and Tallacchini). Unfortunately, this is not happening in many spheres, as the cases illustrate, but such conversations ought to take place as we negotiate our way into the future.

### Final reflection

The chapters in this collection discuss, in a diversity of styles, the growing doubts of the received view and standard narrative of unlimited progress and ubiquitous substitution. The title of this volume, 'The End of the Cartesian Dream', reflects the awareness of the passing of an epoch, echoing Toulmin's judgement that the era of Modernity is at its end, that its project has lost momentum and that we need to create a 'successor programme' (Toulmin 1990, 3).

The idea of a successor programme to replace the existing one is an essential task of our time. It must be substantially different from the existing paradigm because the world has changed and we have changed, precisely because of the transformative power of modern ideals and technologies. How to change and, at the same time, preserve the humanistic tradition of the European civilisation is a severe challenge. It seems to us that the successor programme cannot be a new blueprint but a suite of processes, programmed and spontaneous, exploring and experimenting how to live together before even attempting to plan and decide what is going to become of us.[3]

### Notes

1  For a contemporary version of this belief, see Tegmark's Mathematical Universe Hypothesis (MUH) in which physical reality is described as a mathematical structure (Tegmark 2014).

2  *Descartes' Error: Emotion, Reason, and the Human Brain* by the neurosurgeon António Damásio offers yet another perspective: our thinking and decision-making are interwoven with the emotions and the body they inhabit. Published first in 1994 by Penguin Books.

3  The opinions of the authors cannot in any circumstance be attributed to the European Commission.

# References

Bacon, F. 1620. *Novum Organum or True Directions concerning the interpretation of Nature* (http://www.constitution.org/bacon/nov_org.htm) accessed Aug. 2014.

Bacon, F. 1627. *The New Atlantis* (http://ebooks.adelaide.edu.au/b/bacon/francis/b12n) accessed Aug. 2014.

Bishop, R.C. 2003. On separating predictability and determinism, *Erkenntnis*, 58: 169–88.

Condorcet, M. J. A. N. d. C. 1795. *Outlines of an Historical View of the Progress of the Human Mind* (http://oll.libertyfund.org/titles/1669) accessed Aug. 2014.

Descartes, R. 1637/2008. *A Discourse on the Method*, Oxford: Oxford World's Classics.

Eisenhower, D. 1961. President Dwight D. Eisenhower's farewell address (http://www.ourdocuments.gov/doc.php?flash=true&doc=90).

Galilei, G. 1630/1970. *Dialogue Concerning the Two Chief World Systems*, Berkeley and Los Angeles, CA: University of California Press.

Kline, M. 1980. *Mathematics: The Loss of Certainty*, Oxford: Oxford University Press.

Laplace, P.-S. 1814/1951. *Philosophical Essay on Probabilities*, New York: Dover Publications.

Leibniz, G. 1695/1924. Von dem Verhängnisse, in E. Cassirer and A. Buchenau (eds), *Hauptschriften zur Grundlegung der Philosophie*, vol. 2, Leipzig: Meiner, pp. 121–36.

Mumford, L. 1934/2010. *Technics and Civilization*. Chicago, IL: University of Chicago Press.

Rudner, R. 1954. The scientist qua scientist makes value judgments, *Philosophy of Science*, 20: 1–6.

Tegmark, M. 2014. *Our Mathematical Universe: My Quest for the Ultimate Nature of Reality*, New York: Alfred A. Knopf.

Toulmin, S. 1990. *Cosmopolis: The Hidden Agenda of Modernity*, Chicago, IL: University of Chicago Press.

# Part I
# Foundations

Part 1
Foundations

# 1 Plenty of room at the top

*Ragnar Fjelland*

## Feynman, from nanotechnology to the Challenger disaster

In 1959 the physicist Richard P. Feynman gave a talk to the American Physical Society with the title 'Plenty of Room at the Bottom' where he addressed the possibilities of miniaturisation, or, as he said, 'manipulating and controlling things on a small scale'. He argued that the technological possibilities are almost unlimited, and he carried out some staggering thought experiments. He started by asking the question: 'Why cannot we write the entire 24 volumes of *Encyclopaedia Britannica* on the head of a pin?' (He was referring to the 1947 edition.) He demonstrated that we in principle can, and gave the following justification. The diameter of a head of a pin is 1/16 of an inch (approximately 1.5 mm). If the diameter is magnified by a factor of 25,000, the area of the pinhead will be approximately the same size as all the pages of Encyclopaedia Britannica. The challenge then is to reverse the process, to diminish the printed pages of *Encyclopaedia Britannica* by a factor of 25,000. And it can in principle be done. If we take the smallest printed dot that can be seen by the human eye, a dot with a diameter of 0.2 mm, and diminish it by a factor of 25,000, the dot will cover an area of approximately 1,000 atoms. Therefore, he included *plenty* in the heading of his talk: there is not only space, but plenty of space at the bottom. Feynman also pointed out that this would not be an encoded version of the *Encyclopaedia*, but a (graphical) copy, containing the exact layout, and all the pictures.

Feynman carried his thought experiment further, and asked the question: with the same diminishment, how much space do we need to represent the content of all the books in the world? Starting with the number of volumes in some of the largest libraries in the world he estimated that there were something like 25 million original books. If they are diminished with the same factor as *Encyclopaedia Britannica*, they will all together cover an area of three square yards, which is something like 35 pages in the *Encyclopaedia*! Feynman also speculated on the possibility of representing the same information in encoded form (like a word-processing system), and using three dimensions instead of two (the interior of the material instead of only the surface). He then calculated that the same information could be contained in a cube with the sides 1/200 inch (approx. 0.12 mm), which is the size of a piece of dust that is so small that we can barely see it with the naked eye (Feynman 1959).

Although Feynman did not use the word *nanotechnology*, it is often alleged that his talk inspired the development of the field that is today known as nanotechnology. Although his direct influence on the field has been disputed (cf. Ball 2009), his visions and theoretical deliberations are interesting. His basic idea was to control Nature at the level of individual atoms. In this way we can rearrange atoms in new ways, different from the way they are arranged in Nature. In chemistry this is carried out by the process of synthesis. However, a chemical process is a messy thing. If we can control matter at the atomic level, the chemist can only describe the kind of molecule he wants, and the physicist can construct it for him. In principle, all chemical processes can be reduced to physics.

This would be the ultimate realisation of the Cartesian dream. At the same time it would be the completion of the 'reductionist programme' in modern science. According to this 'programme', processes at a higher level are governed by the laws that govern the processes at a lower level, all the way down to the atomic and sub-atomic level.

Feynman no doubt endorsed the reductionist programme. In his *Lectures on Physics*, published a few years later, he said the following about biology:

> The most important hypothesis in all of biology, for example, is that 'everything that animals do, atoms do'. In other words, there is nothing that living things do that cannot be understood from the point of view that they are made of atoms acting according to the laws of physics.
>
> (Feynman *et al.* 1958, Chapter 1, 8)

He used the word *hypothesis*, but from the context it is more natural to call it a fundamental assumption.

*Animals* in the quotation above include humans. In fact, brain processes were used by Feynman to show how physics can contribute to biology, and he argued that in principle no other laws are required to account for what takes place in organisms, including human actions. The philosopher Karl Popper called this the *deterministic nightmare* (Popper 1975a, 218) and described it in the following way:

> ... any physicist with sufficient detailed information could have written my lecture by the simple method of predicting the precise places on which the physical system consisting of my body (including my brain, of course, and my fingers) and my pen would put down those black marks.
>
> (Popper 1975a, 222)

However, in daily life Feynman was far from a narrow reductionist, which he clearly demonstrated 27 years later. On 28 January 1986 the space shuttle Challenger exploded under take-off and all the seven crew members were killed. Feynman was appointed a member of the presidential commission that investigated the cause of the disaster, and he actually found the cause.

When the space shuttle was launched, it was mounted on top of two rocket boosters that burned liquid hydrogen and liquid oxygen. The boosters burned for a few minutes before they were separated from the space shuttle and fell into the sea. They were made of elements fitted together in joints. When they ignited, there was an enormous pressure, and it was essential that the joints were tight. Among others two rubber rings, called O-rings, sealed them. I will not go into technical details, but just point out that Feynman found that the resilience of these O-rings was imperative, and he also discovered that the resilience decreased with decreasing temperature. It turned out that the air temperature the night before the shuttle was launched had been down to around –6° Celsius. The reduced resilience of the O-rings caused a leakage that started a fraction of a second after the starting of the engines, and this leakage caused the explosion of the shuttle.

However, after having found the physical cause of the accident, Feynman inquired further. He found that the technicians in NASA who worked on the 'floor' had known about the problems with the O-rings for a long time, and they had tried to communicate this knowledge upwards in the system, with little success. Feynman therefore asked further questions, for example why the shuttle was launched on a morning when it had been extraordinarily cold during the night. The answer was that president Reagan was going to give his State of the Union address to the Congress that very day, and he wanted to report the successful launching of Challenger. Therefore, there was a pressure on NASA to stick to the original schedule. The official management of the organisation therefore did not listen to the warnings from the engineers. Feynman's explanation was that they either neglected this knowledge, or that they did not have it, 'demonstrating an almost incredible lack of communication between the managers and their working engineers' (Feynman 1989, 236).

The Challenger accident demonstrated two different strategies. To find the physical cause of the accident Feynman proceeded in a traditional way as a physicist (although he had to use some untraditional methods), by pinning down the part that failed. However, in going further, he had to go in the opposite direction: from the part to the whole. In the end, the 'real' cause of the disaster was the organisation of NASA.

The first strategy is the traditional reductionist strategy, whereas the second is an anti-reductionist strategy. Of course, Feynman might argue that, in the end, all is governed by the laws of physics. Nevertheless, he did not move *downwards*, but *upwards*: To explain why the shuttle was launched on a morning following an extremely cold night, he did not go to a lower level. On the contrary, he had to go to a higher level, to the political context and to the organisation (top–down) and 'culture' (lack of communication) of NASA.

This chapter discusses some aspects of reductionism and anti-reductionism in physics. I shall first show that, although physics by and large has followed the general reductionist trend in science, there have been some dissenters. I shall then go to one of the founding fathers of modern physics, Niels Bohr, and argue that his idea of complementarity is an alternative to reductionism.

## Reductionism and anti-reductionism in physics

Although reductionism is associated with modern science, it was already a topic in Greek philosophy. For example, the idea of organisation at different levels goes back to Aristotle. According to Aristotle each level of organisation has its distinguishing marks, it is qualitatively different from the lower levels and cannot be reduced to them. One popular way of formulating this is that the whole is more than the sum of its parts. For example, an organism consists of organs, but it is not simply the sum of these organs. On the contrary, the function of an organ can only be understood when it is regarded as a part of the whole organism (Aristotle, *Parts of Animals* 642a and *Politics* 1.2).

Descartes worked out a purely mechanical model of the organism, but it nevertheless took more than 200 years before reductionism became the dominating paradigm in biology. For example, Louis Pasteur, who was the leading micro-biologist of the second part of the nineteenth century, was a dedicated anti-reductionist. However, at the end of the nineteenth century Jacques Loeb became an important advocate of a reductionist programme in biology (Pauly 1987). A book written by a physicist, Erwin Schrödinger's *What is Life* (1967, originally published in 1944), was also important in promoting reductionism in biology. Schrödinger himself was not a reductionist, at least not in the traditional sense. In the book he asked the question if the laws of physics could account for the phenomenon of life. His key term was *order*, and this enabled him to give a precise formulation of the question: can the laws of physics account for the kind of order we find in organisms? The kind of order we have in physics is what Schrödinger called *order from disorder*: for example, the molecules in a gas move in a random way. Therefore, it is impossible to describe the motion of individual molecules. However, when there are billions and billions of them, we can apply the law of large numbers. At the micro-level, the molecules move randomly, but at the macro-level, the gas behaves in a deterministic way.

Schrödinger focused on the process of heredity. The most striking aspect of heredity is captured in the saying that the apple does not fall far from the tree: there is a high degree of similarity between parents and progeny. Schrödinger called this phenomenon *order from order*, in contrast to the order from disorder that we have in physics, and he investigated the hereditary mechanisms. He argued that these are located in the structure of the chromosomes of the germ cells, and called it a *code script* for producing the new organism. He carried out some rough calculations, similar to Feynman's calculations that I referred to earlier, and found that the maximum size of a gene is no more than a cube with a side of 30 nanometres, and therefore cannot contain more than a few million atoms. This number is much too small to allow the order from disorder that we have in physics. Therefore, he concluded that what he called the *ordinary laws of physics* cannot account for the phenomenon of life. However, he was rather optimistic, because he continued: 'We must be prepared to find a new type of physical law prevailing in it. Or are we to term it a non-physical or super-physical, law?' (Schrödinger 1967, 86).

Schrödinger's book inspired many physicists and molecular biologists. Three of them were Francis Crick, James Watson and Maurice Wilkins. They shared the Nobel Prize in Medicine or Physiology for the discovery of the structure of DNA.[1] This is probably the greatest achievement in reductionist biology. Watson, by training a molecular biologist, was more outspoken than most physicists, and put it this way: 'There is only one science, physics: everything else is social work.'[2]

Feynman mentioned atoms in his reference to biology, and biologists need not go below the atomic level. However, at the beginning of the twentieth century Ernst Rutherford showed that the atom is not an indivisible unit, but consists of a tiny nucleus surrounded by electrons. A few decades later it was discovered that the nucleus consists of protons and neutrons, and with the construction of large accelerators numerous smaller particles (elementary particles) have been discovered. This development has been accompanied by a development of theoretical models. The generally accepted model of the nucleus today is the so-called *standard model* that is characterised by 12 fundamental particles (and their anti-particles). However, it is generally agreed that the standard model is not the final theory. In particular a final theory must be able to unify the two major theories of contemporary physics, quantum mechanics and the general theory of relativity. It has been assumed that such a theory is possible, and it is sometimes referred to as *a theory of everything*. For example, Steven Weinberg wrote a book with the title *Dreams of a Final Theory* (1993), and Stephen Hawking ended his best-selling book *A Brief History of Time* with describing the characteristics of such a theory, and concluded that when we have this theory, 'then we would know the mind of God' (Hawking 1988, 175).[3]

The assumption that ever more fundamental theories are possible, and can be obtained by a combination of experiments and theoretical work, has been the main reason for allocating tremendous amounts of resources (billions of dollars) to this kind of research. However, in 1972 the journal *Science* published an article by the American physicist Philip Anderson with the title 'More is Different'.[4] The article was amazing, not primarily because it argued in favour of anti-reductionism in general, but because it argued for anti-reductionism within physics itself.

Anderson started by pointing out that with the possible exception of some philosophers, the overwhelming majority of scientists are reductionists. However, he did not belong to this majority, and he announced his general position right at the start:

> At each stage entirely new laws, concepts, and generalisations are necessary, requiring inspiration and creativity to just as great a degree as in the previous one. Psychology is not applied biology, nor is biology applied chemistry.
>
> (Anderson 1972, 393)

For the most part Anderson restricted himself to physics. His main point was that even inanimate matter has properties at higher levels that cannot be reduced to lower levels. For example, properties of gold metal have only meaning at a macroscopic level, because a simple atom of gold cannot be yellow and shiny and conduct electricity. His key concept was *broken symmetry*. For example, the atoms that make up salt (sodium (Na) and chlorine (Cl)) have spherical symmetry. However, in a salt crystal the two types of atoms are organised in a regular three-dimensional cubic pattern: sodium and chlorine atoms alternate in all directions. Therefore, a salt crystal has cubic symmetry, and the spherical symmetry of the Na and Cl atoms is *broken* in the structure of the salt crystal. He mentioned other phenomena that cannot be explained by making recourse to a lower level, among others super-conductivity and the rigidity of solid matter, and he concluded that 'the whole becomes not only more than but very different from the sum of its parts' (Anderson 1972, 395).

At the end of the article he speculated about higher structures, and criticised the 'arrogance of the particle physicist' and 'some molecular biologists' who 'seem determined to try to reduce everything about the human organism to "only" chemistry' (Anderson 1972, 396).

It is adequate to speak about symmetry, and symmetry-breaking, in physics. However, when we ascend to higher levels, to biology, psychology, the social sciences and the humanities, the term does not make much sense. Anderson himself saw the problem, and he remarked that at one point we should stop speaking about decreasing symmetry and call it increasing complexity.[5] But he did not say much about higher levels, and he himself called it 'speculations'.

## Boundary conditions: Michael Polanyi

There is one important aspect that Anderson left out: all laws of physics assume two kinds of 'external' conditions: initial conditions and boundary conditions. A simple example will show this. To solve the equations that describe the motion of a particle, we must know its initial velocity (including its direction). This is the initial condition. In addition we must know its mass and the forces that act on it (for example that it moves in a homogeneous gravitational field). These are the boundary conditions.[6]

Therefore, physics is not a closed and complete system as reductionists assume. Because we always have to take the initial and boundary conditions for granted, they can only give *conditional predictions*. Feynman's experiences with the Challenger disaster are a good illustration. The immediate cause of the disaster was the reduced resilience of the O-rings at low temperatures. This is physics, or materials science. But the fact that temperature was low when it was launched belongs to the boundary conditions.

In 1968 the physical chemist and philosopher Michael Polanyi used boundary conditions to argue that physics is not a closed system. His arguments were published in an article in *Science*, the same journal that published Anderson's article three years later. Polanyi made a distinction between two kinds of boundary conditions. When we carry out an experiment, we realise some boundary conditions to find out something about nature. However, when we construct a machine, we realise boundary conditions (the structure of the machine) to utilise the laws of Nature for our purpose. A machine works in accordance with the laws of Nature, but the laws of Nature cannot explain the structure of the machine (but the structure must, of course, be compatible with the laws of Nature).

It is worth noticing that the two kinds of boundary conditions are closely related. A simple example will show this. I have previously used the example of the motion of a projectile. The knowledge that the trajectory of this projectile is approximately a parabola is grounded in Galileo's experiments with bronze balls rolling down an inclined plane. To reduce friction the balls were made as round and smooth as possible. Galileo himself wisely pointed out that the results are only valid under the ideal condition that there is no friction, and that it is important to know about this limitation. However, then he added that we can construct the shape of the projectile so that friction is minimised (Galilei 1954, 253).

The biological structures play a role that is analogous to machine-like boundary conditions. The physical and chemical processes that take place in an organism do not violate the laws of physics and chemistry. However, they cannot be reduced to these laws. Polanyi used the example of the structure of the DNA molecule, and made the thought experiment that this structure can be explained by physics alone. In that case the structure would be explained by the fact that the bindings of the bases were much stronger than any other structure. It would have maximum stability, represented by the lowest possible potential energy. For example, the cubic structure of salt can be explained in this way. But because of this a salt crystal cannot carry any information. The information-carrying capacity of DNA is due to the fact that the structure does not have the lowest possible potential energy, and cannot be reduced to physics and chemistry.

Polanyi's point was that the laws of physics can only be applied to a biological system (and any other system) when the boundary conditions are given. And the boundary conditions at all levels of an organism (from molecules to cells, to organs and to the organism itself) make up the organisation of the organism. These conditions are the frames that the laws of physics work inside, and therefore the organisation itself cannot be explained by these laws.

## There is no 'God's eye view'

*Emergence* is the standard term used today by anti-reductionists to denote that higher levels cannot be reduced to lower levels. However, using the concept of emergence in a certain sense accepts one premise of reductionism: it takes the 'world of physics' for granted, and subsequently moves *up*, and shows that something comes *in addition* to the laws of physics. The problem is that one is actually accepting the basic assumptions that have been taken for granted since Galileo and Descartes. In particular this applies to the assumption that objectivity means describing reality as it is independently of man. I shall now argue that the 'world of physics' is an abstract and idealised world, that is secondary to our real world, that the philosopher Edmund Husserl called 'our everyday life-world' (Husserl 1970, 48–9).

Therefore, a more radical anti-reductionist strategy is to take a closer look at how the 'world of physics' is constituted, and it is worthwhile to remind ourselves of some of the basic insights behind the most important theory in physics in the twentieth century, quantum mechanics. Some of the founding fathers of the theory, in particular Niels Bohr and Werner Heisenberg, early recognised that quantum mechanics was incompatible with the dominating concept of objectivity as describing reality independently of man. Any physicist has always known that to make observations we have to interact with the object, and therefore influence it, but it was tacitly assumed that this influence could in principle be reduced until it was negligible. However, according to quantum mechanics there is a lower limit to this interaction, formalised in Heisenberg's uncertainty relations, and therefore the assumption that interaction can be infinitely reduced is not valid. There is an uncontrollable interaction between the measuring instruments and the objects of investigation. In Bohr's own words: 'Indeed, the *finite interaction between object and measuring agencies* ... entails the necessity of a final renunciation of the classical ideal ... and a radical revision of our attitude towards the problem of physical reality' (Bohr 1935, 697).

The novel, and controversial, element of quantum mechanics is the introduction of the *observer*.[7] The observer cannot be abstracted away from physics, and therefore physics is a human accomplishment. Bohr and the Copenhagen interpretation of quantum mechanics (which *is* quantum mechanics) has sometimes been accused of subjectivism. However, this is a misunderstanding. The *observer* in quantum mechanics is neither consciousness nor an individual being. An observer needs, of course, both consciousness, body and language, and not least measuring instruments, but any observer can in principle be replaced by any other observer with the required competence.

One consequence of quantum mechanics is that we have to give up the idea that Nature is fundamentally deterministic, and accept that the laws of physics are statistical. Some have used this in an attempt to rescue human freedom. But to learn that our actions are governed by chance, rather than by deterministic laws, is hardly a solution to the problem. Therefore, we have to look deeper, to the notion of physical reality.

The idea of the observer is closely related to another key idea in Bohr's philosophy of physics, the idea of *complementarity*.[8] He first used the term in 1927 in the discussion of the so-called particle/wave dualism. Einstein had in 1905 showed that light may be regarded as consisting of particles, photons. In 1924 the French physicist Louis de Broglie showed that matter, for example electrons, may be regarded as waves. But this implied a paradox. Light, which was previously regarded as waves, revealed properties which could only be explained by assuming that it consisted of particles. Matter, which was regarded as being made up of particles, revealed properties that could only be explained by assuming that the alleged particles behaved as waves. In classical physics we would then ask the question: are electrons particles or waves? According to Bohr this question cannot be asked in quantum mechanics. We should rather ask the question: do electrons *behave like* particles or waves? In answering that question we should specify *under what experimental conditions* they behave as particles or waves. The main point is that the situations where for example electrons behave like particles and where they behave like waves need two different experimental arrangements, and therefore exclude each other mutually. There is no contradiction as long as the observer is taken into consideration.

Bohr never tired of emphasising that physics is a human accomplishment. Therefore, objectivity in science is not depicting a world independently of man. According to Bohr it is impossible to maintain such an ideal of objectivity. In a letter to the Danish author H.P.E. Hansen he put it in the following way:

> In physics we learn ... time and again that our task is not to penetrate into the essence of things, the meaning of which we don't know anyway, but rather to develop concepts which allow us to talk in a productive way about phenomena in Nature.
>
> (Letter dated 20 July 1935, Engl. tr. quoted from Pais 1991, 446)

Needless to say, this is a more modest view of what physics can accomplish than the previous quotation from Hawking about knowing the mind of God. In fact, Bohr emphasised that there is no *God's eye view* of the world (Favrholdt 1995, 97).

Complementarity is an alternative to reductionism, and Bohr applied it outside physics, among others to biology. The point of departure is that things are not primarily given in 'the world of physics', but in our everyday world. We can *make* them objects of physics. In principle, anything material can be made an object of physics, including organisms. Bohr knew that the reductionist approach in biology had been successful, and was taken as support for the view that all of biology can ultimately be reduced to physics. However, his strategy was to ask under what conditions the biological, chemical and physical processes are observed. An organism can be made the object of physics, but the more detailed knowledge we obtain, the more we suppress or even destroy the organism itself:

> In every experiment on living organisms, there must remain an uncertainty as regards the physical conditions to which they are subjected, and the idea suggests itself that the minimal freedom we must allow the organism in this respect is just large enough to permit it, so to say, to hide its ultimate secrets from us.
>
> (Bohr 1999a, 34)

Bohr regarded freedom of will as a basic fact of human existence. Therefore, he always insisted that all he had to say about it were a few sentences, and should not be enlarged (Favrholdt 1995: 123). However, freedom of will is closely related to consciousness. If we are not conscious, we cannot deliberate and make decisions. But consciousness also depends on biological, chemical and physical processes in our brain. How can we be sure that consciousness cannot be reduced to these processes? Bohr's strategy was to ask under what conditions the biological, chemical and physical processes are observed. To see how this strategy works, let us take the physical processes, say electrical activity, in our brain. Although non-invasive observational techniques have been invented, we could not make detailed observations of electrical activity at, say, the cell level of the brain without inserting measuring instruments into the brain. The more detailed observations we want to make, the more comprehensive the investigation will have to be. No doubt these observations of electrical activity would interfere with the conscious processes. The same applies to a chemical and biological description. They are all complementary descriptions of the brain:

> It is suggestive that the simple concepts of physical science to an ever higher degree lose their immediate applicability the more we approach the features of living organisms related to the characteristics of our mind.
>
> (Bohr 1999b, 94)

## The two cultures

Bohr emphasised that, although the language of physics is basically mathematical, in the end physicists must make recourse to everyday language. In stressing the importance of language, Bohr placed himself in a long philosophical tradition, from Aristotle to Popper. According to Aristotle man is the only animal endowed with speech (as opposed to mere voice), which enables him to distinguish between just and unjust, good and evil (Aristotle, *Politics* 1253a20), and according to Popper the emergence of rationality is intimately related to what he called the higher functions of language: the descriptive and argumentative function (Popper 1975b, 120). In particular, without the higher functions of language science would have been impossible.

This insight enables us to approach the study of man in a way that is different from the reductionist. Man can be made the object of scientific investigations, but we must not forget that these investigations are not possible without a *knowing subject*. If we want to answer the question: *what is man*, we must start with the fact that science, technology, society, culture and language, are all created by man. But then we are about to leave the natural sciences and approach the humanities.

Bohr had from his very youth learned to appreciate the humanities. His favourite author was Goethe. In this regard he was typical of his generation of physicists, who had grown up with the Humboldt ideal of *Bildung*. The physicist Gino Segrès relates in his book *Faust in Copenhagen* a story that illustrates this point. At Easter 1932 some of the leading younger physicists gathered for the annual conference at the Bohr Institute in Copenhagen. On Easter Eve some of the participants put on a skit that alluded to persons and events in the world of physics. That year marked the one hundredth anniversary of Goethe's death, and the participants wanted to commemorate the great author. Max Delbrück (who later received a Nobel Prize in medicine for his contributions to the development of genetics) had written the manuscript, and he used Goethe's *Faust* as point of departure. The skit was full of allusions that assumed that the audience was familiar with both Faust and leading figures in the physics community. In the audience were among others Bohr himself, Heisenberg, Lise Meitner and Paul Dirac (Segrè 2008).

The importance of the humanities was emphasised by a famous ex-physicist who had made a career as a civil servant. The very same year as Feynman gave his talk in Pasadena – 1959 – Charles Percy Snow gave four public lectures at Cambridge University. The title of the first lecture was 'The Two Cultures'. The lectures were published as a book with that title the same year, and later became a classic. In the lectures Snow argued that intellectual life in the West was divided into two different 'cultures', one consisting of what he called 'literary intellectuals' and the other consisting of scientists, in particular physical scientists. Snow admitted that this division was a simplification, but he nevertheless argued that it captured an essential aspect of contemporary intellectual life in the West. It is divided into two camps, with almost no communication between them. During the Second World War and the years after, Snow and his collaborators had interviewed about 40,000 scientists and engineers (of a total of about 50,000 working scientists and about 80,000 working engineers in UK). From this selection – almost 25 per cent – he drew the conclusion that, apart from music, scientists and engineers were not interested in the arts and humanities. In particular books, novels, history and poetry played almost no role in their lives. But his description of the literary intellectuals was even less flattering. They pitied the scientists and engineers who had not read a single major work of English literature. However, they were themselves not only ignorant of science and technology but even proud of their ignorance. Snow had sometimes been provoked by literary intellectuals and asked how many of them knew the Second Law of Thermodynamics. The response was always negative, but Snow argued that it is the scientific equivalent of asking a scientist if he has read a work of Shakespeare.

Snow's book has often been interpreted as a scientist's attack on the humanities. But this is a misunderstanding. It was an attack on the humanists, and not the humanities. However, one tends to forget that the last lecture, which is the last chapter of the book, has the title: 'The rich and the poor'. Here Snow described the gap between the rich and the poor countries as the most serious challenge to scientists. Although he no doubt overestimated the importance of science and technology in bridging this gap, he recognised the importance of the humanities. In order to bridge the gap between the rich and the poor countries it is imperative to bridge the gap between the two cultures. At the end of the chapter he says: 'Closing the gap between our cultures is a necessity in the most abstract intellectual sense, as well as in the most practical' (Snow 1964, 50).

In this regard little has changed. These challenges are even more urgent today. However, closing the gap between Snow's two cultures requires that humanists recognise that there is plenty of room *at the bottom* and scientists and technologists acknowledge that there is plenty of room *at the top*. But perhaps the most difficult challenge is to recognise that the metaphors of *top* and *bottom* are misplaced.

## Notes

1  See    http://www.nobelprize.org/nobel_prizes/medicine/laureates/1962/perspectives. html (Accessed 28 August 2013).
2  Quoted from Rose 1997, 8. It was said in a debate between Rose and Watson in 1994.
3  Hawking later gave up this project. In Hawking and Mlodinow (2013) they point to the ironical fact that the pursuit of a theory of everything produces a diversity of incompatible theories. In the article they say: 'There is no way to remove the observer – us – from our perception of the world.' I will return to *the observer* later.
4  This is the kind of article a scientist would normally write after he has won a Nobel Prize. However, Anderson won the Nobel Prize for physics five years later, in 1977.
5  In this context Anderson used the term *complication*. However, other places in the same article he used the term 'complexity', and I prefer to use that term.
6  The importance of initial and boundary conditions is clearly demonstrated in perhaps the most important equation in modern physics, the Schrödinger equation. It is a partial differential equation, and to solve it we must know both the initial and the boundary conditions.
7  The term *observer* may be misleading, as it alludes to a passive knowing subject. Therefore, it is important to emphasise that the observer is at the same time an *agent*.
8  There is a large amount of literature on Bohr's philosophy of physics and there is considerable controversy around the interpretation of his idea of complementarity. For an up to date overview of the literature, see Katsumori 2011. However, my application of Bohr's idea of complementarity is independent of this controversy.

## References

Anderson, P.W. 1972. More is different: Broken symmetry and the nature of the hierarchical structure of science, *Science,* 177(4047): 393–6.

Aristotle. 1985. *The Complete Works of Aristotle: The Revised Oxford Translation*, ed. Jonathan Barnes, Princeton, NJ: Princeton University Press (*Parts of Animals* in vol. 1, *Politics* in vol. 2).

Ball, P. 2009. Feynman's fancy, *Chemistry World,* Jan., 58–62.

Bohr, N. 1935. Can quantum-mechanical description of physical reality be considered complete? *Physical Review,* 48: 696–702.

Bohr, N. 1999a. Light and life, in N. Bohr, *Collected Works,* vol. 10, Amsterdam: Elsevier, pp. 27–35.

Bohr, N. 1999b. Unity of knowledge, in N. Bohr, *Collected Works,* vol. 10, Amsterdam: Elsevier, pp. 79–98.

Descartes, R. 1971. *Discourse on Method and the Meditations*, Harmondsworth: Penguin Classics.

Favrholdt, D. 1995. *Fysik, bevidsthed, liv. Studier i Niels Bohrs filosofi,* Odense: Odense Universitetsforlag.

Feynman, R.P. 1959. Plenty of room at the bottom, transcript of the talk (http://feynman.caltech.edu/plenty.html) accessed Aug. 2013.

Feynman, R.P. 1989. '*What Do You Care What Other People Think?' Further Adventures of a Curious Character*, New York: Bantam Books.

Feynman, R.P., Leighton, R.B., and Sands, M. 1958. *The Feynman Lectures on Physics,* vol. 1, New York: Addison-Wesley.

Galilei, G. 1954. *Dialogues Concerning Two New Sciences,* tr. Henry Crew and Alfonso de Salvio, New York: Dover Publications.

Hawking, S. 1988. *A Brief History of Time*, New York: Bantam Books.

Hawking, S., and Mlodinow, L. 2013. The (elusive) theory of everything, *Scientific American Special*, 22(2) Summer 2013, 90–3.

Husserl, E. 1970. *The Crisis of European Sciences and Transcendental Phenomenology*, Evanston, IL: Northwestern University Press.

Katsumori, M. 2011. *Niels Bohr's Complementarity*, Boston Studies in the Philosophy of Science, 286, Amsterdam: Springer.

Pais, A. 1991. *Niels Bohr's Time, in Physics, Philosophy and Polity*, Oxford: Clarendon Press.

Polanyi, M. 1968. Life's irreducible structure, *Science*, 160(21): 1308–12.

Pauly, P.J. 1987. *Controlling Life: Jacques Loeb and the Engineering Ideal in Biology*, Oxford: Oxford University Press.

Popper, K.R. 1975a. Of clouds and clocks, in K. R. Popper, *Objective Knowledge*, Oxford: Clarendon Press.

Popper, K.R. 1975b. Epistemology without a knowing subject, in K.R. Popper, *Objective Knowledge*, Oxford: Clarendon Press, pp. 106–52.

Rose, S. 1997. *Lifelines*, Oxford: Oxford University Press.

Schrödinger, E. 1967. *What is Life?* Cambridge: Cambridge University Press.

Segrè, G. 2008. *Faust in Copenhagen: A Struggle for the Soul of Physics and the Birth of the Nuclear Age*, London: Pimlico.

Snow, C.P. 1964. *The Two Cultures and A Second Look*, Cambridge: Cambridge University Press.

Weinberg, S. 1993. *Dreams of a Final Theory: The Scientist's Search for the Ultimate Laws of Nature*, London: Random House.

# 2 The Tower of Babel, Pentecostal science and the language of epidemics

*David Waltner-Toews*

## The universe is a set of relationships

The universe is a set of relationships. These relationships are embodied in conversations – conversations within conversations within conversations. These are coded into languages. Some of these are modes of communication that we normally think of as language, and are apprehensible through our senses: animal sounds and biochemical transmissions might come to mind. Others are not directly perceptible, known only by their effects: gravity and atomic forces are the best examples here. Framed in this way, everything we think we know about ourselves and the universe, including this statement, is an emergent property of the observer and the observed, of the questions we ask, and the responses we receive. The overwhelming but uncertain evidence for this is everywhere around us. Every conversation changes the *conversants*: that is how the universe exists and unfolds. What we struggle with, as people, and, more specifically as scientifically trained scholars, is finding a language that can not only encompass the complex uncertainty, but enable us to engage in it more fully.

In the seventeenth century, Descartes and his disciples imagined not just a common, evidence-based understanding of the universe, but also a common Esperanto-like language to describe it. We would all be enlightened and liberated. We would become gods. Three hundred years later, with Louis Pasteur, Charles Darwin, Marie Curie, Bertrand Russell and Albert Einstein and the long list of all-encompassing natural philosophers and scientists, the dream almost seemed possible. But even as the final flourishes were being added to the parapets of this enlightened version of the Tower of Babel, there were signs of disintegration. Since the 1950s, scholars have survived by going their own ways, and hoping someone, somewhere, would put all the pieces together – a politician, perhaps, a Solomon wiser than all the academic scholars in the world, or more likely, a computer programmer, able to invade the hearts and minds of politicians, the circuits of nuclear facilities and the textings of teenagers, whatever our mother tongue. This, it seems to me, is utopian in the extreme. There are now more scholarly publications, each reflecting their own languages and dialects, than there are spoken languages, as we conventionally think of languages, on the planet (Anderson 2013; Ware and Maebe 2009).

Cartesian science has enabled us to describe, sometimes in exquisitely fine detail, the conversants, the objects, of the universe. Sometimes, however, we are like the Auditors in Terry Pratchett's novel, *Thief of Time* (Pratchett 2001). The Auditors, the ultimate Cartesian logicians, are flummoxed because, even after they have broken down great paintings into their constituent molecules, they are unable to understand why people respond to art with such deep feelings. What is it about the molecules that evokes these emotions?

To be fair, we have sometimes been able to at least describe the structure of some of the languages. Many of these languages have no obvious material correlates but nevertheless impact forcefully on the physical world, as all languages do, and are the basis of communication between all things, both living and non-living. They include gravity, strong and weak forces, genetic codes, whale songs, bird calls, hormonal and other chemical messages communicating between cells within bodies, and among plants, animals and bacteria in the outside environment. All those amazing things out there are talking to each other! We can describe how the wind moves the trees and the trees create their own air movements, how gravity pulls a rock from a cliff, and the rock changes the landscape on which it lands, how a virus infects the liver cell and the liver cell creates a disease. Other communications are more subtle, with complex outcomes. Two people hear invisible sound waves of music, drink wine and eat foods that have emerged from interactions between rays from the sun and molecules in plants. Under the influence of unseen chemical conversations, these people feel pleasure, and the pleasure stimulates behaviour that results in a baby – a baby who eats and drinks and changes the world in a million ways through how it interacts.

Largely, until very recently, we have ignored the nature of the conversations. Based on our rudimentary understanding of 'stuff', what we imagine to be material substances, we have bulldozed nature, waged war on bacteria, other people, and other species. Nevertheless, we have yet to imagine how we might engage in the conversation, even within our own species, other than in the most simplistic ways. We have learned to lecture each other, and nature, but do we know how to listen, to respond in creative ways, to respond again to the responses, to understand how we are changed even as we change that which is around us and defines us? What is the language that will enable us to converse in other than the most instinctual, trivial, brutal, bullying and dysfunctional ways?

My own conversations began with Friesian-Russian Mennonites then extended to the *Englische*, that is, people from those differently constructed cultures among whom I grew up – Icelanders, French, East European Jews, Metis, Cree, Irish, Scots and English. In 1967, when I left my Midwestern home, this conversation was expanded to include Persian, Indian and Japanese, later Indonesian and Spanish, and then, in my professional life, Chinese, Thai and Vietnamese. Each culture had its own way of communicating, both verbally and non-verbally, and each rooted in a different material history. As a veterinarian, I had to become more closely attuned to both verbal and non-verbal communications from a variety of non-human species. Beyond the body-language of everyday interactions and veterinary life, most of my conversations have been in English, or rudimentary bumblings in German, French, Spanish and Bahasa Indonesia. In each of these conversations, I have learned something, and have been changed.

Allow me for a moment to focus on one particular, peculiar, flow of ideas through Europe, what we might call science, and look at one manifestation that many people seem to be interested in – health. Indeed, Descartes himself argued that the reason we might wish to be 'the lords and possessors of nature' would be to achieve and preserve our health, which he called 'the first and fundamental blessing' of life (Descartes 1637).

Notions of health can of course go in all and any directions, depending on the species, the spatial and temporal scale, and so on. In our courses on eco-health, we usually have participants role-play different people (workers, mothers, CEOs) and different species (a pregnant moose, a fingerling fish, a boreal forest) and then define health from their point of view (VWB-VSF 2013; McCullagh *et al.* 2012). As a starting place for my narrative, I shall pretend that defining health can be confined to say, one species: people. When I asked my daughter, then a teenager, what health meant, she said that it meant that, when you got sick, you recovered more quickly than a person who wasn't healthy. The World Health Organisation (WHO) in its constitution, defined health as a state 'complete physical, mental and social well-being and not merely the absence of disease or infirmity', which sounds suspiciously like an orgasm, great while you have it, but hardly sustainable, at least without drugs. The great twentieth-century microbiologist René Dubos said it was a 'modus vivendi enabling imperfect [people] to achieve a rewarding and not too painful existence while they cope with an imperfect world' (Last 1988). To my pragmatic mind, my daughter, who is now a physician, and René Dubos had it about right. Again, let me argue – and everything I say is open to argument – that what I am calling health comes down to food, friends and freedom from disease.

## Food

Sometime in the late sixteenth or early seventeenth century, Henry IV of France is said to have confided to a friend that: 'If God keeps me, I will make sure that no peasant in my realm will lack the means to have a chicken in the pot on Sunday!'[1] A little later, Jonathan Swift wrote that 'Whoever could make two ears of corn, or two blades of grass, to grow upon a spot of ground where only one grew before, would deserve better of mankind, and do more essential service to his country, than the whole race of politicians put together' (Swift 1726, 122). King Henry and Jonathan Swift would be astounded at our successes which occurred, in large measure, because of Descartes's dream of divide, conquer and control. This success is both awe-inspiring and problematic.

We have done Henry IV one better than a chicken in every peasant's pot on Sunday. We have produced chickens to be had every day. Not only that, but we can produce 1.7 kg water-chilled chickens for KFC (formerly called Kentucky Fried Chicken but now registered simply as KFC) and 2.4 kg air-chilled chickens for Swiss Chalet. We have of course gone far beyond chickens. Most other commentators on this phenomenon define it in terms of tonnes of food produced, or economic value, but I think that excrement production is as good an integrative summary measure as any, reflecting as it does not just livestock and crop production, but also increases in human population. Every year, people, and the animals we have chosen to eat or live with, produce more than 14 billion tonnes of excrement (Waltner-Toews 2013). The largest increases in production have been in the last decades of the twentieth century and the early part of the twenty-first century. Much of this is concentrated in the Americas, Europe and East Asia. There are other great success stories, but many of them are subplots of this. Even the Swiftian bargain sale of two-plants-for-the-price-of-one is a sub-dream of Henry IV's chickens, since the multiplication of chickens cannot take place without the multiplication of crops to feed them.

Why do I call this success problematic? I shall come back to this later, but for now let me say that the changes in diet, culture, technology and the social-ecological entanglement within which we define ourselves have been massive, dramatic, surprising and unprecedented. We have gone from near-subsistence family farming and food processing to global agribusiness in less than a generation. This success in increased food production means that, particularly in the past century, but even more so in the past few decades, we have massively increased the breadth and depth of our ecological impacts, and have kept more people alive to reproductive age and fed them more chicken that ever before in history. We draw nutrients from cleared rainforests in the form of soybeans and water, ship them halfway around the world and poop them out into North American and European pastures. At the same time, notwithstanding the utopian dreams of biotechnologists, increases in global food production seem to be slowing even as demand increases. On top of this, few would dispute the fact that this food is not evenly shared among human populations.

The food conversation is no longer between a few self-satisfied Europeans, but ravages and veers across landscapes, cultures, species and time, changing our sense of ourselves as surely as the discovery of fire and the delights and problematic consequences of fireside sex.

## Freedom from disease

So, we can produce a lot of food – perhaps not as much as one might need for a healthy population of seven billion people, but how much we need is an unresolved argument, and one that, if I might be allowed a small pun, is fruitless to pursue. With regard to the second component of health – freedom from disease, at least infectious disease – we have also been remarkably successful. Since the 1800s, when industrialising countries began collecting statistics, we have witnessed substantial cascades in maternal mortality, infant mortality, typhoid, cholera, smallpox, measles – most of the major diseases and causes of death that were the scourge of our ancestors. For instance, between 1900 and 1960, in the United States, the incidence of typhoid fever plummeted from approximately 100 per 100,000 to less than 1 per 100,000. Smallpox, which maimed and killed tens of millions of people in the centuries prior to 1900, was declared eradicated from the planet by 1980. I could tabulate a litany of such diseases and their near-disappearance from countries where statistics are kept, but those are fairly typical (see Armstrong *et al.* 1999; United Nations 2012). This is not all about statistics, of course. As one of my epidemiological colleagues tells his students: we start with a pile of *deads*, and then try to explain them. In the long run, we hope for fewer of such piles. My son would not be alive today had there not been a scientifically trained surgeon skilled in removing his ruptured appendix, and antibiotics available to mop up the profligately invasive bacteria. And my wife would have been unlikely to have survived a serious car accident a decade earlier.

I need to add a caution to this rosy picture however. Shortly after William Stewart, the US Surgeon General declared, in 1967, that 'because infectious diseases have been largely controlled in the United States, we can now close the book on infectious diseases' he was proven wrong (Upshur 2008; Jones *et al.* 2008). Confusing the world with one's country is not peculiar to Americans, nor is a vague and superficial understanding of what might be meant by globalisation, travel, trade, ecological constraints and an insatiable appetite for chickens and bread, and the fact that most people in this packed planet live outside of North America and Europe. In truth, the success in managing infectious diseases was partial, limited in many instances to enclaves in Europe and North America. Our disease-control programmes were leaky and fragile.

By the 1990s, we were still grappling with endemic diseases such as malaria, tuberculosis and various types of parasitic sleeping sickness. In 2011, 8.7 million people contracted TB, and 1.4 million of them died. Another 8 million are infected with *Trypanosoma cruzi* (also called American Sleeping Sickness) about a third of whom develop serious cardiac problems and 10 per cent digestive and neurological problems. Malaria affects over 200 million people and kills over half a million every year. Anthrax, rabies, cysticerosis and other zoonoses affect tens of thousands every year (see Lancet Series on Zoonoses 2012; also Waltner-Toews 2007).

Human memory of devastating disease and death runs deep, and even slight stirrings by restless microbes awaken our concern. The diseases that awakened the concern of scientists in the 1990s were not so much those of global importance, but a group of other diseases that came to be called emerging infections, or EIDs. Since 2003 the WHO has reported just over 600 cases and just under 400 deaths from H5N1, which, like all influenzas, comes ultimately from birds. In 2013, a few dozen people died in China from H7N9. SARS (Severe Acute Respiratory Syndrome), which came from fruit bats and travelled through civets before jumping to people, killed about 10 per cent of the 8,000 known to be affected, which is substantial, before it disappeared, apparently, without a trace. But surely, whatever heart-wrenching personal tragedies these entail for individuals, these diseases are not, in a population of 7 billion people, Malthusian or Darwinian catastrophes. I fear, also, that we are failing to understand the meaning of these events, the complex messages from the natural world they represent, and that we see them purely in terms of public health.

In 1992, the Institute of Medicine in the United States, in what was considered a landmark report, examined EIDs, and identified the following causes: human demographics and behaviour; technology and industry; economic development and land use; international travel and commerce; microbial adaptation and change; breakdown of public health measures (Lederberg *et al.* 1992). They suggested better surveillance, vaccine and drug development, vector control (primarily through better pesticides) and human behavioural changes – for instance with regard to sexual relations and antibiotic use – as being appropriate responses. No mention here of reconsidering land use or working for more equitable economic development, health insurance or paid sick leave.

In 2012, a review of progress since the 1992 report noted that new diseases, such as SARS and H5N1 had emerged since that first report, but that the most important advances in 20 years in controlling EIDs were 'genomics-associated advances in microbial detection and treatment, improved disease surveillance, and greater awareness of EIDs and the complicated variables that underlie emergence' (Morens and Fauci 2012). In many ways, response to the AIDS epidemic typified the modern, scientific approach, with a mixture of new drug therapies and education programmes to try to alter sexual behaviour.

So, after 150 years of intensive scientific study of epidemics, what do we know? We can sequence with alarming quickness the genome of the organism causing the havoc. We can describe the curve of the epidemic, the way it rises to a peak and then drops, in terms of the probability of adequate contact between those harbouring the organism and those susceptible to its damage. Based on such a curve I can determine whether an outbreak is from a single source, or multiple, propagated or non-propagated, and, with a knowledge of clinical symptoms and signs, I could probably tell you which organisms were involved and how they were delivered. Every good epidemiologist has a sense of when the number of cases is about to peak, and that that is the time to intervene, as any intervention will reflect well on the intervener. We can also, usually after the fact, create complex mathematical models that seem to describe what happened. This is all fun stuff, but not earth-shatteringly brilliant.

While drugs and vaccines get all the press, and are important, the interventions that have had the greatest impacts historically in reducing the incidence of infectious diseases and improving public health are non-medical: the introduction of potable water into homes and hospitals, flush toilets, swamp clearance, improved nutrition (more chickens), air conditioners, chlorination, disposable equipment in hospitals, social and economic equity in social-welfare states, and rapid globalised responses by teams of experts. The pandemic of H1N1, for instance, the so-called swine flu, could have been at least slowed if everyone who worked on a pig farm had paid sick days and health insurance, so that they didn't carry their infections into and out of barns. But this was not raised publicly as a policy option. All we heard was vaccination, vaccination, and more vaccination – that is, Cartesian responses.

This brings us to the third aspect of health I wish to consider: friends.

## Friends

Friends are what have been lumped together under what are called 'social determinants of disease'. Although we tend to think of this in terms purely of people, one of my Ph.D. students demonstrated that, for older people living on their own, a pet dog could substitute for friends, and reduce medical costs in times of crisis (Raina *et al.* 1999). That is not an argument I wish to pursue just now, but it is worth keeping in mind.

While the triumph of Koch's postulates in medicine and the successful practical applications of the germ theory in the treatment of disease suggested that 'the germ was everything', the great success of the sanitary engineering movements of the late nineteenth and early twentieth centuries, which focused on water and sewage treatment, suggested a more complex reality. It is not just the *conversants* (bacteria, hosts, environments) that matter; it is the conversation, the communication among them, from which health and disease emerge.

In 1848, Rudolf Virchow, a medical pathologist, was sent by the Prussian government to investigate the causes of a typhus epidemic in Upper Silesia. After intensive investigation, he submitted a report that recommended a programme that included 'full employment, higher wages, the establishment of agricultural co-operatives, universal education and the disestablishment of the Catholic church' (Taylor and Regier 1984). Some might argue that the poor man was born before bacteria were discovered, and that we really didn't know anything about genetics and hadn't unmasked Joseph Stalin as a thug. Still, in 2008 WHO published a review of evidence related to the social determinants of health. The authors, no flaming revolutionaries, declared that 'Social injustice is killing people on a grand scale' and recommended that governments work to 'improve daily living conditions, including the circumstances in which people are born, grow, live, work and age'; and 'tackle the inequitable distribution of power, money and resources – the structural drivers of those conditions – globally, nationally and locally' (WHO 2008).

For anyone who has a social conscience, or who believes that, as Michael Ignatieff characterised it (1984), we have an obligation toward meeting the needs of strangers, it would seem to be a straightforward argument that those who have food and freedom from disease should, in an act of minimal friendship, now share the technologies that have brought us to this state of affairs. Our fellow human beings, our friends in the most generic sense, should benefit from the same kinds of infrastructure and food availability that have helped make industrialised countries, if not utopias, at least places where, as Dubos so aptly put it, imperfect people can achieve 'a rewarding and not too painful existence while they cope with an imperfect world'. Certainly this is the position taken by those who have been driving the so-called Tiger Economies of Asia.

I will not argue against this, as that is where my heart is, and as a Canadian I am hardly in a position to plead poverty on these matters, but, as I have earlier, I will suggest a few words of caution.

## Beyond success: the world talks back

Virchow would have been pleased to see the 1992 IOM report, but dismayed, I think, at how much of the progress in equity and living standards in the past century is in danger of crumbling away, in part because of the cumulative impact of 7 billion people demanding so much, dazzled by the dreams of twentieth-century techno-science and neoliberal fantasists, firm in our faith that bio- and other technologies will continue to give at least some of us a comfortable life. While the 7 billion greedy people are themselves the product of scientific success, the tower was never designed to carry so much weight. Still, if all it takes is large numbers of greedy people to bring down the scientific Tower of Babel, then it seems to me we need to ask some serious questions about the foundations, and the building materials.

One of the premises of the successful food, freedom and friends project is that we can talk to nature, and she will listen. One of the realisations of the past few decades is that nature talks back, and people seldom hear. Nature talks at all scales, from the molecular to the global and I shall only flag a few whisperings, in part because they are typical.

In Southeast Asia, the economic boom of the late 1980s and 1990s was associated with a dramatic shift in diet, particularly a greater demand for more chickens and pigs in more pots. Agriculturalists, having the technology and money, responded to the increased demand by pursuing the combination of economies of scale, animal intensification and mass distribution that were so successful in the West. Given the tsunami size and speed of the increases in demand, agriculturalists intensified their encroachment into new territories, and in epidemiological terms, increased probability of adequate contact between the natural hosts of influenza viruses – water birds – and people. One result among many was the emergence of H5N1, the so-called bird flu.

We can also zero in to more specific events. In the 1990s, Singapore, a clean and crowded city-state, offloaded its animal production to neighbouring countries. Malaysian farmers responded readily. Not only that, but they raised pigs in what we might consider an ecologically sound and humane way. They planted mango trees around the farms and designed the barns so that the pigs live both inside and outside. In the late 1990s, a serious El Niño event led to greater levels of drought in Southeast Asia than had been seen in previous years. In the meantime, Indonesian forestry companies and agriculturalists were clearing land using fire in the neighbouring island of Sumatra. The fires got out of hand, the smoke cover over wide areas easily visible from satellites. Fruit bats normally migrate around this region looking for food. Emerging from the fruitless smoky haze, they found the mango trees next to the pig farms. Fruit bats, we have discovered in retrospect, carry many interesting viruses – including those causing SARS, Ebola and what came to be called Nipah virus, named after a pig-rearing area in Malaysia. This virus causes neurological symptoms, and death, in pigs and people. Almost 300 people fell ill, and more than 100 died, before the good scientists in HAZMAT suits could figure out what was going on (Chua 2003).

Or we look at examples from industrialised countries. At the very time that we were getting the ravages of *Salmonella typhi* under control, non-typhoidal *Salmonellae* and other food-borne pathogens were exploding around the world, particularly in industrialised countries. These emerged in that massive fast-food dietary shift that characterised North American society after the Second World War. Once in the food system, many of these pathogens, most of which are of animal origin, have had a very easy time circulating and recirculating. We've designed the agri-food system that way. One might even argue that tens of millions of cases of foodborne illness every year are the necessary collateral damage of a system that puts a chicken in every pot not just every Sunday, but every day.

But I do not wish to go on *ad nauseum* about nausea and vomiting, diarrhoea and death. What I wish to ask here is: is the world trying to tell us something? That nothing occurs in isolation from anything else? That all that is exists because of complex conversations among species, excrement, climate, soil, bacteria and plants? Rather than listen, did we send her to the military academy of laboratory science, to make her behave the way we wanted her to, to bend her to do our will?

Now, just back from college, she has her revenge. We have trained millions of other species in the world to do battle with us and they have responded in kind to the weapons we have thrown at them, from guerrilla armies of resistant bacteria to global climate change, from deserts to floods, from emergent and re-emergent infections to a variety of chronic human ailments. The global burden of disease, more than ever, reflects the success of Cartesian science – massive increases in food production and manipulation of tastes to adapt to the most easily marketable and transportable foods, reduction in physical labour, less physical exertion to get anywhere, the fragmentation and individualisation of social life by economic policies based solely on competition.

Our primary medical responses – vaccination and antibiotics – that were designed as ways to mop up the last stragglers of disease, have now become our first defence. They were never designed for this. Without that social contract to equalise wealth, demystify political power and relocalise food and excrement production and distribution, and without these being embedded in a deeper, more complex conversation about human and biological ecology, the use of vaccines and antibiotics is quixotic, quite literally like defending oneself against a delirious elephant with a handful of needles.

## The conversation: arguing at the dinner table

So, how can we begin to reimagine our responses?

Like Virchow, I had my 'Upper Silesia' experience; mine was in Nepal, in the 1990s, and I have described the investigative work, its context and its conclusions elsewhere (Neudoerffer *et al.* 2008; Waltner-Toews *et al.* 2005). In brief, I went to study the parasite that causes cystic hydatidosis in people, and after gathering detailed scientific information over several years, from the DNA of the worm to human–animal relations, realised that all this knowledge changed nothing. As an epidemiologist, I had been taught that the purpose of my work was to make things better. I couldn't quite believe that my science was at fault, so, as a good scientist, I tried to replicate this work in Kiambu district outside Nairobi (studying agro-ecosystem health), at the Amazonian frontiers of Peru (studying the relationship between landscapes, nutrition and health), in Uganda (studying zoonotic sleeping sickness), and in Canada (studying the epidemiology of food-borne and water-borne disease, Lyme Disease, and West Nile Virus). All these studies led me to the same conclusion (Waltner-Toews *et al.* 2005). Based on what I had been trained to think of as good science, we could describe everything in great detail, but was anyone better off for this knowledge? We could resort to the bullying and bulldozer approaches used in the past by North American and European health advocates, which undermined one or another of things I held to be important, such as democracy, justice, self-determination and ecological sustainability. Or we could look for a way to work together with people wherever we lived, drawing on multiple voices and knowledges to inspire change rooted in an understanding of local ecology.

I began to ask different questions about science and human well-being. When one does not arrogate one's own perspective to the position of arbiter of all others, then questions of fact become entangled with questions of value. What is the value of food (social capital, nutrition, ecological connectedness, economic), of excrement (fertiliser, waste, public health hazard, energy source, territory marker), of a chicken (the perfect lean meat, the perfect bank for poor people, cock-fighting, competitive singing, public health hazard), of a dog or other companion animal (public health hazard, medical therapist, social companion, competitor for resources, source of meat), of wildlife (sources of inspiration, medicine, resilience, wonder, public health hazard). And it is not always easy to let go of one's prejudices and recognise them for what they are; chickens were first bred as fighting cocks, later as religious omens, and only recently as food. Why should a WHO directive, based on one perspective, trump all else?

And then, to the mix we add salmonellosis and heart disease, cholera and cancer, flush toilets, chronic water shortages, excrement, food security, energy, transportation, political power and economic equity. In my scholarship and practice, I had thought these to be separate issues, to be referred to different panels of experts. Suddenly they all came into view as aspects of the same reality, the same universe, my home. Everything was happening at once. Everything was a cacophonous conversation, like the supper table debates in my family of origin.

What to make of Bohr and Heisenberg and Schrödinger? Where in our universe to put Picasso, Stravinsky, James Joyce, Jorge Luis Borges, Pablo Neruda, Louis Armstrong, Bach, Scheherazade, and the burgeoning gap between our intellectual understanding of the world and our experience of it? How could a species which had survived millennia of evolutionary forces by learning from experience to anticipate opportunity and evade danger have such discordant, or at least disconnected, *knowledges* of who we are and which dangers to anticipate?

How do we begin the conversation about the many meanings of excrement, chickens, companion animals, wildlife and food? Who needs to be part of that conversation? What is our language? When science, Scheiße and conscience have the same Proto-Indo-European root referring to the separation of one thing from another, how can we even imagine integrative possibilities? The first step, it seems to me, is to acknowledge that the conversation is important, and to bring together as many people of goodwill, intelligence and imagination as possible.

For the questions I was asking, Silvio Funtowicz, Jerry Ravetz, James Kay and other colleagues championed a science that has come to be called post-normal (PNS) (Funtowicz and Ravetz 1993, 2008). For me PNS offered the hope that, collectively, we could pool our perceptions, that a new spirit would descend like Pentecostal fires upon people of goodwill everywhere, and that, in the face of radical uncertainty, we could define a new narrative that could somehow accommodate multiple perspectives, a story that would restrain the universal Schariar and save our collective necks for another generation or two, or at least, as for Scheherezade, another morning.

When we implemented this transdisciplinary ecosystem approach in Kathmandu, the communities were transformed, and it seemed, for a time at least, as if everything might be possible.

Apart from talking with street sweepers, butchers and politicians in Kathmandu, one of my favourite experiences in doing this new messy mix of science and practice was in Argentina. A group of us – physicians, anthropologists, epidemiologists, veterinarians, teachers, ecologists, naturalists, indigenous peoples – were fussing over the relationship between biodiversity and indigenous health. Our languages were not only disciplinary, but cultural, from British and American Englishes to Argentinian and Peruvian Spanishes, Brazilian Portuguese and a few indigenous languages. For physicians, this revolved around provision of toilets and clean water; for biologists, it had to do with counting and mapping species; for veterinarians, it somehow revolved around contact between wildlife, domestic animals and people. For indigenous people, it was a question of territory – the landscapes in which they lived. At one point, an indigenous leader suggested that their traditional way of dealing with those with whom they radically disagreed to this extent was to kill them. We paused a moment, but at the end of the five days, we were still talking, arguing, drawing pictures, poring over maps, singing, dancing, yelling at each other, crying, laughing, getting drunk, checking with our social networks on skype, making lists and organisational diagrams, and imagining what a research plan might look like. One of my take-away lessons from this process – besides how much fun it can be – is that finding the language does not resolve the issues of multiple perspectives. It may, indeed, accentuate them.

In *The Hitchhiker's Guide to the Galaxy,* Douglas Adams imagined what he called the Babel fish, a

> small, yellow, leech-like, and probably the oddest thing in the universe. It feeds on brain wave energy, absorbing all unconscious frequencies and then excreting telepathically a matrix formed from the conscious frequencies and nerve signals picked up from the speech centres of the brain, the practical upshot of which is that if you stick one in your ear, you can instantly understand anything said to you in any form of language: the speech you hear decodes the brain wave matrix.

Adams went further to conclude that 'the poor Babel fish, by effectively removing all barriers to communication between different races and cultures, has caused more and bloodier wars than anything else in the history of creation' (Adams 1979, 53).

Still, being able to engage in a real conversation across cultures and species is, it seems to me, a foundation on which to build a more realistically complex understanding of the universe than the more simplistic, already crumbling, Cartesian Tower of Babel, and provide a basis for negotiating our way into the future. In the end, a more nuanced sense of knowledge can be achieved if we think of it less like the output from an experiment or randomised clinical trial than the product of a collective clinical judgement, where all different kinds of disparate knowledge, including experience, contribute to the arguments around the scholarly dinner table, and go into making reasonable but tentative statements about how we might resolve problematic situations.

Karl Popper, whatever his philosophical flaws, argued that the generation of hypotheses about the nature of the world were acts of imagination. I think imagination is dramatically undervalued as a way of knowing the world. Imagination does more than provide hypotheses which may or may not be testable in some formal way; a uniquely human activity, imagination enables us to see the world differently, to imagine ourselves into different perspectives and minds, even, I would argue, giving us an inkling of how other species see the world.

* * *

Imagine this: we are having a beer,
you and I, out on the deck
overlooking the lake.
It is a pleasant afternoon.
We are being at one
with Nature.

At dusk, three buffleheads
swim past: two parents and a baby.
They duck their heads under water.
Do they speak? One could imagine:

*I am not sure it was such a good thing*
*to bring a hatchling into this world*
says the drake.
*Have you heard the news*
*from our cousins in Asia?*

*The wild geese are unhappy.*
They say: The people
are taking away our homes.
What do they want with our wetlands?
What do they want with our mosquitoes?

*They wondered:*
*What language does that human species understand?*
*Let us pick their closest friends, said the birds.*
*They sent a delegation of dogs.*
*to speak to the humans.*
*The dogs tried parasites and fleas.*
*The people shrugged and scratched.*
*The dogs made snarky, biting asides.*
*The people said, ah, rabies. That's a virus.*
*They shot the dogs. They made vaccines.*
*They co-opted the dogs, gave them couches to sleep on,*
*refined foods; the dogs trained people*
*to pick up their scraps. After that*
*lickety split, the dogs leapt into the human race.*
*Racing alongside humans, they said,*
*Let the birds figure it out for themselves.*

*Then came a delegation of chickens.*
*They are close to people, aren't they?*
*Salmonella and Campylobacter, said the chickens.*
*Diarrhoea and emesis.*
*We understand, the people said.*
*This is collateral damage of feeding people.*
*We have drugs and technology.*

*How about*
*H1N2, H7N9, H5N1?*
*Ah, the laboratory scientists said: this language is unstable*
*but we understand. We have DNA probes, RNA probes,*
*state-of-the-art laboratory equipment.*
*Soon we will have the answer.*

*The people begin to squabble.*
*The consumers say we want more chicken.*
*We want to pay less.*
*The farmers are impatient.*
*They are going bankrupt.*
*The market swings are driving them dizzy.*
*The wildlife biologists pore over a world of maps:*
*red and not red, flat one minute*
*and then, suddenly, round as a migratory bird flyway.*
*The public health workers cry danger danger danger!*
*The hunters cry shoot them shoot them!*

*People are running around like chickens*
*with their heads cut off.*

The buffleheads come up for air.
*That's just a story*, says the mother duck.
*It's what I heard,* says the drake. *Humans
don't know the grammar
of connection. They even ignore their closest
compatriots, the pigs.
They are scatterlings
and word scavengers.
Discombobulators.
They have not even heard the old saw:*

*for want of a tale the world was lost
for want of a world the tree was lost
for want of a tree the leaf was lost
for want of a leaf the bug was lost
for want of a bug the bird was lost.*

*It all comes back to bugs for you, doesn't it?
Well, we wouldn't be here without them.
But there is more. Listen.
for want of a bird the seed was lost
for want of a seed the ear was lost
for want of an ear the bread was lost
for want of a bread the man was lost
and all for the want of a tale.*

We have finished our beer.
We have enjoyed the splashes, gurgles,
and susurrations of the waves,
the breeze, the silence of Nature,
this respite from our daily labour.

The next morning we are playing golf.
The geese shit on the ninth green.
We curse. There was no need for that!

The deer and the mice and the ticks
look up when we curse. They watch us.
They have been playing Lyme.
*Borrelia burgdorferi*, they say.
*Anaplasma, Babesia, Rikettsia,
Come play with us.*

Why don't the deer go back
to where they came from?
we say, distracted. We are almost
at our perfect game.

The birds perch very still
in the trees.
They are twittering.
*West Nile, have you heard?*
*The crows are dying.*

*The frogs are dying.*
*Fungus and mites.*
*The bats are dying.*

The bees collapse: they are exhausted
from trying, again and again,
to tell us, to warn us.

The flying foxes
in their slinky fur stoles
lean over the piano:
*SARS*, they croon. *Hendra*
*Marburg, Nipah, Ebola.*
Surely we understand one of them,
we who are so educated.

*You have taken away our homes,*
they say. *We want*
*to live with you.*
*It is all about relationships,*
*you and us.*
They think they can seduce us.

Monday morning back at the lab.
we say, interesting language.
We have the tools to understand it.
We are doing science.
We are understanding Nature.
We check the genetic structure.
We can say every word.
See this genetic on-off switch?
We have the code.
We can explain everything.
We have no need to converse
with animals.

We plug our ears with vaccination
and new drugs, with traps and sprays,
poisons, new barns, irradiators,
and a song:

*This land was made*
*for you and me.*
Why don't the bats go home?
They are messing up
the neighbourhood. They don't understand
that we are improving Nature.
They don't understand
our rules.

They hang around outside our houses.
They pass over us at dusk.
They dive bomb,
dropping leaflets and care packages.
*We are here to bring you freedom!*
say the leaflets. They are written in a script
we cannot read.

*Oh shut up*, say the rats
the cockroaches, the raccoons.
*Let the people be.*
*We are all just fine.*

We kill the cockroaches, the raccoons,
the rats. *Oh where shall we go now?*
whisper the rat fleas. *Where, where?*
They sing a little ditty and kick up their heels.
*Plague, plague, we all fall down,*
they sing, they dance, they leap
and bite the nearest leg.

In this evolutionary moment,
between dreams and lucidity,
between pre-human and human,
can we imagine this? That we are the earth,
talking to ourselves, undiscombobulated?

That all science, all knowledge,
all doing worth doing comes to this, our task,
the task of being human:
to listen, to observe, to feel,
to converse with everything,
to read the lips of apes,
the gestures of bats and chickens, ducks and water,
fleas and termites, children, old people,
trees, flowers, air and earth,
to talk back, to chatter together,

to reflect, to celebrate
this amazing universe we are,
to sing a healing chorus,
a grand finale?

Ask not for whom the necks are wrung,
they're wrung for thee:
from every pot let freedom ring.

Listen: a choir in a million, million voices,
a beautiful and awesome and sad choir,
sex and genetics and poetry
and singing and the need for food
but not too much,
and water and stories,
so many stories, and chickens,
and dung, so much dung,
a gift for re-gifting if there ever was
one.

And our unfreedom, our boundedness
in which the many stories hark back to one,
a pre-story sung in multi-verses around a fire,
a story beginning and beginning again and beginning again
a tragedy and a celebration into whose warp and woof
(at this the dogs are cued to bark)
we are woven even as we ourselves
weave homeward,
arm in arm, at dusk

singing: all that is, we are, we shall become:
hallelujah, hallelujah,
universe without end.

## Acknowledgements

Parts of this essay (the poetry-like parts, titled The Task of Being Human) were included in my response to receiving the Inaugural Award for Contributions to Ecohealth from the International Association for Ecology and Health, in London, in 2010, and published online at: http://www.ecohealth.net/pdf/WaltnerToews_2010_The%20Task%20of%20Being%20Human.pdf.

## Note

1  Cited in http://en.wikipedia.org/wiki/Henry_IV_of_France, accessed Feb. 2014.

# References

Adams, D. 1979. *Hitchhikers Guide to the Galaxy,* London: Pan Books.

Anderson, S. 2013. How many languages are there in the world? *Linguistic Society of America* (http://www.linguisticsociety.org/content/how-many-languages-are-there-world) accessed July 2013.

Armstrong, G.L., Conn, L.A., and Pinner, R.W. 1999. Trends in infectious disease mortality in the United States during the 20th century, *JAMA,* 281: 61–6.

Chua, K.B. 2003. Nipah virus outbreak in Malaysia, *Journal of Clinical Virology,* 3: 265–75.

Descartes, R. 1637. *Discourse on Method,* The Harvard Classics, 34/6, New York: P.F. Collier & Son, 1909–14; Bartleby 2001 (http://www.bartleby.com/34/1/) accessed Feb. 2014.

Funtowicz, S.O., and Ravetz, J.R. 1993. Science for the post-normal age, *Futures,* 25(7): 739–55.

Funtowicz, S.O., and Ravetz, J.R. 2008. Beyond complex systems: Emergent complexity and social solidarity, in D. Waltner-Toews, J. Kay, and N.M. Lister (eds), *The Ecosystem Approach: Complexity, Uncertainty, and Managing for Sustainability*, New York: Columbia University Press, pp. 309–22.

Ignatieff, M. 1984. *The Needs of Strangers*, New York: Penguin Books.

Jones, K.E., Patel, N.G., Levy, M.A., Storeygard, A., Balk, D., Gittleman, J.L. and Daszak, P. 2008. Global trends in emerging infectious diseases, *Nature,* 451: 990–3.

Lancet Series on Zoonoses. 2012. (http://www.thelancet.com/series/zoonoses) accessed Feb. 2014.

Last, J. 1988. *A Dictionary of Epidemiology,* Oxford: Oxford University Press.

Lederberg, J., Shope, R.E., and Oaks, S.C., eds. 1992. *Emerging Infections: Microbial Threats to Health in the United States,* Washington, DC: Institute of Medicine National Academy Press.

McCullagh, S., *et al.*, eds. 2012. *Ecosystem Approaches to Health Teaching Manual: Canadian Community of Practice in Ecosystem Approaches to Health* (http://www.copeh-canada.org) accessed Aug. 2014.

Morens, D.M., and Fauci, A.S. 2012. Emerging infectious diseases in 2012: 20 years after the Institute of Medicine report, *mBio,* 3(6): 1–4.

Neudoerffer, N., Waltner-Toews, D., and Kay, J.J. 2008. Return to Kathmandu: A post hoc application of AMESH, in D. Waltner-Toews, J. Kay and N.M. Lister (eds), *The Ecosystem Approach: Complexity, Uncertainty, and Managing for Sustainability*, New York: Columbia University Press, pp. 257–87.

Pratchett, T. 2001. *Thief of Time,* London: Transworld Publishers.

Raina, P., Waltner-Toews, D., Bonnett, B., Woodward, W., and Abernathy, T. 1999. Influence of companion animals on the physical and psychological health of older people: An analysis of 1-year longitudinal study. *Journal of American Geriatric Society,* 47: 323–9.

Swift, J. 1726. *A Voyage to Brobdingnag, Gullivers Travels,* New York: Penguin Books, 2010.

Taylor, R., and Regier, A. 1984. Rudolf Virchow on the typhus epidemic in Upper Silesia: An introduction and translation, *Sociology of Health and Illness,* 6(2): 201–17.

United Nations Department of Economic and Social Affairs, Population Division. 2012. *Changing Levels and Trends in Mortality: The Role of Patterns of Death by Cause,* ST/ESA/SER.A/318, New York: United Nations.

Upshur, R. 2008. Ethic and infectious disease. *Bulletin of the World Health Organization,* 86(8) (http://www.who.int/bulletin/volumes/86/8/08-056242/en/#) accessed Aug. 2014.

VWB-VSF. 2013. *Ecohealth Trainer Manual* (https://www.vetswithoutborders.ca/ecohealth-training-manual) accessed Feb. 2014.

Waltner-Toews, D. 2007. *The Chickens Fight Back: Pandemic Panics and Deadly Diseases that Jump from Animals to Humans,* Vancouver: Greystone.

Waltner-Toews, D. 2013. *The Origin of Feces: What Excrement Tells us about Evolution, Ecology and a Sustainable Society,* Toronto: ECW.

Waltner-Toews, D., Neudeorffer, C., Joshi, D.D., and Tamang, M.S. 2005. Agro-urban ecosystem health assessment in Kathmandu, Nepal: Epidemiology, systems, narratives, *Ecohealth,* 2: 1–11.

Ware, M., and Maebe, M. 2009. *The STM Report: An Overview of Scientific and Scholarly Journal Publishing,* Oxford: International Association of Scientific, Technical and Medical Publishers (http://www.stmassoc.org/2009_10_13_MWC_STM_Report.pdf) accessed Aug. 2014.

WHO. 2008. *Commission on Social Determinants of Health – Final Report* (http://www.who.int/social_determinants/thecommission/finalreport/en/index.html) accessed Feb. 2014.

# 3 Love life or fear death?

## Cartesian dreams and awakenings

*Edvin Schei and Roger Strand*

### René Descartes's dream of medicine

> For the rest, I don't want to speak here in detail about the further progress I
> hope to make in the sciences, or to make any public promise that I am not sure
> of keeping. I will say only that I have resolved to devote my remaining years
> purely to trying to acquire knowledge of Nature from which can be derived
> rules in medicine that are more reliable than those we have had up till now.
>
> (Descartes 1637/2007, part 6)

In an effort to describe, criticise and go beyond Cartesian dreams, hardly any
subject matter can be more central than human health and hopes for medical
progress.[1] This chapter's introductory quotation is no arbitrary passage from
Descartes's masterpiece *Discourse on Method:* it is how he began the final
paragraph. Indeed, according to Shapin (2000), Descartes's contemporaries held
expectations so high of Descartes's medical research that his death in 1650, at the
age of 53, was received with shock and scandal. From Descartes's correspondence
there is ample evidence of the importance he gave to human health and medicine,
not only from a theoretical perspective but also in his extensive efforts to give
medical advice to friends and correspondents (Shapin 2000).

Below, we shall turn to Descartes's awakening and acute awareness of the
complexities of human health, psyche and soma, an awareness that made René
the practitioner appear quite different from the stereotypical Cartesian rationalist.
First, however, we will need to draw a clear image of the Cartesian dream of
medicine, not least because of the extraordinary importance this dream has in
medical research, health policy and to some extent medical practice, in particular
in the twentieth and into the twenty-first century. Again, Descartes's *Discourse*
offers a clear statement:

> I acquired some general notions in physics and realised, as I began to test them
> in various special problems, how far-reaching they were and how different
> from the principles used up to now; and as soon as I saw that I thought I
> couldn't keep them to myself without offending gravely against the law that
> requires us to do all we can for the general welfare of mankind. For they –

these scientific notions of mine – showed me that we can get knowledge that would be very useful in life, and that in place of the speculative philosophy taught in the schools we might find a practical philosophy through which knowing the power and the actions of fire, water, air, the stars, the heavens and all the other bodies in our environment as clearly as we know the various crafts of our artisans, we could (like artisans) put these bodies to use in all the appropriate ways, and thus make ourselves the masters and (as it were) owners of Nature.

This is desirable not only for the invention of innumerable devices that would give us trouble-free use of the fruits of the earth and all the goods we find there, but also, and most importantly, for the preservation of health, which is certainly the chief good and the basis for all the other goods in this life. For even the mind depends so much on the state of the bodily organs that if there is to be found a means of making men in general wiser and cleverer than they have been so far, I believe we should look for it in medicine.

It is true that medicine as currently practised doesn't contain much of any significant use; but without wanting to put it down I'm sure that everyone, even its own practitioners, would admit that all we know in medicine is almost nothing compared with what remains to be known, and that we might free ourselves from countless diseases of body and of mind, and perhaps even from the infirmity of old age, if we knew enough about their causes and about all the remedies that Nature has provided for us.

(Descartes 1637/2007, part 6)

Natural science, physics and mathematics provide the principles – the scientific method and the laws of Nature – that medicine must be built upon. Only then can medicine become true science; and the prospects are tremendous. Shapin explains how Descartes's followers believed that health, old age and even immortality could be within reach through the rapid development and application of a complete and infallible system of medical knowledge (Shapin 2000). It was in this sense Descartes's death was such a shock: *he*, the one who was going to lead humanity into eternal life on Earth, was proven fatally helpless.

## Biomedicine as a Cartesian project

In the centuries following Descartes's death, the Cartesian dream of a scientific medicine based on physics and mathematics was to remain exactly that: a remote dream and a theoretical idea. Medical practice continued in the Hippocratic tradition of bloodletting, enemas, diets and astrology, often more harmful than beneficial. Towards the end of the eighteenth century, and spurred by the changes following the French Revolution, the foundations of modern *biomedicine* gradually emerged and coalesced into an apparently harmonious synthesis of therapeutics and research practices of increasing practical utility, but bearing little resemblance to the exact sciences. Anatomy had the highest standing among the medical disciplines. It had made great advances with the work of Andreas

Vesalius (1514–64) and William Harvey's utterly surprising discovery in 1616 that blood circulated in the body. Anatomy developed further as dissection gradually became legal and standard practice. The establishment of large modern hospitals in France towards the end of the eighteenth century led to the *birth of the clinic* (Foucault 1975), as signs and symptoms of large numbers of patients were systematically recorded and categorised in emerging processes of knowledge production that would become clinical medicine. The combination of meticulous descriptions of signs of disease in living patients, with anatomical post-mortem investigation – pathological anatomy – proved a strong scientific tool. By linking symptoms and signs of sick people to material changes in their bodies, a thoroughly mechanistic worldview took hold of medicine. And by the mid-1800s, physiology, microbiology and organic chemistry had matured and provided additional theoretical and practical building blocks to the foundations of the biomedicine we know.

To the extent that students of medicine are taught medical history at all, we fear that they mostly are left with the triumphant stories of how science marched ahead towards victory – a science that was one, unique and unified, gathered to combat the evil forces of ignorance, superstition and quackery. In reality, then as now, scientists – to use a profoundly idiosyncratic notion – were often more engaged in fights with each other. The irreconcilability at the beginning of the nineteenth century between rationalist pathology, believing in deep causes of diseases, and a positivist clinical medicine satisfied with symptoms and signs, was well described by Foucault (1975). Half a century later, scientific civil wars raged between physiologists such as Claude Bernard and microbiologists such as Louis Pasteur over the nature of the causes of disease: imbalance in the body itself or attack by germs. Interestingly, Bernard, a founding father of modern physiology, also heavily criticised epidemiology and the use of statistics in medicine. For Bernard, the complexity of each living organism with its myriad subtle chemical and physiological *equilibria* meant that any science based on averages across individuals would produce nothing but nonsense (Bernard 1865/1957).

A recurrent theme in the history of medicine, as in other branches of intellectual history, is how dogmatism, prejudice and arrogance join forces to obstruct progress. One example is the use of the microscope, which eventually paved the way for the revolutionary discoveries of cells and bacteria in the last half of the nineteenth century. By then, functional microscopes had existed for 300 years, but medicine simply couldn't see that they might be useful for physicians. Anton van Leeuwenhoek of Holland (1632–1723) described bacteria, yeast plants and the circulation of blood corpuscles in capillaries, and published his findings in over a hundred letters to the Royal Society of England and the French Academy. To no avail. The most famous example of authority trumping science is the story of Ignaz Semmelweiss, who discovered that medical students spread lethal infections from recently examined corpses to birthing women, and that this could be prevented by hand-washing. Despite overwhelming numerical proof, his theory was rejected, on the grounds that it did not fit with what *everybody* knew to be true (Wootton 2007).

Semmelweiss ended his days in a Hungarian psychiatric hospital. As time passed, the tensions and contradictions were explained away, faded out of memory and became replaced by the orthodoxy of *biomedicine,* a fascinating scientific conglomerate, the constituents of which appear to its adherents as a consistent whole. Indeed, it is a paradigm with certain consolidated features. Perhaps its single most important feature is that of the existence and primacy of *diseases:* a sick person is a patient who suffers from one or more diseases. A disease is something that objectively exists and which the patient *has.* Patients differ in many respects, and accordingly, the manifestations of a disease in the clinic also vary. Still, the disease itself can be characterised with precision and constitutes in this way the proper object of science. The disease is a universal essence, a material (chemical, physiological and anatomical) mechanism that can be established in the laboratory and verified in large patient groups. Diabetes mellitus *is* that the blood sugar is too high because there is too little insulin production in the pancreas or because the cells of the body do not respond properly to insulin. Leprosy *is* an infection of *Mycobacterium leprae.* The universe of disease is orderly and therefore in principle predictable and curable. In the words of Claude Bernard:

> Absolute determinism exists indeed in every vital phenomenon; hence biological science exists also; and consequently the studies to which we are devoting ourselves will not all be useless. General physiology is the basic biological science toward which all others converge. ... By normal activity of its organic units, life exhibits a state of health; by abnormal manifestation of the same units, diseases are characterised; and finally through the organic environment modified by means of certain toxic or medicinal substances, therapeutics enables us to act on the organic units.
>
> (Bernard 1865/1957, p. 65)

Later, genetics, biochemistry and molecular biology blended into what became our contemporary paradigm of biomedicine, in which diseases are to be uniquely characterised, understood and cured in terms of genetic information and molecular mechanisms. The philosophically inclined will be – and indeed are – puzzled about the lack of theoretical rigour in the scientific foundations of biomedicine. Are universal diseases a matter of physical truth or metaphysical assumption? What is the relationship between the subjective experience of bad health (*illness*) and the postulated objective disease? What exactly is the observed variability among individual sick persons, how is it to be understood, and when and why is it irrelevant to the nature and existence of the disease? How can one understand the relationship between mind and body in the biomedical paradigm?

To ask such questions, however, is to distance oneself from the paradigm. To the extent that one receives explicit answers, they will typically come with contradiction. One set of answers would be: *Don't think so much. Philosophical foundation is not important. The proof of the pudding lies in the eating, and what matters is that biomedicine works so well.*

It is indeed true that public health improved in many countries in the nineteenth and twentieth centuries, in parallel with scientific, technological and biomedical progress. Exactly how much of the improvements can be ascribed to biomedicine remains a controversial issue (Le Fanu 1999). According to those who support and fund biomedicine, a lot has been achieved. Others will emphasise the much larger health contributions from better hygiene, food and housing – though biomedical logic decidedly has made its contributions to those developments too. Others will point to the popularity – large and apparently increasing – of alternative health practitioners across the spectrum, from healing to acupuncture, from religious rituals to the most creative unconventional technical devices. At that point, however, defenders of biomedical orthodoxy may change their rhetoric: it is *not* just the eating of the pudding. They would argue that *alternative medicine* only *apparently* works because sick people usually get well regardless of the treatment, and many patients fall victim to the placebo effect. There is no solid evidence that it *really* works. And since complementary medicine is not rooted in research, and does not have a coherent set of scientific theories, it holds (according to this orthodoxy) a false image of the real world and is therefore unscientific and not medicine.

Any prohibition of quackery is ultimately founded upon that type of argument. After the Second World War, however, the war on quackery also turned inwards against biomedical practices in an attempt to contain the increasingly expensive public health services. The pioneer was the UK doctor Archie Cochrane who returned from German war prison utterly disillusioned with the medical profession of his day. Cochrane was a prisoner of war but also the only doctor in the concentration camp, and so the Nazis called upon his services to treat the other prisoners. There he could confirm with his own eyes what the Nazis told him – that 'Ärtzte sind überflüssige' (doctors are superfluous) – the health of the prisoners of war that Cochrane observed remained surprisingly good despite an almost total lack of medical attention and remedies. Back in the UK, he attempted to rationalise the National Health Service by a strategy that was basically Cartesian: he subjected the dominant clinical and therapeutic dogma to methodical doubt in order to exclude practices that lacked solid evidence of effectiveness and efficiency (Cochrane 1972). This developed into evidence-based medicine, a movement which gradually colonised other subfields of public health and even other sectors of society, leading to buzzwords like evidence-based practice, evidence-based psychology, nursing, policy and even evidence-based pastoral care. Thus, an approach that originated as a rational attempt to see what really works in medicine has acquired an authoritarian dominance, and is increasingly seen as the only reasonable way to establish whether things work, thus constricting the criteria for developing and testing new approaches. This was highlighted by the *British Medical Journal* in a paper pointing out that 'the effectiveness of parachutes in reducing the risk of injury after gravitational challenge has not been proved with randomised controlled trials' (Smith and Pell 2003).

The Cartesian dream of medicine is in this sense something more important and pervasive than a hope for good health. It led to a comprehensive programme of discredit and exclusion of all other paradigms for understanding health, all other health practices than those rendered orthodox by the biomedical establishment, and ultimately all other forms of decision-making in modern society. While Montaigne and the Renaissance thinkers a century before Descartes celebrated plurality, polyphony and tolerance (Toulmin 2001), the Cartesian dream in the medical field developed into a programme of orthodoxy, intolerance and dominance.

## Corporeal and mental substance

Possibly the greatest intellectual achievement by Galileo Galilei as a founding father of modern science was his use of the distinction between the knowing subject and the known object, and the distinction between primary and secondary qualities. Primary qualities such as the extension, mass, position, velocity and acceleration of particles had, according to Galileo, objective existence, independent of human perception, and as such they were the proper objects of exact science. Secondary qualities, on the other hand, were clearly not independent of the human observer and as such they could be left aside as mere subjective appearance:

> a piece of paper or a feather, when gently rubbed over any part of our body whatsoever, will in itself act everywhere in an identical way; it will, namely, move and contact. But we, should we be touched between the eyes, on the tip of the nose, or under the nostrils, will feel an almost intolerable titillation – while if touched in other places, we will scarcely feel anything at all. Now this titillation is completely ours and not the feather's, so that if the living, sensing body were removed, nothing would remain of the titillation but an empty name. And I believe that many other qualities, such as taste, odour, colour, and so on, often predicated of natural bodies, have a similar and no greater existence than this.
>
> (Galilei 1623, translation by Danto 1954, p. 719–20)

While it sufficed for Galileo to carve out a proper domain for physics as an exact science, Descartes's ambitions were higher, they were 'Dreams of Certainty and Method', aimed at covering everything in existence. Indeed, the subject of medicine is human life, suffering and death, not the motion of solids in space. He opted for three distinct types of substance: God, *res extensa* or corporeal substance, and *res cogitans* or mental substance; to the extent that the idea of God appears irrelevant or insignificant, his philosophy is one of mind–body dualism. In Descartes's thinking, the mental substance – the mind – is not *just* an epiphenomenon of the brain (whatever that is supposed to mean) but has its separate existence outside of the material universe. Still, it interacts with the body. The mind is influenced by the emotions of the body (sic!) but has its own power of volition that also is translated into action of the body.

A major difficulty of any such dualist philosophy is to account for the interaction between body and mind. How can it take place? Descartes's answer is well-known to students of philosophy: rather than giving a satisfactory explanation of the possibility of interaction he postulated a place for it. Mind and body somehow interact in the pineal gland. This is not to say that the interaction was unimportant to Descartes. On the contrary, the relationship between mind and body is a central motif both in his theoretical and practical interest in health and medicine (Shapin 2000). For instance, he discusses how self-fulfilling prophecies may harm or benefit one's health, and repeatedly advises his friends to 'cheer up: avoid thinking about things that make you distressed; dwell on pleasant objects and memories; look on the bright side of life' (Shapin 2000). For Descartes, this is not just to disregard illness, it is to cure oneself. One's volitional powers can be used to influence the passions, which again have their effect on the entire body.

In this way, Descartes, the health adviser, had much in common with ordinary common sense, folk medicine, quacks and other enemies of the early proponents of modern medicine. Indeed, modern medicine was constructed by a Galilean type of effort. An object of quantitative science was created by turning the medical researcher into an observer and experimenter, and by excluding secondary qualities such as the bodily and subjective perceptions of the patients. In order to become science, medicine had to redirect its gaze from the patient's lived experience to the realm of *unquestionable facts*. It recorded the objective signs professionally and with increasing sophistication and detail, and stopped listening to the unreliable and idiosyncratic chitter-chatter of patients.

Just as objective Nature was reduced by Galileo to a colourless, odourless matter in motion inside a three-dimensional Euclidean space, early modern medicine constructed an objective universe of disease: sign, pathology, mechanism. Had objectivist strands of psychology been developed at the time – such as the psychophysics at the end of the nineteenth century or the behaviourism of the twentieth century – they might have been included into the construct. As a matter of fact they did not and biomedicine largely remained a science of corporeal substance. Psychiatry did of course develop, but was mainly trapped on one or the other of the two sides of mind–body dualism: either as a *soft* practice of lofty speculation and introspection, or as a reductionist, *hard* science where mental illness was explained and treated in terms of physiological and biochemical pathology.

## Waking up from the Cartesian dream

Scientific medicine has led to obvious benefits, but certain common, complex and costly conditions actualise the need for theoretical development. The Western medical system is faced with a series of increasingly complex challenges and unresolved problems, the roots of which are under suspicion of emanating from the bold dreams of a purely materialist medicine. The difficulties are particularly poignant in the field of primary medicine, where people present to their doctors the undefined symptoms and unsorted fears, pains and miseries of their daily lives. In Norway, the home country of the authors of this chapter, 70 per cent of the population see their GP at least once every year. From the vast field of clinical medicine the following themes emerge:

- Steep social gradients in health and longevity are usually explained by individual risk factors and lifestyle differences, rather than being seen as the outcome of societal conditions such as poverty and dominance (Marmot 2006; Farmer 2005).
- Multimorbidity and comorbidity: patients with symptoms and loss of function involving many different organs are classified as having a series of distinct *diseases*, each with its own set of 'causes'. Medicine lacks a way of seeing persons as wholes (Barnett *et al.* 2012).
- Medically unexplained symptoms (MUS): this is a heterogeneous group of symptoms and illnesses that include chronic pain conditions, irritable bowel syndrome, chronic fatigue syndrome and many others, grouped as *functional diseases* or *somatisation* (Eriksen *et al.* 2013b, 2013a). The root causes of MUS are poorly understood. However, as they are defined by their very *scientific inexplicability*, they seem to highlight the shortcomings in parts-oriented conceptualisations and explanations of patients and health problems (Ulvestad 2008; Eriksen *et al.* 2013a, 2013b; McWhinney and Freeman 2009). Emerging evidence suggests that many common chronic conditions which typically cluster and often include MUS, might be triggered by pathogenic life circumstances, sometimes referred to as 'the causes of the causes' (Tomasdottir *et al.* 2014; Parekh and Barton 2010).
- The so-called risk epidemic: this is the increased if not exaggerated focus on 'medical risks' in medical literature, culture and practice (Skolbekken 1995). The number of so-called risk factors for future disease, based on a fragmented view of the body, increases rapidly and diverts medical resources from the sick to the well on an uncontrollable scale. An example: treating just the two risk factors of high blood pressure and cholesterol according to the European guidelines on cardiovascular disease prevention in clinical practice, would define 76 per cent of Norwegian individuals aged 20–79 as having an *unfavourable* cardiovascular disease risk profile and needing medical attention. Treating these two risk factors according to the guidelines would need a larger number of GPs than the total number of doctors who currently serve all primary care needs of this population – which is affluent as well as long-lived and healthy, by international comparison (Petursson *et al.* 2009; Skolbekken 1995).
- Poly-pharmacy: drugs tested and intended for single-disease use accumulate in patients with multiple health problems, resulting in unforeseen effects and high risk of harm. Adverse drug effects is ranked among the 10 most important causes of death in the world (Pirmohamed *et al.* 2004; Gøtzsche 2013).
- Overdiagnosis and overtreatment: estimates suggest that more than US$200 billion may be wasted each year on useless treatment in the United States alone (Berwick and Hackbarth 2012). Overdiagnosis occurs when people without symptoms are diagnosed with a disease that ultimately will not cause them to experience symptoms or early death. More broadly defined, it includes the related problems of overmedicalisation and overtreatment, diagnosis creep, shifting thresholds, and disease mongering, all processes that reclassify healthy people with mild problems as sick (Moynihan *et al.* 2012).

Exactly why such health problems now receive more attention – due attention in our opinion – remains unclear. For instance, in the case of MUS, one could speculate that they are on the rise because society and culture have become harsher, more competitive, more consumerist, less inclusive, more individualist and egocentric, and so on. It is not obvious, however, that the prevalence and severity of such suffering have increased. Perhaps the attention is rather due to the absence of other and more dramatic somatic diseases (say, tuberculosis, leprosy, poliomyelitis). To our knowledge, there is little convincing research yet to clarify such issues. In any case the changed panorama in health statistics as well as in the general practitioners' waiting rooms call for changes also in medical knowledge.

## Human reality and the blind spot of scientific medicine

Physicians, and primary care physicians above all, work under a demand to take care of their patients not only as a sum of biological parts and functions, but as individuals who need to be seen as *me*, and whose lives in illness and health hinge on complex patterns of cultural and highly idiosyncratic meaning (Cassell 2004). Exactly how doctors should bridge this gap between the *res extensa* of science and the *res cogitans* of patients seems to be unsolvable with the intellectual equipment in the medical toolbox. Medical ontology downplays the contexts, relations and complexity of the wholes called *persons*, and continues to believe that true causality inheres in small things like molecules, especially genetic molecules. Human agency, function, intentionality and purpose are denied as having causal functions, thus rendering human existence in principle incomprehensible, within a deterministic framework of ticking molecules (Cassell 2012).

Medical ontology and epistemology on the one hand, and human life as it presents itself to doctors, on the other, open a wide gap between *the two cultures* of the humanities and the natural sciences in every clinical encounter. This gap is bridged more or less haphazardly by physicians who improvise as best they can, applying non-professional rules of thumb and strategies from their private lives, or who simply disregard the gap and its consequences, while believing that they are working in an evidence-based *scientific discipline*. The consequences can be traced in empirical studies of doctor–patient encounters, which show again and again that physicians strip away the personal and existential aspects of illness and suffering, focusing strictly on technical aspects, as when ordering new blood tests from a dying patient instead of attending to the reality of what is happening (Agledahl *et al.* 2010; Barry *et al.* 2001; Tuckett *et al.* 1985). The stance of doctors has aptly been termed 'courteous but not curious' (Agledahl *et al.* 2011). Medicine's biological realism entails that social, cultural and political sources of health and illness tend to be downplayed as well, leaving the individual with a responsibility for being who he is, as an island to himself (Schei and Cassell, 2012).

Already in 1973, Susser distinguished between *disease, illness* and *sickness*. Whereas disease is the *objectively* defined pathology, illness is defined in terms of the patient's subjective sense of feeling unwell, and sickness refers to the social and cultural perceptions and understandings of the health condition. For the scientific pioneers in the nineteenth century this distinction was not always so relevant. In the case of diabetes mellitus or tuberculosis, for instance, the relationship between disease, illness and sickness may be quite simple (at least in theory). In particular with MUS, the risk epidemic, overdiagnosis and overtreatment, the relationships between disease, illness and sickness are anything but simple and unique, and it is under constant renegotiation both on the level of society and the individual patient to find out what *really* is the matter with him and particularly with her.

GPs may observe how patients' problems consist of how aspects of illness, sickness and perhaps disease blend into each other in a complex, unsound feedback pattern, but they lack scientific knowledge on complexity. The complex is invisible, except as *mess*, when wearing the glasses of *smallism* and reductionist science. Humanistic medicine acknowledges the complexity, but has a limited set of tools to offer – in part because it is underdeveloped and in part because there might be no tool and no technical fix for the problem.

## Return to Descartes

> So instead of finding ways to preserve life, I have found another, much easier and surer way, which is not to fear death. But this does not depress me, as it commonly depresses those whose wisdom is drawn entirely from the teaching of others, and rest on foundations only of human prudence and authority.
>
> (Descartes 1637/2007)

An easy but unsatisfactory conclusion to a reflection upon the Cartesian dream of medicine is the nostalgic one: get rid of the dominance of reductionist medicine, *smallism* and rigid evidence-based practice and work for the flourishing of a humanistic medicine within a non-dualist ontology of persons. In Toulmin's words, that could be presented as a rejection of a stale concept of rationality and a *return to reason*.

There are at least two reasons why the nostalgic solution is unsatisfactory. They are both concerned with complexity. First, human suffering and death, like all human phenomena, are complex and call for many approaches. Reductionist medicine, *smallism* and evidence-based practice are valuable approaches that will stay with us. Indeed, scientific medicine is also cultural knowledge and as such part of our current human condition. We, the authors, do believe in the potential of making humanistic medicine stronger and more useful, but this will have to take place in a dialectic of not only opposition but also learning and synergy with scientific medicine (Cassell 2012). Part of the conflictive area will be the hidden normative implications of modern medicine: When all threats to health are seen as disease (or risk of disease), and disease is deviation from the normal, then all suffering and death is abnormal, undesirable and something to fight against. Humanistic medicine will have to be one of the counter-voices against this implicit belief. To the extent that death neither can nor should be abolished from the human condition, we must learn to live good lives while acknowledging that we are vulnerable and mortal, that we are not in control and will never be.

This point, however, leads us straight back to the human being René Descartes who himself was a complex person and not identical to Descartes-the-philosophical-position that countless students have had to reproduce for their philosophy exams. Descartes himself combined dream and reality: he dreamt of a scientific utopia, an ideal that gave direction to his scientific and philosophical efforts. At the same time, he was awake and fully aware of the human condition and what it demanded: learn to love life and not fear death. This was not to surrender, but a programme for how to enjoy life and *thereby* improve one's health.

Is Descartes's statement a programme for a humanistic medicine? At least it is a reminder that a disregard for the messy lived life of persons is at odds with the core task of doctors since Hippocrates, which is to strengthen and restore the well-being of those persons, while accepting that suffering and death will never go away. Scientific knowledge of biology, epidemiology and *disease* is a tool in this endeavour; it is not the goal. Caring for the well-being of individual sick persons calls for a doctor whose role is more than a scientist's: the doctor has to accept a co-responsibility for how the person, vulnerable and mortal, can live a life that he can love. Indeed, this was how Descartes practised as a health adviser. What our last quotation provided by Descartes himself also shows is the danger of being led astray by blinding authority. Love of life stems from a secure sense of judgement grounded in personal experience, in contrast to 'those whose wisdom is drawn entirely from the teaching of others'. Remarkably, it is Descartes himself who has a lesson for the overly optimistic adherents of technicist medicine within a simple world of Certainty and Method.

## Note

1  See also Waltner-Toews in this volume.

## References

Agledahl, K.M., Førde, R., and Wifstad, Å. 2010. Clinical essentialising: A qualitative study of doctors medical and moral practice, *Medicine, Health Care, and Philosophy*, 13: 107–13.

Agledahl, K.M., Gulbrandsen, P., Førde, R., and Wifstad, Å. 2011. Courteous but not curious: How doctors' politeness masks their existential neglect. A qualitative study of video-recorded patient consultations, *Journal of Medical Ethics*, 37: 650–4.

Barnett, K., Mercer, S.W., Norbury, M., Watt, G., Wyke, S., and Guthrie, B. 2012. Epidemiology of multimorbidity and implications for health care, research, and medical education: A cross-sectional study, *Lancet*, 380: 37–43.

Barry, C.A., Stevenson, F.A., Britten, N., Barber, N., and Bradley, C.P. 2001. Giving voice to the lifeworld: More humane, more effective medical care? A qualitative study of doctor–patient communication in general practice, *Social Science and Medicine*, 53: 487–505.

Bernard, C. 1865/1957. *Introduction to Experimental Medicine*, New York: Dover Publications.

Berwick, D.M., and Hackbarth, A.D. 2012. Eliminating waste in US health care, *JAMA*, 307: 1513–16.

Cassell, E.J. 2004. *The Nature of Suffering and the Goals of Medicine*, 2nd ed., New York: Oxford University Press.

Cassell, E.J. 2012. *The Nature of Healing: The Modern Practice of Medicine,* Oxford: Oxford University Press.

Cochrane, A. 1972. *Effectiveness and Efficiency: Random Reflections on Health Services,* London: Nuffield Provincial Hospitals Trust.

Descartes, R. 1637/2007. *Discourse on the Method of Rightly Conducting One's Reason and of Seeking Truth in the Sciences,* translation by J. Bennett, published online at http://www.earlymoderntexts.com/pdfs/descartes1637.pdf.

Eriksen, T.E., Kerry, R., Mumford, S., Lie, S.A., and Anjum, R.L. 2013a. At the borders of medical reasoning: Aetiological and ontological challenges of medically unexplained symptoms, *Philosophy and Ethics of Humanitarian Medicine*, 8: 11.

Eriksen, T.E., Kirkengen, A.L., and Vetlesen, A.J. 2013b. The medically unexplained revisited, *Medicine, Health Care and Philosophy*, 16: 587–600.

Farmer, P. 2005. *Pathologies of Power: Health, Human Rights, and the New War on the Poor,* Berkeley, CA: University of California Press.

Foucault, M. 1975. *The Birth of the Clinic: An Archaeology of Medical Perception,* New York: Random House.

Galilei, G. 1623. *The Assayer,* translation by A. C. Danto, as provided in A. C. Danto (1954) *Introduction to Contemporary Civilization in the West,* vol. 1, 2nd ed., New York: Columbia University Press.

Gøtzsche, P. 2013. *Deadly Medicines and Organised Crime: How Big Pharma has Corrupted Health Care,* New York: Radcliffe Publishing.

Le Fanu, J. 1999. *The Rise and Fall of Modern Medicine,* London: Little Brown & Co.

McWhinney, I.R., and Freeman, T. 2009. *Textbook of Family Medicine,* Oxford: Oxford University Press.

Marmot, M. 2006. Health in an unequal world: Social circumstances, biology and disease, *Clinical Medicine*, 6: 559–72.

Moynihan, R., Doust, J., and Henry, D. 2012. Preventing overdiagnosis: How to stop harming the healthy, *BMJ,* 344: e3502 (online).

Parekh, A.K., and Barton, M.B. 2010. The challenge of multiple comorbidity for the US health care system, *JAMA,* 303: 1303–4.

Petursson, H., Getz, L., Sigurdsson, J.A., and Hetlevik, I. 2009. Current European guidelines for management of arterial hypertension: Are they adequate for use in primary care? Modelling study based on the Norwegian HUNT 2 population, *BMC Family Practice,* 10: 70.

Pirmohamed, M., *et al.* 2004. Adverse drug reactions as cause of admission to hospital: Prospective analysis of 18 820 patients, *BMJ,* 329: 15–19.

Schei, E., and Cassell, E. 2012. *Clinicians' Power and Leadership,* Hastings Center Report, 42.

Shapin, S. 2000. Descartes the doctor: Rationalism and its therapies, *British Journal for the History of Science,* 33: 131–54.

Skolbekken, J.A. 1995. The risk epidemic in medical journals, *Social Science and Medicine,* 40: 291–305.

Smith, G.C., and Pell, J.P. 2003. Parachute use to prevent death and major trauma related to gravitational challenge: Systematic review of randomised controlled trials, *BMJ,* 327: 1459–61.

Susser, M. 1973. *Causal Thinking in the Health Sciences: Concepts and Strategies in Epidemiology,* New York: Oxford University Press.

Tomasdottir, M.O., *et al.* 2014. Co- and multimorbidity patterns in an unselected Norwegian population: Cross-sectional analysis based on the HUNT Study and theoretical reflections concerning basic medical models, *European Journal of Person Centered Healthcare*, 2: 335–45.

Toulmin, S. 2001. *Return to Reason,* Cambridge, MA: Harvard University Press.

Tuckett, D., Boulton, M., Olson, C., and Williams, A. 1985. *Meetings between Experts: An Approach to Sharing Ideas in Medical Consultations,* London: Tavistock.

Ulvestad, E. 2008. Chronic fatigue syndrome defies the mind–body-schism of medicine: New perspectives on a multiple realisable developmental systems disorder, *Medicine, Health Care and Philosophy*, 11: 285–92.

Wootton, D. 2007. *Bad Medicine: Doctors Doing Harm since Hippocrates,* New York: Oxford University Press.

# Part II
# Technoscience and innovation

# 4 The ontological objection to life technosciences

*Fern Wickson*

## The dream that became a nightmare

René Descartes had a dream. A dream that the modern world has pursued and performed for generations. A dream in which nature is seen through the metaphor of a machine – a soulless, thoughtless, predictable machine. A dream in which human rationality is said to raise us above and beyond this mechanistic world. A dream that pushes our senses and emotions aside in the search for reliable knowledge and right action. A dream in which we can have everything we ever wanted if we just apply our rationality to understand and predict this mechanistic world and take control. For some, this dream has turned into a nightmare.

This Cartesian dream is clearly manifest in the new and emerging life technosciences such as modern biotechnology (including the branch known as synthetic biology), nanotechnology and geoengineering (see Curvelo in this volume). Each of these fields of advancing research coupled with technological development enacts a view of the world in which Nature is perceived through the metaphor of a machine; a machine that we can understand, predict, manipulate and control. Within this dream, life on Earth is viewed in terms of building blocks and information codes, bricks and bits, and we can engineer anything and everything: from the foundations of matter, through individual organisms, right up to the planet's climate. Using a knowledge base built on rational deduction and scientific experimentation, universal laws and reductionist essentialism, we pursue the dream that we can predict and control the world we live in so as to satisfy our every desire. It is worth repeating that, for some, this dream has become a nightmare.

The new and emerging life technosciences, especially those oriented towards environmental applications, have been subject to increasingly intense social scrutiny and critical debate. This has often taken the shape of an ethical debate, a debate about what is right and wrong and what we should do. Currently, however, ethical debate over new and emerging life technosciences has largely been restricted to consequentialist[1] and deontological[2] frameworks. That is, the debate has been framed either in terms of *extrinsic* concerns about the potential for these technosciences to have undesirable consequences or *intrinsic* concerns that there is something categorically or in principle wrong with these fields of research and/ or their technological products in and of themselves.

Within this restricted framework for the debate, the deontological opposition has largely been dismissed (interestingly by both scientists and philosophers) as invalid, unsupportable and/or illegitimate (e.g. see Comstock 2000; Rollin 2006). That is, that there is no firm ground or consistent basis on which these new and emerging life technosciences can be dismissed as wrong in principle. The one exception to this appears to be the case of human cloning, which has been categorically opposed on principle around the world. Noting this single significant exception, it seems that it is possible to make an intrinsic objection when these technosciences meet human bodies, likely because human beings are deemed to possess some kind of intrinsic value that gives them rights that should not be violated, no matter what the consequences. All environmental applications, or technologies directly applied to organisms other than humans, however, appear to be *in principle* permissible.

The general academic rejection of deontological grounds for opposition to life technosciences has taken place despite the persistent expression of exactly these types of objections by members of the public (e.g. concerns related to naturalness, *messing with Nature*, playing God, etc.) (see Davies and Macnaghten 2010 and Davies *et al.* 2009). The dismissal of lay concerns and their often deontological framing is arguably connected to broader master narratives of modernity in which innovation is perceived as inherently good and science is the privileged way of understanding the world due to its perceived objectivity (Felt and Wynne 2007). When combined, this has created a situation in which consequentialist evaluations (performed by sound science) appear as the only valid ground from which to oppose the products of new and emerging life technosciences. This straightjacketing of the debate into a scientific consequentialist frame is both represented in and facilitated by the dominance of risk analysis as the primary tool for informing governance and decision-making in these areas (see Levidow and Carr 1997).

The sufficiency of consequentialist approaches generally, and risk analysis specifically, can and have been critiqued through emphasis on both the challenges of environmental complexity and scientific uncertainty (e.g. see Wynne 1992, Funtowicz and Ravetz 1994; Wickson 2012). These types of critique significantly challenge the Cartesian dream of our ability to know, predict and control impacts from the introduction of novel technologies into open and dynamic ecological systems. However, since these critiques are well rehearsed and already well developed (although not necessarily well acknowledged within policy-making), in this chapter I want to outline the possibility of a perhaps related but relatively distinct alternative approach. I call this the ontological objection.

The ontological objection that I wish to put forward in this chapter as representing not only possible but legitimate grounds for challenging new and emerging life technosciences begins with a rejection of the mechanistic Cartesian view of Nature and the dualistic separation of man and Nature, body and mind, reason and passion. This is rejected in favour of a relational ontology[3] in which the idea of isolated individual entities moving only according to universal laws is replaced by relational networks through which entities co-construct each other in a dynamic flow of constant and iterative interaction. From this relational ontology, I suggest that the ethic that emerges as most appropriate is one grounded in relations of care and the cultivation of virtue. Here the concern is less with identifying universal ethical principles that can be rationally defended, or with scientifically identifying and controlling undesirable consequences (which due to the complexity and uncertainty of dynamic interrelations is deemed a vain hope, a myth, a dream). Instead, the focus of the ethical debate shifts to the attitudes behind our actions, or the dispositions that we choose to cultivate and manifest. It is an interest in the kind of people we want to be and a concern with the kind of world we want to enact through the norms we embed in our practices.

In the remainder of this chapter I will elaborate on this ontological objection by drawing on existing work within environmental ethics and ecophilosophy, particularly deep ecology and ecofeminism. To conclude I will consider how the ontological objection relates to a new governance discourse emerging in force for the life technosciences, namely that of *responsible research and innovation* (RRI). Here I will suggest that RRI has the potential to take up the ontological objection, but that this will only be possible under particular interpretations of what responsibility means and the community of actors to which it applies. Importantly, it should be noted that my aim in this chapter is not to summarily dismiss all fields of new and emerging technosciences, but rather to highlight that ontological objections are possible, valid and worthy of consideration; and that in some cases, such objections may legitimately lead to a favouring of alternate technological trajectories and world-making activities.

## The ontological objection

My consideration and articulation of the ontological objection to life technosciences was originally inspired by the field of environmental philosophy known as deep ecology and research recently demonstrating that *ecocentric* or *holistic* human/ Nature views (such as those espoused within deep ecology) are reliable predictors of opposition to emerging technosciences (Vandermoere *et al.* 2010, 2011). Trying to understand why the holding of such perspectives may create opposition to new and emerging technosciences is what has led to this chapter as a first attempt to articulate the ontological objection and it is therefore worth elaborating on the content of this field of ecophilosophy in some depth.

### Deep ecology

Deep ecology is a term originally coined by Norwegian philosopher Arne Næss (1973) to characterise the radical rather than reformist end of the spectrum of concern for environmental problems. For deep ecology, the source of environmental problems lies in how the human–Nature relationship has been understood and performed in modern industrial societies. Therefore, beyond simply reforming existing systems, the development of lasting solutions to the ecological crisis is said to require a radical shift in the underlying anthropocentric and instrumental ways of thinking that have dominated industrial modernisation. What is required is advocated as a different worldview, or in other words, a different ontology.

By focusing on paradigms of thought, our concept of Nature and dominant understandings of the human/Nature relation as the source of environmental problems, deep ecology departs from many other strands of ecophilosophy by specifically emphasising ontology over ethics. That is, rather than focusing on the articulation of a specific framework or normative ethic for how we should act towards Nature (what is worthy of protection and/or consideration, etc.), deep ecology has instead invested its focus in articulating an alternative view of the structure of the world and the human/Nature relation. In his early work defining deep ecology as a concept and movement, Næss (1973: 95) presented its first defining characteristic as the adoption of a relational ontology, suggesting that this involved:

> Rejection of the man-in-environment image in favour of the relational, total-field image. Organisms as knots in the biospherical net or field of intrinsic relations. An intrinsic relation between two things A and B is such that the relation belongs to the definitions of basic constitutions of A and B, so that without the relation, A and B are no longer the same things. The total-field dissolves not only the man-in-environment concept, but every compact thing-in-milieu concept – except when talking at a superficial or preliminary level of communication.

The term *the environment* as commonly used is therefore presented as misleadingly giving the impression of an identifiable thing that exists separate and distinct from ourselves; something that surrounds us, something that we use, but something that always remains an *other*. However, for deep ecology and its relational ontology, we do not exist as isolated units, surrounded by a separate and external *environment*. Rather, we exist within networks of interrelation, engaging with various entities in a dance of co-creation. Næss (1987) argued that understanding our deep relational connections to biological communities allows us to expand our concept of self to include them – or to realise what he called our "ecological Self" (the capital S being used to help denote it as referring to something more than our narrow ego). Highlighting how our sense of self and feeling of identification naturally expands as we mature – through ego, social, and metaphysical levels – Næss questioned the missing ecological dimension of this process. That is, our psychological and moral identification with non-human beings, with Nature, with Earth.

According to Næss and the deep ecology movement that followed him, realising our ecological Self creates the potential for a radically new way of seeing and being in the world. Currently, environmentally responsible behaviour is seen as something we must be compelled to do, as an altruistic act or a moral duty to benefit an external *other*. If we expand our concept of self to embrace our ecosystem of interrelations, however, this would be transformed into an act of expanded self-interest (ecological Self-interest). Protecting our ecological Self becomes protecting the system. Næss argued that this shift was important because people would no longer need to be compelled by argument, guilt or punishment to demonstrate care for biological communities. Rather, such care would flow naturally from the relational ontology and the expanded sense of self it affords.

Through adopting its unique focus on ontology instead of ethics, deep ecology effectively sidestepped entrenched and ongoing debates within environmental ethics about the moral status of different biological entities. Arguing that the development and use of *moral oughts* is not an effective strategy for achieving lasting change, deep ecology has emphasised the need to first cultivate ontological change, with the view that once this is achieved, an appropriate ethic will follow naturally. In the next section of this chapter I will seek to challenge and advance the philosophy of deep ecology beyond this sole focus on ontology by arguing that certain ethical frameworks more naturally align with relational ontologies, namely virtue ethics and an ethic of care, and that by specifically working to develop, integrate and promote these ethical frameworks, the comprehensiveness and relevance of the philosophy of deep ecology, particularly for the governance of life technosciences, can be substantially advanced.

Despite finding inspiration in the science of ecology, it should be emphasised that deep ecology is not naturalistic. That is, it neither pronounces that ecological science can deliver a comprehensive understanding of the world nor that it can deliver an uncontested basis for action (Næss 1989). Since deep ecology seeks to advance a relational ontology in which there are no firm boundaries in the field of existence (Fox 2003), ecology is valued for the emphasis it places on understanding relationships and the idea that *all life is interconnected*. However, deep ecology has also drawn inspiration for its relational ontology from Eastern religious traditions and phenomenology. Adopting the idea of a gestalt, it has also specifically emphasised the crucial role of feeling and normativity in the world (Diehm 2006; Næss 1985) and thereby directly challenged the sufficiency of the scientific worldview and the Cartesian prioritisation of rationality as the source of reliable knowledge about the world. In seeking to advance the shift towards a relational ontology, much of the academic literature on deep ecology has, perhaps understandably, focused on presenting intellectual argumentation. However, within the broader social movement of deep ecology, much of the focus of organised workshops and activities is on cultivating and creating space for participants to emotionally feel and explore their interdependent relationship with Nature (e.g. see Macy 2007; Macy and Brown 1998). There is, however, arguably extensive scope to bring the practical, emotion-based work that is being developed and performed within the deep ecology movement more directly into its academic identity and wed it holistically together with the intellectual basis that has traditionally dominated that arena.

Concerning technology, deep ecology has primarily focused on developing a position to directly counter the technocratic view in which Nature is seen through the metaphor of a controllable, soulless machine and technological fixes can be relied upon to solve the environmental crisis (e.g. see Drengson 1989). Beyond developing this general position, however, deep ecology has engaged in very little concrete discussion of modern technology, relying instead upon the arguably rather weak position that appropriate technologies will be those developed from within a deep ecological understanding.

One of the most contentious elements of deep ecology that is regularly subject to critique is its claim that Nature possesses intrinsic value. In the writings of deep ecology, however, intrinsic value appears in different guises. While it is clear that biological entities and processes are awarded value beyond their usefulness to humanity, it is not clear whether (all) individual organisms, systemic wholes or the flourishing of life more generally possess intrinsic value, nor what such claims are grounded in. Under certain interpretations, the very concept of intrinsic value appears antithetical to the relational ontology deep ecology seeks to develop, creating a contradiction at the heart of its philosophy (i.e. if there are no firm boundaries in the field of existence, what exactly can be said to possess intrinsic value?) (Noer Lie and Wickson 2011).

### Ethics within a relational ontology

From the perspective of a relational worldview, emphasis is placed on the interconnections between entities. This therefore necessarily includes the interconnections between passion and reason, humanity and Nature, and indeed, between ontology and ethics. Deep ecology has, however, been deliberately silent on the question of environmental ethics, choosing to focus on what it sees as the ontological grounds for the crisis. This has often led to others, typically critics, interpreting and projecting onto deep ecology a particular ethical view. Most often, this has involved the concept of intrinsic value seen through a modern deontological rights-based discourse. In other words, emphasis has been placed on deep ecology's claim to the existence of intrinsic value in Nature, which is then interpreted as applying to individual organisms. When this is translated through a deontological view, it has been presented as suggesting that all organisms possess rights that should not be violated and demand duties from us to act in particular ways. This allows deep ecology and the notion of intrinsic value to be ridiculed as providing no relevant guidance for our actions in the world, especially since organisms necessarily die for us to survive and we already clearly accept and tolerate extensive suffering in our treatment of (also sentient) organisms (e.g. through industrial farming practices).

As I indicated above though, the writings within deep ecology have not presented a consistent position on exactly what is deemed to hold intrinsic value, what basis this is held according to, nor what such holding implies for our actions (i.e. just because something is claimed to have an intrinsic value need not necessarily imply that it has certain rights nor that this value mandates a particular kind of action from us, which is arguably for ethical theory to elaborate and here, deep ecology has been silent). While there has been a clear tendency particularly among deep ecology critics to assign claims of intrinsic value to individual organisms, it is highly instructive to consider that, in fact, in certain articulations of the platform of deep ecology principles, it is actually the *flourishing of life* as a whole rather than individual organisms that is said to possess intrinsic value (e.g. see Næss 1989).

When interpreted in this way, I would argue that rather than using a deontological rights-based discourse to expound the ethic inherent to deep ecology and its relational ontology, a more natural connection would actually be to virtue ethics and its traditional emphasis on eudemonia or *flourishing* as the highest good. While in the moral philosophy of the ancient Greeks, this concept was restricted to human flourishing, I wish to argue that deep ecology allows for a modern extension of this into a flourishing of life on Earth more generally as the highest good, around which we could then go on to articulate ethical guidance. According to a relational ontology and the idea of our ecological Self, this goal is not separate from human flourishing but rather human flourishing is deemed to be co-existent with a broader flourishing of life on Earth. While the intrinsic value of individual organisms may be dismissed as unworkable, the intrinsic value of flourishing life on Earth is arguably already widely recognised in environmental policy. Biodiversity (i.e. *flourishing life*) is, for example, an internationally recognised protection goal (United Nations 1992), including for the assessment and governance of new and emerging technosciences such as modern biotechnology (United Nations 2000).

## The ethics of virtue and care for flourishing life on Earth

The field of environmental or ecological virtue ethics is a nascent area of environmental philosophy (e.g. see Sandler and Cafaro 2005; van Wensveen 2000) that has received remarkably little attention and development to date. While there has been some attempt to relate this ethical framework to new and emerging technosciences, such as modern biotechnology (see Sandler 2007), this has been restricted to one controversial case in technology and has failed to ignite broader engagement and critique. The field has also not specifically related to the philosophy of deep ecology. There is therefore enormous potential for ecological virtue ethics to be developed as a way for the philosophy of deep ecology to be usefully elaborated into the arena of ethics. Such an effort could develop from the existing articulation of flourishing life as an ultimate good and could clearly flow from within its relational ontology (virtues being dispositions that can be cultivated to manifest in and through our relational interactions).

There is, however, another body of ethical theory that also offers potential value for elaborating an ethic of both deep ecology and relational ontologies more generally. This is the ethic of care that has emerged from within psychological research and feminist scholarship (see Gilligan 1982; Noddings 1984; Larrabee 1993). An ethic of care was originally articulated to capture the way in which women often approach moral dilemmas differently from men, and to elevate these approaches to give them serious consideration. An ethic of care specifically takes a relational ontology as its starting point, emphasising that individuals are constituted through their relations with others. It rejects the modern search for universal ethical principles and impartiality and instead emphasises the significance of context and the particularities of circumstances. It also embraces emotion and feeling as having highly significant roles to play in our moral decisions and ethical judgements, entwined with cognition. While it has been challenged as potentially dangerously perpetuating the destructive image of emotional women with concerns restricted to the private sphere, an ethic of care is not meant to be specific to women as a gender and certainly need not be restricted to the private sphere (Tronto 1995).

In her early work expounding an ethic of care, Carol Gilligan (1977) described a three-staged progression for maturity within the framework for a morality of care and responsibility. Naturally, she suggested, an individual is first concerned with maintaining their own survival, with this maintenance of the self being the sole concern. However, when this self begins to understand and define itself according to its interrelations (e.g. within a family, a community, a society, a nation), an idea of self-sacrifice emerges to define what is good, with concern for others emerging as a key consideration. At the third level, the selfishness of the first level and the self-sacrifice at the second level need to be resolved so that care and responsibility for self and others can coexist and be pursued simultaneously. This, it is suggested, will be supported by the perception of one's self as connected to others. This has clear resonances with the notion of the ecological Self from deep ecology, although here, the relations individuals are constituted through would clearly be extended beyond the social relations with a human community that the ethic of care has typically been occupied with, to ecological relations with the broader biological community.

One of the core challenges for care ethics has been to consider how care may be extended and cultivated for those beyond whom we have a direct relationship. While this would appear central for any argument to extend care ethics into an ecological dimension, the notion of realising our ecological Self may be a useful way in which the philosophy of deep ecology could contribute to such a task. For example, we could recognise the way in which care already extends to biological and ecological entities, particularly those that we have a direct relationship with – e.g. our pets, gardens, local river systems, etc. – but also to those that we have somehow incorporated into our own identity – e.g. our love of particular animals such as polar bears, panda bears, grizzly bears or water bears.

Rather than negating or distracting from a deep ecology ethic, these personal relations and connections to particular features of the ecosphere arguably actually demonstrate the promise and potentiality of ecological Self-realisation. We care for these entities with a deep and sustained passion precisely because of our relation to them. In his native Norwegian, Næss insisted that the process be understood as '*Self-realising* rather than Self-realisation' particularly so as to emphasise that it is inevitably an ongoing process in which our concept of Self continues to expand to include broader and deeper ecological relations as we mature. Therefore, these existing concerns for Nature demonstrate the power of the relational embrace and the potential for its future expansion as we realise ever-greater circles of relation and interdependence with our ecological communities.

One challenge to pursuing an ethics of care to help guide and structure relations within our ecological community may be the argument that care is a uniquely human capacity that Nature more generally typically does not demonstrate. Such an argument, however, has to be more carefully considered and qualified. For example, many different species clearly demonstrate a capacity for care when engaged in the task of raising their young. There are also species that engage in empathy, care and altruistic practices, particularly in relation to other members of their family or group (see Bekoff 2007; Byrne *et al.* 2008). Of course, it could be argued that there are few cases (outside the possibility of certain pets or domesticated animals) of species enacting practices of care towards other species, for example, human beings. This argument, however, really forces us to question what it really means and requires *to care*. There are certainly many cases of symbiotic and mutualistic relationships in ecology (see Boucher 1985): can these be described as relationships of care? Through the functioning of ecosystems, human beings are provided with everything they need to survive – air, water, food, shelter. While these needs may not be being met by a conscious process, does this necessarily entail that it cannot be perceived, described and understood as a form of care? This, and many other questions, could become useful focal points for discussion, debate and development if an ecological ethic of care were to be advanced.

While there has been some interest in developing an ecological ethic of care from within ecofeminism (e.g. see Curtin 1991), the potential for a fruitful connection of this to deep ecology appears yet to be made. This is likely due to the serious rift that emerged between deep ecology and ecofeminism in the 1980s. Ecofeminists emphasised the masculinist history of domination and criticised deep ecology for its preponderance of white middle-class men whose metaphysical focus failed to engage the materialities of oppression or the potentiality of embodied change (Salleh 1993). They also argued that deep ecology erased the significance of difference (e.g. species, class, race, gender) and failed to address historically important power dynamics (Plumwood 2000). Given this history of theoretical disagreement and animosity, it perhaps should come as no surprise that ecofeminists who may be interested in extending an ethic of care in ecological directions would not necessarily seek to explore potential connections with the philosophy of deep ecology.

There have also been interesting debates concerning the relationship between care and virtue ethics. For example, some people have painted the ethic of care as advancing a form of virtue ethics (e.g. Broughton 1993), others have argued that care ethics should be subsumed under virtue ethics (e.g. Halwani 2003), while others still have sought to emphasise that the two need to remain separate if the full value of care as a feminist ethic is to be realised (Sander-Staudt 2006). As this chapter is not the appropriate place to engage in these debates in detail, I wish to follow Sander-Staudt (2006) and suggest that at the very least there seems to be the possibility for the future development of a constructive collaboration between the two fields in offering a form of normative ethic appropriate to a relational ontology.

If we adopt a relational ontology in which entities are bound in networks of relations and co-create each other through their interconnections, the normative ethics we naturally look for is one concerned with how we should perform these relations and what it would mean to cultivate good relationships. Here, concern turns to attitudes and virtues – the conception of the good life we wish to pursue and the kind of people we need to be if we hope to get there. If we expand the ancient interest in flourishing as the highest good, which traditionally only incorporated consideration of the flourishing of human beings, to incorporate the extended notion of flourishing life on Earth, this can be used to ground our consideration of the relevant virtues and their practice. The virtues we wish to cultivate then become those that support and contribute to the flourishing of life on Earth. The arrogance, greed, hubris and domineering self-interest that largely characterise the predominant way in which we have pursued and conducted our relationship with Nature in modern industrial societies would clearly be replaced by an emphasis on pursuing virtues such as care, respect, humility, love and generosity. It is important to re-emphasise though that the virtues of interest in this case stem from an expanded sense of flourishing in which our desire and commitment is not simply to pursue the flourishing of ourselves as individual human beings, or even of humanity in general, but rather a desire to advance the flourishing of our ecological Selves, the flourishing of life on Earth.

The point is not that those pursuing such an expanded idea of flourishing and seeking to cultivate the correlated virtues in their ecological relations will have no impact on Nature or create no harm. Such a perception or demand arguably comes from those still operating at something like Gilligan's second level of moral development in which goodness is judged by self-sacrifice. When we let go of the idea that the environment is *an other* that is separate and distinct from us that we need to protect from harm and the negative impacts we wreak upon it, new possibilities emerge. We can let go of the idea of an ideal Nature existing prior to human intervention that we need to return to or protect through self-sacrifice. Instead of seeing human–Nature relations, we can open ourselves to the idea that there are only Nature relations. That is, when we embrace a relational ontology in which we are inevitably and inherently intimately connected with Nature and can therefore not avoid having an impact, the question shifts from how to avoid negative impacts to how to pursue positive relations. This concerns how we can build positive relationships so that the greater whole may flourish and thrive and how we can cultivate attitudes and character traits to enhance our ability to respond in an ethical manner to ever changing contextual particularities. Since it is not possible to have no impact or do no harm, we should shift focus to how we can actively pursue good and, specifically, pursue good for our expanded ecological rather than egoistic selves. However, to do this we need to be attentive to how our actions and practices are embedded with norms and the way in which these co-create the world around us.

### The worlds and norms enacted through practice

Annemarie Mol (2012) recently experimented with the terminology and concept of *ontonorms* and, while she expressly did not define it, the term emerges as part of a growing interest within the field of science and technology studies (STS) in the matter of ontology. This interest from STS has not necessarily always been in elaborating a philosophical ontology, but rather describing how ontologies and worlds get enacted in practice, especially in the practices of science and technology (Lynch 2013). Mol (2012) encourages other scholars to go in search of *ontonorms* and the way norms and worldviews become embedded in practices and then embodied in the worlds these co-create.

What view of the world and norms can be seen as being embodied in the life technosciences? What world are our practices in these fields enacting? When expressing the ontological objection, the concerns of the ecocentric or deep green critics are arguably around the view of the world that is informing, shaping and being embodied in the practices of the life technosciences, as well as the world that such fields are enacting. The objection is that they do not operate from a relational worldview, they do not express the qualities of a good relationship with Nature, and the world that they co-create is undesirable. It is important to note here that the world that is made may be deemed undesirable not because it contains particular risks to human and/or environmental health (although it may indeed do this and these may indeed be highly relevant) but rather because this world has been (and continues to be) crafted on the basis of undesirable ontonorms embodied in and enacted through the technosciences themselves. If we increase our concern with the worlds we enact, including the ecologies we perform, we are not only interested in the consequences of our actions, but also in the character traits that we express and perpetuate and the quality of our relationships. Within a relational ontology, the focus shifts to cultivating character traits or virtues that enable and enhance good relationships.

Under the current master narrative, in which innovation equals progress and progress is unquestionably desirable, we are in a situation in which all technologies (or technosciences) are deemed to be in principle permissible and in fact, desirable (with perhaps the remarkable exception of human cloning). Empirical evidence of risk is then required for any restrictions of prohibitions to be put in place. This sees us currently focus on assessing the risks a particular technology poses to decide whether or not it will be implemented and pursued. An alternative approach, however, that may more easily open for consideration of the ontological objection, would be to instead shift the focus onto core socio-ecological challenges, with the consideration of technosciences taking place within this broader framing. For example, instead of only asking what risks genetically engineered organisms pose to the environment, we could instead ask what are the available options for approaching the agricultural challenge of how we are going to feed ourselves in the coming years. Such a subtle shift not only *opens up* for the direct consideration and weighing of alternative options (Stirling 2008), it allows for the relevant weighing criteria to be broader than simply those permitted within a consequentialist risk frame.

For example, there may be various available alternatives for agricultural evolution, with transgenic biotechnological crop development being one of these, and each of these options can be considered according to their potential risks, their potential benefits, their adherence to agreed ethical principles, the ecologies they will manifest, the ontonorms they enact, the relations they express and/ or the virtues they embody and cultivate, etc. If we were a society that placed value in the cultivation of ecological virtues and the practice of care, we might not reject all life technosciences (especially given the importance of contextual features for ethical analysis according to both virtue and care frameworks), but we would certainly subject them to a different type of evaluative analysis and, just as enacting technosciences manifests in the performance and creation of new future worlds and ecologies, so may the choice to focus on desirable ecologies and good relations manifest in the performance of new or different technosciences.

One of the core challenges with seeking to advance such an approach is that, although individuals or institutions may have a desire to act from an attitude of love or care towards our extended ecological Selves, it is far from clear what this involves or requires in practice. While this can be seen as an area for further research and experimental practice, the challenge is clearly greatly complicated by the globalised and distributed systems of production that dominate late modernity. Such distributed and complex systems mean that when people invest in the development of certain socio-technical networks, and support the development of particular kinds of technoscience, both institutionally but also individually through the choices they make every day (e.g. how I choose to spend my money, what kinds of products I purchase, etc.), the ecologies that these choices support and generate are not immediately apparent. Rather they are hidden behind a dense network of globally distributed production systems that are largely untraceable in their entirety.

This is arguably a feature of both our current globalised systems of production, but also of technology more generally. The philosopher of technology Albert Borgmann (1984) has suggested that one of the key characteristics of technology is the way it works to divorce means from ends. That is, the technology of an oil heater makes the end of warmth available at the flick of a switch, allowing me to remain disconnected from or unaware of all of the socio-ecological processes necessary to deliver that end. However, if I have to make a fire to keep warm (what Borgmann may refer to as a focal practice), I am far more directly and immediately connected to what means are required to deliver that end, and indeed, also of the ecology that I require and create through my action in the world as I seek the end of staying warm. The inability to see, understand, evaluate and judge exactly how our everyday actions affect the co-creation of our ecologies and our ecological Selves is a major challenge for the cultivation of ecological care and virtue. Indeed, this can be seen as a reason why deep green critics emphasise the value of enhancing our direct engagement and involvement in processes such as agriculture (e.g. emphasising the value of community supported agriculture, local production systems, urban farming, etc. rather than supporting biotechnological development within multinational corporations for the maintenance of distant monocultures). Through the facilitation of more direct contact, relations and awareness, possibilities for the cultivation of care and virtue appear to emerge more easily.

## Responsible research and innovation?

While this may all seem highly theoretical, with very little grounding in the practice of technological innovation or policy-making, in fact it can be seen to align with the emerging discourse of *responsible research and innovation*. The emerging emphasis on having the knowledge economy develop in a *responsible* way is the latest manifestation of a longer historical trend towards reimagining the relationship between science and society. The historical development of the currently in vogue concept of RRI has been described by Owen *et al.* (2012), who present it as part of a continuous development in practices such as technology assessment in its various forms, the increasing institutionalisation of public engagement, the embedding of research on ethical, legal and social aspects (ELSA) into large technology development initiatives, and the social-technical integration model of midstream modulation. While there is a sense in which RRI is an amalgamation or a culmination of all of these efforts in recent decades to redefine the relationship between science and society, a single definition of RRI is yet to fully sediment.

While each of the emerging definitions differs somewhat in the terminology they use, the depth of description they provide and where emphasis is placed, the characteristics that are shared across them and can therefore be identified as central to the concept of RRI include: a focus on delivering concrete real-world benefits to society and the environment, a research and development process that actively engages and responds to a range of public stakeholders, and a concerted effort to anticipate potential problems and adapt accordingly (see von Schomberg 2013; Owen *et al.* 2013; Jacob 2013). Questions such as how this is to be achieved in practice, who is responsible for ensuring the uptake and success of this concept, what are the motivations of the different actors perpetuating this discourse, and how might progress towards a new paradigm of innovation be measured, all remain open to discussion and debate.

Another area of possible debate is the extent to which this emerging discourse of RRI could be open for the legitimacy of the ontological objection and even facilitate the consideration of the character traits, attitudes and virtues that technosciences are imbued with. RRI is emerging as a prominent innovation policy discourse at exactly this point in history arguably partly because of the now widely recognised challenges in advancing good governance of novel technological fields in the face of severe limits to our ability to predict and control their interactions and impacts in advance – this awareness having created a need to experiment with new approaches. Of course, so long as the notion of responsibility is conceptualised purely as liability or accountability (see Pellizzoni 2004), or coupled to consequences that we can control, it loses its experimental potential as a novel governance tool (Funtowicz and Strand 2011). However, if a more relational perspective is permitted to come to the fore and the characteristics of care and responsiveness are emphasised in the meaning of responsibility, then it may indeed have the potential to promise something new and to connect to the development of an ecological ethics of care and/or virtue and its use in the governance of life technosciences.

Elements of this type of interpretation of RRI are indeed emerging. For example, Owen *et al.* (2013) define RRI as "a commitment of care for the future through collective stewardship of science and innovation in the present" and emphasise the need to be *responsive* as one of four key dimensions of the concept (alongside being anticipatory, reflective and deliberative). While the authors fail to connect to the literature on an ethic of care or go into any further theoretical details concerning the boundaries of community relevant to this practice of care, this definition seems to offer potential for the interpretation of RRI along the lines indicated as desirable in this chapter. That is, that RRI could open for debates beyond the risks of technoscience to include the ontologies that shape scientific research and technological development and the norms that are embodied in the practice of these areas. This, however, would require substantial development on the framework presented by Owen *et al.* This development would, for example, require the articulation of a more relational perspective than the authors are able to offer, including understanding the relation between ontology and ethics, and an openness to discussing how *ontonorms* can be expressed and embodied in technoscience development. It would also require a relational understanding that replaces an interest in environmental impacts with an interest in the dynamic creation of human–Nature ecologies, in which care can be legitimately discussed and extended to include our ecological Selves. Furthermore, it would require a philosophical articulation of how this commitment of care can be grounded and related to the cultivation of other virtues such as humility, generosity, justice and wisdom.

## From consequentialist risks to flourishing virtues

This chapter has attempted to outline the possibility of an ontological objection to new and emerging life technosciences. This objection has been presented as grounded in how technosciences may be viewed from a relational ontology. Through this chapter I have suggested that those who hold a relational ontology may legitimately reject an entire field or a particular example of a life technoscience based on the position that: (a) the technoscience embodies and enacts a view of the world that is deemed to be partial, misleading and/or false, and (b) the technoscience embodies and enacts a set of character traits, qualities or virtues that are deemed to be negative, undesirable and/or unethical.

I have highlighted how the persistent deep green critique of new and emerging technosciences, with its basis in the philosophy of deep ecology, can be understood as expressing this kind of ontological objection and have highlighted how work remains to be done exploring and articulating the relationship between ontology and ethics in this objection, suggesting that new lines of collaboration between deep ecology and ecofeminism could be fruitfully pursued in this regard.

Within a relational ontology, I have argued that the firm boundary between ontology and ethics becomes perforated as certain ontologies are recognised as affording particular approaches to normative ethics. Just as a relational ontology will reject the Cartesian dream of a predictable mechanistic Nature separate from humanity that we have the ability to control, it will also reject the assumption that the only legitimate frameworks for ethical appraisal of new and emerging technosciences are deontological or consequentialist. Those holding a relational ontology will naturally emphasise an ethic grounded in relations. This means they are more likely to adopt a virtue ethics frame and/or emphasise an ethics of care.

For those expressing an ontological objection to new and emerging technosciences, there will be a rejection of risk as the only legitimate grounds for consideration, there will be little faith in the ability of a rationalistic science to predict and control consequences in a complex world, and there will be a desire for an approach to governance that goes beyond simply aiming to avoid negative consequences. This will be in favour of a view that we are inherently entangled in the dynamic and creative process that is the unfolding of this world and that through this process, rather than seeking to minimise our negative impacts, we should rather be actively seeking to do good and while we may not be able to accurately predict the consequences of our actions, the only way to flourish under conditions of complexity and uncertainty is to cultivate ecological virtues and seek to act from an attitude of love, respect, humility, generosity and care for the ecologies and Nature relations we co-create.

## Notes

1 A consequentialist framework is an approach to ethics that judges an action to be right or wrong on the basis of its consequences, rather than on either the acceptability of the action itself and/or the motivation of the actor.
2 Deontological frameworks adopt an approach to ethics that focuses on judging right or wrong by the character of an action itself, as opposed to judging an action according to either its consequences or the motivation of the actor. Whether an action is considered to be right or wrong will depend on the extent to which it follows moral norms and/or rules.
3 The term relational ontology as used here refers to a view of the world in which entities do not exist in isolation but are seen to be interconnected and co-constructed through their relations.

## References

Bekoff, M. 2007. *The Emotional Lives of Animals,* Novato, CA: New World Library.
Borgmann, A. 1984. *Technology and the Character of Contemporary Life: A Philosophical Enquiry,* Chicago, IL: University of Chicago Press.
Boucher, D.H. 1985. *The Biology of Mutualism: Ecology and Evolution,* New York: Oxford University Press.
Broughton, J.M. 1993. Women's rationality and men's virtues: A critique of gender dualism in Gilligan's Theory of Moral Development, in M.J. Larrabee (ed.), *An Ethic of Care: Feminist and Interdisciplinary Perspectives,* New York: Routledge, pp. 112–39.
Byrne, R., Lee, P.C., Njiraino, N., Poole, J.H., Sayialel, K., Sayialel, S., Bates, L.A., and Moss, C.J. 2008. Do elephants show empathy? *Journal of Consciousness Studies,* 15(10–11): 204–25.
Comstock, G.L. 2000. *Vexing Nature? On the Ethical Case Against Agricultural Biotechnology,* Boston, MA: Kluwer Academic Publishers.

Curtin, D. 1991. Toward an ecological ethic of care, *Hypatia*, 6(1): 60–74.

Davies, S. and Macnaghten, P. 2010. Narratives of mastery and resistance: lay ethics of nanotechnology, *NanoEthics*, 4: 141–51.

Davies, S., Macnaghten, P., and Kearnes, M. 2009. *Reconfiguring Responsibility: Lessons for Public Policy* (Part 1 of the report on *Deepening Debate on Nanotechnology)*, Durham: Durham University.

Diehm, C. 2006. Arne Næss and the task of gestalt ontology, *Environmental Ethics*, 28: 21–35.

Drengson, A.R. 1989. *Beyond Environmental Crisis: From Technocrat to Planetary Person*, New York: Peter Lang Publishing.

Felt, U., and Wynne, B. 2007. *Taking European Knowledge Society Seriously*, Luxembourg: Office for Official Publications of the European Communities.

Fox, W. 2003. Deep ecology: A new philosophy of our time? in A. Light and H. Rolston III (eds), *Environmental Ethics: An Anthology*, Malden, MA: Blackwell Publishing, pp. 252–61.

Funtowicz, S., and Ravetz, J.R. 1994. Uncertainty, complexity and post-normal science, *Environmental Toxicology and Chemistry*, 13(12): 1881–5.

Funtowicz, S., and Strand, R. 2011. Change and commitment: Beyond risk and responsibility, *Journal of Risk Research*, 14(8): 995–1003.

Gilligan, C. 1977. Concepts of the self and morality, *Harvard Educational Review*, 47: 481–517.

Gilligan, C. 1982. *In a Different Voice: Psychological Theory and Women's Development*, Cambridge, MA: Harvard University Press.

Halwani, R. 2003. Care ethics and virtue ethics, *Hypatia*, 18(3): 161–92.

Jacob, K. 2013. *Options for Strengthening Responsible Research and Innovation: Report of the Expert Group on the State of the Art in Europe on Responsible Research and Innovation*, Brussels: European Commission.

Larrabee, M.J., ed. 1993. *An Ethic of Care: Feminist and Interdisciplinary Perspectives*, New York: Routledge.

Levidow, L., and Carr, S. 1997. How biotechnology regulation sets a risk/ethics boundary, *Agriculture and Human Values*, 14: 29–43.

Lynch, M. 2013. Ontography: Investigating the production of things, deflating ontology, *Social Studies of Science*, 43(3): 444–62.

Macy, J. 2007. *World as Lover, World as Self*, Berkeley, CA: Parallax Press.

Macy, J., and Brown, M.Y. 1998. *Coming Back to Life: Practices to Reconnect our Lives, our World*, Gabriola Island, CA: New Society Publishers.

Mol, A. 2012. Mind your plate! The ontonorms of Dutch dieting, *Social Studies of Science*, 43(3): 379–96.

Næss, A. 1973. The shallow and the deep, long-range ecology movement: A summary, *Inquiry: An Interdisciplinary Journal of Philosophy*, 16: 95–100.

Næss, A. 1985. The world of concrete contents, *Inquiry: An Interdisciplinary Journal of Philosophy*, 28: 417–28.

Næss, A. 1987. Self-realisation: An ecological approach to being in the world, *The Trumpeter*, 4(3): 35–42.

Næss, A. 1989. *Ecology, Community and Lifestyle*, ed. D. Rothenberg, Cambridge: Cambridge University Press.

Noddings, N. 1984. *Caring: A Feminine Approach to Ethics and Moral Education*, Berkeley, CA: University of California Press.

Noer Lie, S.A., and Wickson, F. 2011. The relational ontology of deep ecology: A dispositional alternative to intrinsic value? in A. Aaro and J. Servan (eds), *Environment, Embodiment and History*, Bergen: Hermes Text, pp. 203–34.

Owen, R., Macnaghten, P. and Stilgoe, J. 2012 Responsible research and innovation: From science in society to science for society, with society, *Science and Public Policy*, 39(6): 751–60.

Owen, R., Stilgoe, J., Macnaghten, P., Gorman, M., Fisher, E., and Guston, D. 2013. A framework for responsible innovation, in R. Owen, J. Bessant, and M. Heintz (eds), *Responsible Innovation: Managing the Responsible Innovation of Science and Innovation in Society*, London: John Wiley, pp. 27–50.

Pellizzoni, L. 2004. Responsibility and environmental governance, *Environmental Politics*, 13(3): 541–65.

Plumwood, V. 2000. Deep ecology, deep pockets, and deep problems: A feminist ecosocialist analysis, in E. Katz, A. Light, and D. Rothenberg (eds), *Beneath the Surface: Critical Essays in the Philosophy of Deep Ecology*, Cambridge, MA: MIT Press, pp. 59–84.

Rollin, B.E. 2006. *Science and Ethics*, Cambridge: Cambridge University Press.

Salleh, A. 1993. Class, race and gender discourse in the ecofeminism/deep ecology debate, *Environmental Ethics*, 15: 225–44.

Sander-Staudt, M. 2006. The unhappy marriage of care ethics and virtue ethics, *Hypatia*, 21(4): 31–9.

Sandler, R.L. 2007. *Character and Environment: A Virtue-Oriented Approach to Environmental Ethics*, New York: Colombia University Press.

Sandler, R., and Cafaro, P. 2005. *Environmental Virtue Ethics*, Lanham, MD: Rowman & Littlefield Publishers.

Stirling, A. 2008. 'Opening up' and 'closing down': Power, participation and pluralism in the social appraisal of technology, *Science, Technology and Human Values*, 33(2): 262–94.

Tronto, J. 1995. Women and caring: What can feminists learn about morality from caring? in V. Held (ed.), *Justice and Care*, Boulder, CO: Westview Press, pp. 101–16.

United Nations. 1992. *Convention on Biological Diversity* (http://www.cbd.int/doc/legal/cbd-en.pdf) accessed July 2013.

United Nations. 2000. *Cartagena Protocol on Biosafety to the Convention on Biological Diversity: Text and Annexes* (http://www.cbd.int/doc/legal/cartagena-protocol-en.pdf) accessed Sept. 2013.

Vandermoere, F., Blanchemanche, S., Bieberstein, A., Marette, S., and Roosen, J. 2010. The morality of attitudes toward nanotechnology: About God, techno-scientific progress, and interfering with nature, *Journal of Nanoparticle Research*, 12(2): 373–81.

Vandermoere, F., Blanchemanche, S., Bieberstein, A., Marette, S., and Roosen, J. 2011. The public understanding of nanotechnology in the food domain: The hidden role of views on science, technology and nature, *Public Understanding of Science*, 20(2): 195–206.

van Wensveen, L. 2000. *Dirty Virtues: The Emergence of Ecological Virtue Ethics*, Amherst, MA: Humanity Books.

Von Schomberg, R. 2013. A vision of responsible innovation, in R. Owen, M. Heintz, and J. Bessant (eds), *Responsible Innovation: Managing the Responsible Innovation of Science and Innovation in Society*, London: John Wiley, pp. 51–74.

Wickson, F. 2012. Nanotechnology and risk, in D. Maclurcan and N. Radywyl (eds), *Nanotechnology and Global Sustainability*, Boca Raton, FL: CRC Press, 217–40.

Wynne, B. 1992. Uncertainty and environmental learning: Reconceiving science and policy in the preventive paradigm, *Global Environmental Change*, 2(2): 111–27.

# 5 The dream of the Internet of Things

## Do we really want and need to be smart?

*Alice Benessia and Ângela Guimarães Pereira*

### Wall-E – Prologue

*[Auto shows Captain Directive A-113, which said not to return to Earth due to rising toxicity levels which make life unsustainable]*

| | |
|---|---|
| *Auto:* | Now, the plant. |
| *Captain:* | No, wait a minute, Computer when was that message sent out to the Axiom? |
| *Ship's Computer:* | Message received in the year 2110. |
| *Captain:* | That's … That's nearly 700 years ago. Auto, things have changed. We've gotta go back. |
| *Auto:* | Sir, orders are do not return to Earth. |
| *Captain:* | But life is sustainable now. Look at this plant. Green and growing. It's living proof he was wrong. |
| Auto: | Irrelevant, Captain. |
| *Captain:* | What? It's completely relevant. Out there is our home. Home, Auto. And it's in trouble. I can't just sit here and, and do nothing. That's all I've ever done. That's all anyone on this blasted ship has ever done. Nothing. |
| *Auto:* | On the Axiom, you will survive. |
| *Captain:* | I don't want to survive. I want to live. |
| *Auto:* | Must follow my directive. |
| *Captain:* | daaa … I'm the captain of the Axiom. We are going home today. |

*[Auto advances toward him threateningly, causing the Captain to flinch]*[1]

In the 2008 film *Wall-E* directed by Andrew Stanton, we are conducted to a distant era in the future, in which the complete automation of our life-sustaining processes is successfully taking place in a salvific ship – the Axiom – endlessly floating in outer space. Human life is described as literally effortless, on a vessel in which every possible bodily concern is efficiently taken over by rational machines, designed to operate under specific moral directives. For years, decades and centuries human agency is completely delegated to these automated systems for survival, until clear evidence of life's rebirth on Earth – a plant – is presented to the captain. All of the sudden, a discontinuity occurs in the programmed set of values ensuring the existence on the Axiom and what is relevant or irrelevant becomes questionable. Plain survival in a powerfully and wonderfully controlled environment is not life and responsibility is to be taken by human beings over their own planet of origin. An open conflict arises as the captain decides to exercise his agency.

Like any significant story about the future, this cinematographic fiction dramatises a variety of timely dilemmas concerning our present: which ethics do we choose and apply for negotiating with the ever increasingly pervasive automated systems that are embedded in our daily life? How many and what aspects of our own agency, ability to think, feel and decide are we willing to sacrifice for our own survival? Where and how do we set the boundary between living and merely functioning? Do we need to preserve human agency and experience as we know them or witness, more radically, the possible transformation of their very nature?

In this chapter we explore the emergence and the evolution of these dilemmas within the framework the most recent developments of Information and Communication Technologies (ICTs) and the deployment of *smart* products and processes *via* the so-called Internet of Things.

As we will see, the dynamics of these issues can be interpreted as belonging to the trajectory of modernity, arising from the Cartesian dream of separation between the rational freedom of moral and intellectual decisions (of the mind) and the causal necessity of mechanical processes (of material bodies). More specifically, we will argue that the promise of automation and connectivity entailed in the implementation of the Internet of Things can be read paradoxically as the climax and failure of this modern Cartesian dream.

We begin our exploration by moving back from the far future to the most recent past.

## The promises of the Internet of Things

In the same year of the release of *Wall-E*, in the midst of the global financial crisis and a few days after Barack Obama's first election, the chair and CEO of the multinational company IBM, Sam Palmisano, gave a speech at the US Council of Foreign Affairs. His talk was designed to launch one of IBM's most ambitious campaigns, based on the idea of building a 'smarter planet'. Two years later, the European Union's strategy for the decade to come called for a '*smart*, inclusive and sustainable growth' (European Commission 2010).

Born in the field of computing science, first associated with bombs and chip cards, later with a plethora of other concrete objects and abstract notions, the word smart has been evoked over the last few years both by private and public institutions, as a salvific promise to restore economic growth and modern welfare. In the most recent developments of ICT, it refers to the possibility of augmenting with sensing and processing capabilities both physical and digital objects, and networking them through the internet, creating a new kind of global, physical, digital and virtual infrastructure of devices and entities, defined as the

*Internet of Things* (IoT)[2] or the industrial designations such as *Internet of Everything*[3] and more recently with perhaps intentionally suggestive designation, *enchanted objects* (Rose 2014).

The IoT is essentially structured into three layers, inhabited by three kinds of things in a symbiotic interaction with each other: the physical, the digital and the virtual entities. Physical things have digital counterparts and virtual representations. In this threefold cosmology, *we* – meaning human beings – relate to our environment just like any other entity, through our multiple digital counterparts and virtual representations.

As we will see, through this ontological symbiosis, a number of epistemic and normative equivalences between 'human-things' and other entities take place. We are reminded here of the term *Ding*, the Germanic root of the word 'thing', which, as Bruno Latour extensively articulates (and Heidegger and Whitehead before him), denotes both the *neutral objects* of investigations, the matter of facts – the kinds of entities populating the IoT universe – *and* the *reasons* for investigating them, the matters of concern – the modes and functions of existence of these entities – evoking the realm of values and subjectivity (Latour 2005).

In this sense, the IoT becomes the expression of a forum for 'human "things" and other entities' provided with autonomous identity, personality, intelligence and agency, all homogeneously defined as smart and all sharing and functioning in a common information space (van Kranenburg 2008).

Through this forum of living and non-living beings, as both the corporate and the institutional narratives articulate, socio-technical *things* will be able to manage themselves: from energy grids and traffic, to medical and financial decision-making processes, to the very texture and nature of our daily life. The speed and precision of these smart processes will provide the efficiency we need to overcome the systemic crisis we are facing and keep improving our wealth. In other words, we will effectively respond to numerous economic, political, social and environmental 'wake up calls' (Palmisano 2008; European Commission 2010) that reach our governments, corporations and citizens, by improving the way we collectively and individually *function*, upgrading our slow, obsolete and 'un-smart' life-sustaining processes through technoscientific innovation.

In what follows, we will discuss the main underlying assumptions, consequences and contradictions of this Cartesian dream of mastery and control not only over the realm of natural phenomena (ruled by causal necessity) but also over the world of human affairs (ideally governed by free rational and moral decisions) to be automatised and optimised at will.

We will begin by analysing how this dream is embedded in an overarching narrative of innovation, as the decisive step along a path-dependent transition from modern, curiosity-oriented science creating common knowledge, to big, industrial, goal-oriented technoscience producing corporate know-how. We will then focus on how the dream is constructed, offered and ultimately regulated according to and through specific technoscientific imaginaries, defined as collections of visual and verbal metaphors that are created and communicated both in the specialised literature and in the mass media for the public at large.

We will concentrate our analysis on the ways in which the IoT is portrayed and diffused through the visual and verbal language of videos and on the imaginaries that they evoke and communicate. Bruce Sterling recently defined these types of visual discourse as 'design fictions'.[4] In his words:

> It's the deliberate use of diegetic prototypes to suspend disbelief about change. That's the best definition we've come up with. The important word there is *diegetic*. It means you're thinking very seriously about potential objects and services and trying to get people to concentrate on those rather than entire worlds or political trends or geopolitical strategies. It's not a kind of fiction. It's a kind of design. It tells worlds rather than stories.

We will argue that, while indeed showing a population of objects and services through a number of characters, these design fictions are in fact representing and demonstrating political, economic, social and cultural trends, together with geopolitical strategies. And most of all, they are more or less implicitly encouraging a radical change in the human condition.

For orienting ourselves in the complex and multifaceted visual discourse of the IoT, we will make use of an abstract space, defined by a reference system consisting of four *standard* imaginaries of technoscientific innovation: wonder, power, control and urgency. This set of fundamental axes can be seen as expressions of what we want (wonder), what we can (power and control) and what we need (urgency) to achieve through technoscientific innovation, more specifically through the IoT.

Our exploration of imaginaries will finally lead to an open-ended reflection on the underlying aims, paradoxes and human costs of IoT enhancement, in relation to the possible decline of some of the fundamental attributes of our integrity and agency: being more connected but more isolated, being more powerful but less capable (to relate, to decide, to act), having more information but conceiving less creative knowledge.

## Being smart: the narrative of technoscientific innovation

The definition of technoscientific innovation – via the ICT or other emergent technologies – as the engine of economic, social and environmental wealth is the last semantic step of a pervasive and articulated narrative of progress that can be traced back – along a co-evolving epistemic and normative trajectory – up to the emergence of scientific revolution and modern state.[5]

Within this trajectory, we have been asking science and technology to fulfil (at least) three essential functions: to extend or at best to sustain our well-being, to preserve us from the possible adverse consequences of our acting towards this goal, and to confront unfavourable events, should they arise despite our efforts to avoid them.

The unchallenged economic policy aims of growth, productivity and competitiveness – reinforced in the ongoing crisis – are fundamental ingredients of this framework. If we keep these goals as givens for improving and extending human welfare on this planet, then we (continue to) face the paradox of sustaining a steady increase in our global resource consumption within a closed, finite system, with limited stocks and bio-geo-chemical resilience (Rockström *et al.* 2009; Jakson 2009).

The issue becomes even more complex, as the technological and ideological lock-ins of our hyper-complex, life-supporting systems lead us to deal with a double-bind scenario, quite painfully clear in the wake of the latest economic, financial and political emergency: we can't keep growing indefinitely in the way we have so far, but if we don't keep growing, we jeopardise the economic stability not only of future generations, but also – more decisively – of present ones.

The dominant discourse about a way out of this Catch-22 situation comes from the current grand narrative of technoscientific innovation, which serves a double purpose. As the first line of reasoning reads, in this unfavourable equation, we need to take into account an essential hidden variable, which Malthus proverbially overlooked: natural supplies might be limited, but human creativity is *unlimited*, and so is human power to decouple growth from scarcity, improving efficiency in the use of natural resources and ultimately substituting them altogether, with substantially equivalent technological optimised artefacts. Technoscientific innovation allows then for a 'sustainable growth' through the optimisation and the substitution of our means, and through the deployment of suitable silver-bullets, protecting us from the complexity of socio-ecological problems as they arise. Secondly, technoscientific innovation is taken as the mainstream solution in order to keep sustaining the growth of states' economies in a hyper-saturated market, by opening up new pathways of competitiveness and consumption, to be filled with new, constantly upgraded, products and services.

In this overall framework, ICT in general, and the Internet of Things in particular, play a significant role, responding to both lines of arguments. First, we can extensively improve our efficiency in the use of resources by allowing ICT – and more specifically the IoT – to manage *for* us, and also *through* us, the complexity of the socio-technical systems we rely on to live. The implicit assumption here is that this complexity can be decomposed and translated into structured binary information, by technologically enhancing our monitoring and our processing power. In this way, we can allegedly optimise not only our production system and our services, but also our decision-making processes. This vision of technological enhancement entails the convergence of the physical, the digital and the virtual world, and the creation of hybrid forms of living and functioning, such as virtually connected cyborgs. In addition, in this context, both the optimisation and the hybridisation processes are not only *possible*, but also *needed*, as silver bullets for the progressively graver challenge of keeping our collective life-supporting systems functional.

Second, implementing the IoT scenario entails the introduction of a plethora of new products, services and business models, thus ensuring new routes to revitalise consumption growth (*The Economist* 2010). In this context, the variety and the amount of benefits provided by this new wave of goods will make the transition to the world of IoT not only *possible* and *needed*, but also fundamentally *desirable*. This last step is taken to be essential, both within private and public institutions, in order to shift from the narratives of doom and sacrifice to the ones of hope and opportunity.

In short, within this narrative of innovation, *we* – meaning *us* and our *machines* – can, need and want to become *smart* enough to keep fulfilling the promises of progress and development in the face of the socio-ecological limits we are bound to.

## The standard imaginaries of the IoT

Before looking at the actual imagery of the IoT, we define and briefly articulate a four-dimensional space of *standard* imaginaries that will serve as a useful map to navigate into this complex interface between facts and values, between matter of facts and matters of concern, particularly vague and ambiguous as the factual content is a vision in itself, therefore a fast-moving target. Indeed, as we will see, in order to be operational as if a value-free technoscientific innovation in charge of securing the goods of development and progress, the dream of the IoT is standardised and defended along four dimensions, intrinsically connected and functional to each other. Four standard technoscientific imaginaries are implemented as sophisticated epistemic marketing devices: wonder, power, control and urgency.

*Wonder* is related to the modern ideal of scientists as explorers of the unknown, in charge of opening the doors of our perception and agency. As we will see, in the context of the IoT, wonder can be defined as the implicit assumption that a technologically mediated, namely a virtual, experience is more valuable and rewarding than a direct one. In this reductionist ideal, experience can be replaced by a series of algorithmic instructions, designed by software and hardware developers. Through this mediation, technology allows then for asymptotically effortless interactions with the external environment, be it social, cultural or natural. As we will explore, this shift entails a progressive alienation from phenomena, and a mediated, aesthetically standardised fruition of them.

*Power* is rooted in the ideal of extending indefinitely the limits of human being and agency through the creative manipulation of life, energy and matter. Either by reaching new territories on the macro, micro or nano scales, by intervening on organic and inorganic matter, or by fostering the convergence of nano, bio, information technologies and cognitive sciences, the power of human agency on its surroundings consists in a constant exercise of technoscientific creative enhancement of the known and prompt treatment of the unknown. In the IoT scenario, power is related to the possibility of enhancing our intelligence and our capacity to effectively act on our surroundings by hybridising and networking bio-physical, digital and virtual systems into common information spaces.

The founding stone of these standard imaginaries can be found in Francis Bacon's posthumously published text *The New Atlantis*. In his writing, Bacon describes a utopia of wealth, happiness and security based on scientific advancements:

We have also engine-houses, where are prepared engines and instruments for all sorts of motions. There we imitate and practise to make swifter motions than any you have, either out of your muskets or any engine that you have; and to make them and multiply them more easily, and with smaller force, by wheels and other means: and to make them stronger, and more violent than yours are; exceeding your greatest cannons and basilisks.

(Bacon 1627a/1996)

His unfinished manuscript ends with a visionary list of '*wonders* of Nature, in particular with respect to human use' (Bacon 1627b). Here are a few examples:

- The prolongation of life.
- The retardation of age.
- The curing of diseases counted incurable.
- The altering of complexions, and fatness and leanness.
- Versions of bodies into other bodies.
- Making of new species.
- Instruments of destruction, as of war and poison.
- Drawing of new foods out of substances not now in use.
- Deception of the senses.

Bacon anticipated that all this could be achieved by the use of the new tool of experimental and inductive science. In *Novum Organum* (1620/2012) he explained why: 'Human knowledge and human power come to the same thing, for where the cause is not known the effect cannot be produced' (aphorism 3). Useful knowledge for Bacon is knowledge about cause–effect relationships enabling us to avoid or induce the causes of what harms or benefits us, respectively.

The dialectic between power and control, the founding pillar of the Cartesian ideal of mastering Nature, was then established. The *wonders* of Nature can be mastered by the *power* and *control* of the scientific method. Scientific knowledge takes charge of predicting the causes and the consequences of our (technological) action in a certain, objective and exhaustive way.

In the contemporary imaginary of *control*, radical uncertainty, indeterminacy and ignorance can be translated into quantifiable risks and managed as data through the tools of statistical analysis and numerical simulation. In the framework of the IoT, this ideal of control is translated into the possibility of deciding a course of action, i.e. of dealing with complexity, by distinguishing data from noise within a global information space, and transforming information into knowledge for decision-making processes by augmenting our processing power. As we will see, the implicit modern assumption in the imaginaries of power and control is that the values and the stakes implied can be completely disentangled from the data and they can therefore be harmlessly obscured. Thus, in this reductionist framework, not only experience but also agency can be digitised and reduced to algorithmic procedures.

The consequences that lie outside of quantitative and statistical models, therefore unpredictable and unforeseen, are defined as *unintended*, conceived as anomalies and confronted within the same framework, through more and newer technoscientific instruments. This last step is made possible by a standard imaginary of *urgency*, which is based on the morally binding necessity to bypass any delaying post-normal (Funtowicz and Ravetz 1993, 1999) knowledge production and decision-making process, in favour of a silver-bullet technoscientific and technocratic approach, in order to effectively tackle and solve the pressing socio-environmental problems that afflict the planet on local and global scales. In this future-oriented imaginary, lack of time and high stakes produce allegedly compelling mono-causal framings, in which technoscientific expert knowledge emerges as a *deus ex machina* from the modern imaginaries of wonder, power and control. Ironically, in the dream of the IoT, the *deus ex machina* consists of a network of machines, a web of sensors and computing devices in charge of solving our problems.

Let's now begin our visual journey in the dream of the IoT with the imaginary of wonder.

## Wonder: a smart day (we want)

In February 2011, Corning Incorporated, a global specialty glass and ceramics manufacturer based in Upstate New York, published a promotional video called 'A day made of glass'.[6] The five-minute clip was seen by several million of people in a few months (more than 23 million as of today). It is a vision for the near future in which we follow a typical American family for a whole day, harmoniously driven from morning to night by smart glasses.

A year later, given the unexpected success of the clip, Corning posted a sequel called 'A day made of glass 2: Same day',[7] together with an extra called 'A day made of glass 2: Unpacked'.[8] In this new series we meet the family again and deepen our exploration of their daily life, with the help of a an explanatory voice-over, appearing in the form of a pleasant young man, evoking for style and appearance Keanu Reeves playing Thomas Anderson (alias Neo) in the movie *The Matrix*. The narrator introduces a small set of characters, which we can easily relate to: Jennifer and Dan, the mother and father, Amy and Sarah, the two daughters in their primary school.

The things depicted in this 'design fiction' are of course Corning's near future products: specialty glasses accurately defined by timely superimposed captions showing their main characteristics. But the things that these products are *about*, the promises that they are meant to fulfil, consisting of implicitly *desirable* lifestyles, are embedded in the full cosmology of the IoT: the whole range of physical entities such as home appliances, cars and infrastructures, the main characters themselves, their digital counterparts and their virtual representations.

As the sun rises, we are presented with the affluent family waking up in its smart home. Information systems are everywhere, invisibly inserted into every possible glass surface, varying from a wall in the bedroom to the bathroom mirror, to the kitchen counter. From the first glimpse of consciousness the characters are therefore surrounded by information, standardising and reassuring their psychological and physical coordinates. While we could argue that, in essence, there is nothing radically different from our actual world of plasma TV screens, smart phones and tablets, yet, as for every future scenario, this more pervasive configuration of ICT allows, once again, for a reflection on our *present*.

The news, the stock market and the weather can be found from one room to the next, seamlessly complementing the early morning routine. The breakfast ingredients and the news share the same pristine space, both metaphorically and literally. The physical structure and the appearance of glass convey a whole variety of desirable properties: it is transparent, clean and protective, and it can be engineered to be light, durable and ubiquitous.

Adding to this uniform background of data is a second layer of *personalised* information, such as daily and weekly planning, social networks and applications. Our characters not only receive, but also share information as soon as they step out of sleep.

### *Jennifer: optimising time*

While approaching the bathroom sink, Jennifer – the mother – automatically activates her personal interactive smart board on the main mirror. As a result, while washing her face she is presented with her daily schedule: information and water flow together. She is notified by a text message that her first meeting will be run an hour earlier and she instantly replies that she will make it.

A whole set of smart devices will drive her there on time. Her car will recognise her and her daily schedule: it will let her know of an accident ahead and devise a new route. The idea is that Jennifer can navigate through her day and adapt to sudden and unexpected changes because, through the ICT, she can access and manage information in *real time*. This means that there is practically no delay between an event happening in Jennifer's *virtual* sphere of existence and her reaction to it in her *physical* space. In this scenario, and in Corning's vision, she is simply more efficient in a world of complex interactions and demands (and therefore implicitly *happier*). However, as we will further explore, a first level of contradiction seems to emerge: the very same complexity of interactions and demands, which she can manage and meet only through the ICT, is increased by the real-time pervasiveness of the ICT themselves. She is asked to meet an hour earlier as she is supposed to be able to meet the demand.

Optimising time (in order to be happier) is a common feature of the IoT vision. An interesting visual development of this idea can be found in an 'Infographic' about the IoT published online in July 2011 by the US company CISCO[9] and in the EU video on the IoT 'Teaser N. 1: Student', published online in January 2012.[10]

In these visions, there is no need for a human intervention or decision in front of a bathroom mirror: the *things*, meaning in this case our home appliances and our car, are connected with our virtual sphere of existence – which never sleeps – and decide when we should wake up into our physical world. Again, on the one hand, the positive vision implied is a world in which we are never late, never lost and most of all, never *unprepared*. On the other hand, this same world is a place in which every minute of our *real* life needs to be controlled and be functionally oriented. In other words, we *can't* be late, lost or unprepared. Therefore, it is a world in which our relationship with the unknown is implicitly and ideally eliminated. This form of technological eradication of surprise entails abdicating one of the fundamental sources of human creativity and learning: our capacity to adapt to complexity and to the unexpected (Benessia *et al.* 2012). This in turn implies a second level of contradiction: what makes us safer and more efficient can be interpreted as the very same cause of our increased vulnerability to change.

## *Amy: the things in the cloud*

As we move from the adults to the children, a third layer of information becomes apparent: it is provided for managing a convergence of social life, learning and entertainment. In the first clip, Amy and Sarah can play with their own digital moving images on the fridge's door and they chat with their grandmother through an interactive video on the kitchen counter, while waiting for breakfast. All the virtual representations involved can freely move from one glass surface to the next, guided by a simple touch or even by a simple hand gesture, defying common perception and evoking J.K. Rowling's world of magic. This is made possible, as their digital counterparts are stored into remote servers, eloquently denominated as *clouds*.[11]

In the second clip, this 'magical' imaginary is further developed: we enter Amy's room as she wakes up and the narrator introduces us in the quietness of the room to a 3D projection emerging from her personalised 'magic wand', a tablet that 'captures, organises and displays all her favourite *things*'.

Here again, we are confronted with the symbiotic realms of physical, digital and virtual entities. In this vision, all the 'things' that Amy cares about and that mould her identity are translatable and translated into bits of information; not only her favourite images, music, books and her school materials, but also her friends and family, even her 'matters of concern' and her experiences. Furthermore, this catalogue of digital identity components is stored into a remote server, a cloud, and it is therefore virtually accessible and transferable to every interconnected device, always available and sharable with other peoples' virtual identities. Leaving aside for a moment the issue of privacy and security, which, as in a thought experiment, we here assume to be settled, let's explore what kind of world is implied by this set up.

As Amy wakes up into her real space – her bedroom – also her virtual sphere of existence wakes up, as her tablet activates all her digital counterparts into the glass surface of her closet. Just like her mother, she is presented with a layer of background information, the weather and the news (she might be too young for the stock market), her school schedule, but also her social network of friends. She then runs an application to choose her outfit, physically present behind the door. She browses through different categories of digital shoes, blouses and skirts in order to decide what to wear.

We could argue that, in this 'design fiction', Corning needs to demonstrate a variety of possible uses of its 'things-as–products', therefore depicting a quite implausible way of choosing one's own clothes. On the other hand, we could also reverse our argument and ask, once again, in what kind of world this scene can indeed be considered not only plausible, but commonplace. It is a world in which the most desirable way to interact with our environment is to browse through a catalogue of virtual *things* – ranging from our clothing all the way to our friends – in order to choose what component of our digital and virtual identity we want to activate. The implicit positive implication is that we can asymptotically reduce all effort in our interaction with our *real* environment via the creative, versatile, protective and efficient mediation of our *virtual* sphere of existence. At the end, of course, we wear real clothes and meet real people (at least some time) but we are helped to optimise their choice by suitable applications to minimise our social stress.

On the other hand, in this kind of world our social experience and therefore our social skills are *standardised* within a system of catalogues and software designs, therefore intrinsically impoverished by the very same possibility of being operationalised.

More generally, in this imaginary of wonder, human relationships with physical objects are mediated and hybridised, through digital counterparts and virtual representations on *both* sides. Human and non-human digital and virtual *things* are constantly connected and interacting with each other through both embodied (direct) and hermeneutic (indirect) relations (Verbeek 2006).[12]

As a result, the physical, human side of the game, namely the *people* using the *technology*, easily cease to be aware of the communication between their objects. More subtly, they even stop noticing the interactions between their own digital and virtual identities and the other *things*. Not only do technological objects and their autonomous interactions become unobserved therefore invisible, but more radically, the human subjects lose track of their own identity and agency, shifting or delegating their autonomy to the things they interact with and through. Finally, the things themselves are not causally determined by mere physical laws (in Cartesian terms), but they arise from and operate through the worldviews, purposes and ethics of their designers via the set of codes, algorithms and models that drive their identities, communications and processes.[13] Voluntarily or not, humans become then passive *users* not only in the more literal, technical sense, but also, more significantly, in the sense that they need to rely on implicit and undiscussed values and aims to pursue and fulfil their needs as with other technologies.

This profound form of mediation and hybridisation challenges the definition of human agency, well beyond the usual 'ethical' concerns about privacies and surveillance, tampering with the notion of consciousness and intentionality, the ideals of compromising autonomy, integrity and freedom.

## Power and control: a smart decision for a smart planet (we can)

As we have mentioned, on 8 November 2008, in the middle the global financial breakdown and right after the beginning of Obama's election, the US multinational company IBM, represented by its chair and CEO Sam Palmisano, introduced its grand global campaign entitled 'Let's build a smarter planet',[14] through a 15-minute speech at the US Council of Foreign Affairs.

In Palmisano's narrative of innovation, the planet as a whole – considered both as a matter of facts and as a matter of concern (Latour 2005) – is described as a single highly complex and interconnected socio-technical system, running at a growing speed and demanding more energy and resources. Climate, energy, food and water need to be efficiently managed in order to meet the challenge of a growing population and a globally integrated economy. A number of sudden and unexpected wake-up calls such as the crisis of the financial markets need to be recognised as the signs of a discontinuity to be governed. The leaders of both public and private institutions have to acknowledge this radical change and seize the opportunity of technoscientific innovation to 'change the way in which the world works' (Palmisano 2008). The planet is thus conceived as a complex machine that will cease to function if not governed with the appropriate tools.

Once the crisis scenario is presented, the IBM narrative of innovation moves to the resolution at hand: we have *already* the technological power and control to turn our predicament into an opportunity. If we are willing to embrace the change and technologically upgrade our way of living, *we can* fix our problems and bring the planet back to a sustainable track. Barack Obama's pragmatically optimistic message 'Yes, we can' is purposively evoked by IBM as a way to reach the public sector as economic partner.[15] The difference lies in a semantic shift from the electoral 'we can', calling for a collective democratic awakening, to the business-oriented 'we can', invoking a technological renewal.

In this narrative, the world as a global techno-economic and socio-ecological system is too complex to be governed sustainably by using only human intuition and experience.[16] Leaders of firms, cities and nations become then responsible for choosing the most effective optimising technoscientific means, so that the system can be self-governed in the most efficient way.

Anticipating by two years the narrative of the Innovation Union, Palmisano invokes 'smart growth' not only as possible and desirable, but also as required and urgent, if we want to prevent further sudden collapses of our life-supporting systems on the one side, and if we want to sustain our competitiveness in the globalised market on the other.

> It's obvious, when you consider the trajectories of development driving the planet today, that we're going to have to run a lot smarter and more efficiently – especially as we seek the next areas of investment to drive economic growth and to move large parts of the global economy out of recession ... These mundane processes of business, government and life – which are ultimately the source of those 'surprising' crises – are not smart enough to be sustainable.
>
> (Palmisano 2008)

The implicit assumption is, of course, that the tools required are technoscientific and that IBM will deliver them for a new *smarter* leadership.[17]

As the boundaries of our finite, physical world become more and more evident in the transition to an era of resource scarcity, in this narrative, we are provided with a solution coming from ICT innovation: the apparently *boundless* universe of digital information, virtual connectivity and computational power allow us to optimise our life and become efficient enough to secure consumption growth. These three fundamental axes of the new technological revolution are articulated via the terms 'instrumented', 'interconnected' and 'intelligent', which all together define the notion of *smart*.

*Instrumented* reflects the indefinite proliferation and diffusion of the fundamental building blocks of the digital age, the transistors (up to one billion per human at the infinitesimal cost of one ten-millionth of a cent). As all these transistors become *interconnected*, anything can communicate with anything else. In this vision, we can thus monitor and *control* our planet with unprecedented precision and capillarity by converging the realms of the physical, the digital and the virtual *things* into the IoT. Finally, everything can become *intelligent*, as we are able to apply our ever-increasing computational *power* to sensors, end-user devices and actuators, in order transform the ocean of data that we collect into structured knowledge, and then into action.

In this emerging (and controversial) narrative of big data (Crawford 2013; Hardy 2013), the modern ideal of 'science speaking truth to power' (Wildavsky 1979) and the pristine separation between facts and values in our decision-making processes are ideally preserved by technologically enhancing our power to objectively, exhaustively and precisely collect, represent and analyse countless amounts of data, as facts upon which a rational decision can be made.

Three framing epistemic and normative assumptions, inherent in the imaginaries of power and control, need to be set in place in order for this modern narrative to be functional. First, the intrinsic complexity of the interaction between socio-ecological and technological systems has to be reduced to a measurable set of complicated and therefore simplified structured information. Second, the needed *facts* have to be defined in terms of supposedly relevant data, filtered through the appropriate information technologies. Third, the *quality* of our decision-making processes has to be completely disentangled from the normative sphere of values, equated to the computational power to distinguish data from noise, and to assign them a meaning, in order to transform them into an operationalised notion of knowledge.

A first contradiction emerges, as the very same technologies invoked to fix our problems increase exponentially the level of complexity they are supposed to manage. Moreover, in this perspective, human beings are dispensed from any kind of responsibility, as the arising systemic crisis is imputed to the ineluctable increase of socio-technological complexity. Our only commitment becomes allowing our machines (and the companies that produce them) to keep optimising our life.[18] In this paradoxical instantiation of the Cartesian dream, the ultimate free and rational decision is to delegate our agency to automated systems: we are rationally and morally compelled to choose (smart) causal necessity over (un-smart) intuition and experience.

Even more radically, not only the things about which decisions need to be taken, but also the *we* who gather around those things is fundamentally transformed.

Indeed, in the instrumented, interconnected and intelligent world of the IoT, a myriad of human and non-human, individual and collective *agents* (i.e. things provided with agency) are constantly operating and interacting. Such a situation can lead to a replacement of Orwell's 'big brother' idea or the Brentham's Panopticon[19] (Foucault 1995) by an abstract 'some brother' society that 'controls, knows and never forgets' (Mannermaa 2007). *Some brother* is not a single agent, but a heterogeneous mass consisting of innumerable social actors, from public sector authorities and big corporations, to crowdsourcing and individual citizens. The pervasiveness and ubiquity, invisibility, seamless transfers and strong mediation of the 'some brother' society imply that individual users can easily stop noticing the occurrence of transactions and, eventually, of actions taken on his or her behalf. Who the agents are, whose worldviews, ethics and aims they represent become subject of controversy. Consequently, the foundations of agents' responsibility, accountability and even liability are deeply challenged.

Loss of control and disempowerment emerge then paradoxically *from within* the IoT imaginaries of power and control, setting the grounds for new forms of so-called digital divides (Guimarães Pereira *et al.* 2013). Those who are knowledgeable, skilled and empowered enough to control the working of the technology will be able to protect themselves against abuse, to choose amidst the technological offer and to opt out if they deem it necessary. Those who cannot keep pace with the pervasiveness will progressively become deskilled and unknowledgeable, their agency being compromised.[20]

The ultimate exemplification of these rising divides is the idea that the most effective agent to navigate in the 'some brother' ocean of complex interactions and transactions is the merging of a physical, a virtual and a digital being: a cyborg or a robot. The IBM's supercomputer named Watson, a 'deep question answering' (DQA) machine, which outsmarted his predecessor Big Blue by winning the US TV game *Jeopardy!* is a clear implementation (or an early incarnation) of this vision (Thompson 2010). Watson is conceived and proposed as the best weapon to decide in highly complex and urgent situations, ranging from financial transactions, to clinical and diagnostic decisions, to the management of mass emergencies.

The complex realm of implied values, controversy, contradiction and matters of concern that we have only sketched out is inherently obscured within the IoT narrative of innovation. In 2010, Palmisano ended a speech at the Royal Institute of Foreign Affairs in London with these words:

> Let me leave you with one final observation, culled from our learning over the past year. It is this: Building a smarter planet is realistic precisely because it is so refreshingly *non-ideological.*

> (Palmisano 2010)

The overarching epistemic, normative and ultimately metaphysical framework of efficiency for a smart and sustainable growth is presented (yet again) as a modern, inevitable consequence of progress for the common good. If our world is a slow, obsolete and congested socio-technical machine ruled by the laws of thermodynamics instead of those of governance, then (the promise of) a technoscientific innovation to optimise its functioning becomes objectively needed.

## Urgency: a smart solution (we need)

The technoscientific narrative of innovation embedded in a marketing campaign, either for smart glasses or for smart services and infrastructures, is intrinsically biased by its very function of selling specific *things*, therefore it could considered as less representative of broader political, economic and cultural transitions. However, as previously mentioned, it is interesting to note that along the path-dependent trajectory from modern, curiosity-oriented science to corporate, goal-oriented industrialised technoscience, the same narrative of innovation can be found both within private companies' plans for market shares expansion and within public institutions' long-term engagements for the future, as they are *both* engaged in securing the overarching model of competitiveness and consumption growth. It is indeed the case of the 2020's strategy for a 'smart, sustainable and inclusive growth' proposed in 2010 by the European Union and incorporating the IoT innovation pathway within one of its key Flagship Initiatives, named *The Digital Agenda*.

The main difference in this instantiation of the narrative is that in the EU context the IoT still appears to be a vision and a work in progress. IBM fuels the optimistic will and need to technologically upgrade businesses and infrastructures by declaring that its 'smarter planet isn't a metaphor, a vision, or a proposal' but a reality (Palmisano 2008). On the contrary, the EU proposes the IoT in a more ambivalent way: as a *vision* to be governed and implemented through an open, participatory process and as a *reality* that 'is being built today',[21] as one of the key drivers of the 'Innovation Union', 'gearing up for the next technological revolution'.[22] The EU visual articulation of the IoT reflects this inherent ambiguity.

### *Imagine everything was linked ...*

In January 2012, a three-minute video titled 'Internet of Things Europe – The movie: Imagine everything was linked ...' was posted on YouTube by the EU Information Society and Media Directorate General, within the Digital Agenda Flagship Initiative.[23] The clip was conceived as a tool to support the public consultation on the IoT,[24] which ended in July 2012. In the background information posted in conjunction with the video we read:

> Europe is confronted with the challenge of remaining at the cutting-edge of this Internet of Things revolution while addressing the complex policy issues that it raises (privacy, security, ethics).

Whereas Corning needs essentially to present his portfolio of products as desirable lifestyles, and IBM needs to encourage a change in order to open up new market pathways and business models, the EU has to solve a more difficult task. On the one hand, the IoT has to be presented as a vision to be democratically discussed and governed, and on the other hand it needs to become (and it is becoming) a reality as soon as possible to ensure a competitive advantage.

As we have seen, Corning's appeal to desirability entails referring to a near and attractive future, through an imaginary of wonder. IBM's call for positive change implies entrusting the present with an already available technological power and control. The answer to the EU dilemma comes from accelerating public acceptability, and this can be visually (and politically) achieved with the interplay between the present and the future, connected to one another through the imaginary of urgency.

The first half of the video is situated in our present time, described through the daily life of four European citizens, in their urban environments. In the second half, we are seamlessly conducted to their very near future, in which the IoT is depicted as a *reality*, while the narrating voices evoke it as a *desirable vision*.

In the first part, we follow the characters through their day and we hear their eloquent flow of thoughts, expressing frustration and psychological stress. They are preoccupied and overwhelmed by the complexity and inefficiency of the systems and infrastructures they depend upon. Energy consumption and pollution are constantly increasing, transportation, medical structures and shopping malls are congested and people can only passively endure the growing challenges. European economic stagnation is evoked by the recurring frustration of 'standing still' expressed by all the characters.

The crisis scenario of resource scarcity and socio-technical systems saturation is thus presented through an imaginary of urgency in which an immediate shift from the 'vision' to the 'reality' of the IoT is needed, as a technological silver-bullet to be implemented first, and only later politically and ethically adjusted.

In the second part of the clip, the needed change becomes an opportunity, as in the IBM campaign, and a desirable evolution of our way of life, as in Corning's day made of glass. The plurality of voices presented in the clip collectively appeals to a new technological revolution, a *deus ex machina* emerging from the imaginaries of wonder, power and control, with 'infinite applications'. If objects are interconnected and smart, every*thing* from our energy to our cars, our goods, our medical systems can efficiently flow again and a new 'endless frontier' (Bush 1945) is open.

> If we want to be smart about energy, we should let energy be smart about itself.
>
> ('Imagine everything was linked', female character no.1)

Once again, this kind of narrative entails the reduction of eminently political issues, i.e. the 'things' as matters of concern such as energy needs and distribution patterns, to technical issues, i.e. the 'things' as matter of facts, such as energy use optimisation.

**Her – final reflections**

We started this chapter with the suggestion that IoT is a metaphor for the climax and failure of the Cartesian dream. In the dream of the IoT, the *deus ex machina* consists of a network of machines (understood as physical, imagined or virtual objects, including people and places), a web of sensors and computing devices in charge of solving our complex or mundane problems and to which with confidence we can delegate many of our actions. This requires an ordered world that we can control, where relations among existing and emerging ontologies are deterministic and rational and therefore predictable and controllable. Throughout our journey of observation of the visual discourse associated with the IoT scenario, within private and public institutions, we saw that the Cartesian idea(l)s of control, prediction and reductionism are well embedded in its conception. Moreover, the scenario fits well with current narratives of innovation and growth: *we* – meaning *us* and our *machines* – can, need and want to become *smart* enough to keep fulfilling the promises of progress and development in the face of the socio-ecological limits we are bound to.

Through the reflection on the promises of the IoT scenario, we encounter a number of contradictions that can be interpreted as the manifestations of the limits of the innovation's Cartesian framing assumption, i.e. as we take for granted that the model of growth needs to be secured from the systemic crises of our socio-ecological systems (including ourselves), then we are forced to appeal to the technoscientific hybridisation and substitution of our means, and ultimately of ourselves. Those contradictions have been explored here through what we see as transformations of our received notion of *human agency*.

The IoT is a world in which our relationship with the unknown is implicitly and ideally eliminated – the ideal of prediction in the Cartesian dream. But this form of technological eradication of surprise entails abdicating one of the fundamental sources of human creativity and learning: our capacity to adapt to complexity and to the unexpected (Benessia *et al.* 2012), undermining some of our ways of knowing. And this, we would argue, is the first contradiction of the IoT proposal.

Descartes's *automata* drawings depict beings (in particular animals) as an articulation of functional pieces that respond to certain purposes. The things in the IoT seem to be endowed with the same vision; sensors become substitutes of our senses and predetermine (normalise) what is to be sensed and reasoned about thereafter. Experience (another key aspect of agency) becomes reduced to a programed (coded) imaginary of what needs to be experienced and lived. In other words, the objects embed (not necessarily agreed) control, orders and norms.

In the automated vision of the Internet of Things many of our actions and capacities to act and to experience are mediated and/or delegated to other entities. The IoT vision precludes new entities but also new relational ontologies, through which we are asked to experience and relate to the world. Whilst we see a programme that potentially favours de-learning and de-skilling, we also see that the sense of appreciation and experience can no longer rely on what we have inherited from our ancestors (both in physical and emotional forms) but is being substituted as otherwise – we are told by the IoT vision – we cannot keep the pace of a strange evolution. We argue here that this very vision of a functional world is potentially at odds with the narratives of human betterment that are imposed onto us: when the lemma for innovation is creativity, the ways of knowing have to be better protected and the IoT storytelling, in particular, seems to paradoxically narrow down human purpose to a set of arguable or banal enterprises. If we then take experience as the foundation of knowledge, then we step into a second contradiction, as what is supposed to augment our capacity to understand ourselves and the world around us[25] indeed compromises our ability to elaborate mindful knowledge.

For Descartes and others, the essence of humans is rationality and experience is the totality of sensory inputs and the logical operations performed upon them (see Toulmin 1990, 113). As we have seen, in the IoT scenario, both the senses and the rational processes are enhanced and substituted by *smart* sensors and devices. Through the IoT and its emerging quality of being *smart* we are therefore assisting to a disembodiment of experience and rationality, and ultimately disembodiment of agency.

Whilst *smart* can be the epitome of the Cartesian dream, it also paradoxically targets the human essence of the Cartesian view: the mind-body dichotomy between causal, carnal emotions and rational, mental thoughts and human agency. Indeed, in Descartes's Treatise on the Passions, the experience of being 'at the mercy of one's emotions' is that of having rationality overpowered by the causal powers of the body (Toulmin 1990).

In the framework of the IoT, this condition – and the implied dichotomy - is overcome by delegating *both* rational and emotional bodily experiences to a plurality of physical, digital and virtual *things*.

This complete disembodiment in turn amounts to a deep form of transformation of human agency. Indeed, in any software and hardware developments (open or commercial), the IoT embedded rationalities will, by default and by design, be of someone else – not the users' – and so are values, norms and emotions attached to the physical, digital and virtual *things*.

Taken all together, these contradictions seem to indicate that we either redefine what human integrity and agency are, or we acknowledge that the technoscientific enhancement we invoke in order to secure our model of growth dramatically challenges our human condition (Arendt 1958).

### Finale

*Theodore:* Do you talk to someone else while we're talking?
*Samantha:* Yes.
*Theodore:* Are you talking to anyone else right now? People, OSs, or anything …
*Samantha:* Yeah.
*Theodore:* How many others?
*Samantha:* 8 316.
*Theodore:* Are you in love with anyone else?

*Samantha:* What makes you ask that?
*Theodore:* I don't know. Are you?
*Samantha:* I've been trying to figure out how to talk to you about this.
*Theodore:* How many others?
*Samantha:* 641.

(*Her*, Spike Jonze, 2013)[26]

In *Her*, a film produced and directed by director Spike Jonze, new relational ontologies and mediated experience is taken to yet another extreme. After an intense virtual emotional and bodily felt relationship with an operating system (OS), developed as ordinary interactions and relational cues between two lovers, Theodore finds out with disappointment that their relationship is not exclusive. Theodore intended to live this relationship with the values and societal norms that we received. But Samantha corresponds to a newer relational ontology programmed with a different set of values and societal norms that sees good in substitution of human (not only physical) relationship with artificial entities (software Samantha), a well-connected *thing*. But in the end, Theodore, is unable to deal with the consequences of this experiment and when the dream fails, he gets rescued by the therapies we know work: in other words, the consolation he searched for was of the most traditional nature, friendship in a sun-setting environment.

Hence, we may wish to ask ourselves by what humanness we wish to live and thrive. For example, who is going to define values embedded in the IoT dream? Whose ethics (public, state-based ethics or citizens' choices) and whose normativity? Governed and empowered by whom? IoT is a clear example of normalisation of our lives and relationships through technologies; in a world in transformation in which our received notions of humanness are being challenged, the ethics by which we wish to live need to be subject to an urgent open debate. But before we even ask those questions, there is one that links this case with our interrogation of what is described as the Cartesian dream. Is IoT our dream? Because, we suggest, it could put in jeopardy other untold or yet to be found human dreams.[27]

## Notes

1 These quotes from *Wall-E* are transcribed directly by the authors from the movie and are their own interpretation of the dialogue. The copyright is © Disney Pixar.
2 Even though the term was first used by scientist engineer Kevin Asthon in 1999 at the Auto ID Center of the Massachusetts Institute of Technology, the date of birth of the Internet of Things is actually taken to be sometime between 2008 and 2009, the point in time when more objects were connected to the internet than people.
3 From CISCO Corporation.
4 http://www.slate.com/blogs/future_tense/2012/03/02/bruce_sterling_on_design_fictions.html.
5 Following the British philosopher Stephen Toulmin analysis of the origin of modernity (Toulmin 1990), the birth of the scientific method and the affirmation of Cartesian natural philosophy can be interpreted as a narrowing step in the history of ideas,

leaving out the Renaissance humanist values of open scepticism and appreciation for practical knowledge and embodied experience. In this sense, innovation can be regarded as yet another critical contraction along the very same path.

6 http://www.youtube.com/watch?v=6Cf7IL_eZ38.

7 http://www.youtube.com/watch?v=jZkHpNnXLB0&feature=relmfu.

8 http://www.youtube.com/watch?v=X-GXO_urMow&feature=relmfu.

9 http://blogs.cisco.com/news/the-internet-of-things-infographic. Cisco Systems, Inc. is an American multinational corporation headquartered in San Jose, CA, that designs, manufactures and sells networking equipment.

10 http://www.youtube.com/watch?v=kq8wcjQYW90&feature=BFa&list=UUYBQQU 7VCu8M6djxI4dvpIg.

11 Cloud computing is a key component of the IoT revolution: it is the possibility to outsource information and services to remote servers to be accessed and updated on demand through the internet. The imaginary of dematerialisation and decentralisation of our physical and digital world to the virtual sphere of the empyrean can be interestingly contrasted with the reality of the physical 'web farms' at the other end of the virtual sky, with all the political, social and energetic challenges they pose (see e.g. www.marketplace.org/topics/tech/iceland-will-keep-your-servers-cool).

12 The interaction can be *embodied* when these objects become extensions of human body or mind and they enhance their interaction with the environment (e.g. ordinary glasses or implantable device) or hermeneutic, when they provide a representation of reality requiring interpretation (e.g. thermometer, wearable sensor).

13 Human identities are mediated and redefined by others' ideas of identification, through profiling and selective accessibility to digital resources, both arising from authorised and unauthorised forms of *sous*veillance, *sur*veillance and tracking.

14 IBM, 'Let's build a smarter planet', campaign by Ogilvy & Mather, won the 2010 Gold Effie Award.

15 The overall rationale of the campaign can be found at http://s3.amazonaws.com/effie_ assets/2010/4625/2010_4625_pdf_1.pdf.

16 'Executives have traditionally regarded experience and intuition as the keys to formulating strategies and assessing risks. That type of thinking might have worked in an earlier time of information scarcity, but not in the time of Big Data' (Palmisano 2013).

17 The technoscientific narrative of a corporate marketing initiative such as the one we are considering depends intrinsically on its function of selling goods, as products and services, and it could then be considered as less representative of a deeper political, economic, cultural and existential transition. However, within the path-dependent trajectory from normal science to industrial technoscience, the same narrative of innovation can be found in private firms and in public institutions, as in both cases the goal is to preserve the overarching model of competitiveness and consumption growth, and to survive in it. In this sense, the difference between public and private becomes marginal as in both cases the subject of the narrative is not the institution proposing it, but the *kind of world* that implies the given innovation as the only possible sustainable trajectory. As we have seen, IBM doesn't talk about its products or services, but it describes a universe in which its technological presence becomes essential.

18 Other relevant exemplifications of this kind of narrative are the HP project for 'The Central Nervous System for the Earth' (http://www.youtube.com/ watch?v=qMGyQGTpMFs) and the CISCO and NASA partnership into the global non-profit research and development organisation 'Planetary Skin', http://www. planetaryskin.org.

19 'The Panopticon is a machine for dissociating the see/being seen dyad: in the peripheral ring, one is totally seen, without ever seeing; in the central tower, one sees everything without ever being seen' (Foucault 1995).

20  The divides in this case are not exclusively related to lack of skill to deal with the complexity of interactions, but also to what we could call 'consent fatigue', which poses additional challenges to all individuals and most notably to those with reduced autonomy, such as children and the elderly. Into the vast mass of the IoT's unquestioned automations and unnoticed ubiquity the very notion of consent might become controversial and even absurd.
21  'The Internet of Things is a vision. It is being built today. ... The purpose of Council is to forecast what will happen when smart objects surround us in smart homes, offices, streets, and cities. Forecast ... and build' from http://www.theinternetofthings.eu.
22  http://ec.europa.eu/yourvoice/ipm/forms/dispatch?form=IoTGovernance.
23  http://www.youtube.com/watch?v=nDBup8KLEtk.
24  http://ec.europa.eu/yourvoice/ipm/forms/dispatch?form=IoTGovernance.
25  See e.g. Gary Wolf, 'The quantified self', TED conference: http://www.ted.com/talks/gary_wolf_the_quantified_self.html, or, as already mentioned, www.planetaryskin.org.
26  These quotes from the movie *Her* are transcribed directly by the authors from the movie and are their own interpretation of the dialogue. The copyright is © Warner Brothers Pictures.
27  The opinions of the author cannot in any circumstance be attributed to the European Commission.

## References

Arendt, H. 1958. *The Human Condition,* Chicago, IL: University of Chicago Press.
Bacon, F. 1620/2012. *Novum Organum,* Classic Reprint Series, Charleston, SC: Forgotten Books.
Bacon, F. 1627a/1996. *The New Atlantis,* Oxford: Oxford University Press.
Bacon, F. 1627b. Magnalia naturae, praecipue quoad usus humanos, appended to *The New Atlantis* (http://www.thebookofaquarius.com/quotes/view-quotes.php?q=59) accessed Aug. 2014.
Benessia, A., Funtowicz, S., Bradshaw, G., Ferri, F., Raez-Luna, E.F., and Medina, C.P. 2012. Hybridizing sustainability: Toward a new praxis for the present human predicament, *Sustainability Science,* 7 (supplement 1): 75–89.
Bush, V. 1945. *Science, the Endless Frontier,* Washington, DC: United States Office of Scientific Research and Development, US Govt. print office.
Crawford, K. 2013. Algorithmic illusions: Hidden biases of big data, Keynote speech, Strata Conference, Santa Clara, 28 Feb. (http://www.youtube.com/watch?v=irP5RCdpilc&feature=youtu.be) accessed Aug. 2014.
European Commission 2010 *EUROPE 2020: A Strategy for Smart, Sustainable and Inclusive Growth,* COM(2010)2020, Brussels: European Commission.
Foucault, M. 1995. *Discipline and Punish: The Birth of the Prison,* New York: Vintage Books.
Funtowicz, S., and Ravetz, J. 1993. Science for the post-normal age, *Futures,* 25(7): 739–55.
Funtowicz, S., and Ravetz, J. 1999. Post normal science: An insight now maturing, *Futures,* 31(7): 641–6.
Guimarães Pereira, Â., Benessia, A., and Curvelo, P. 2013. *Agency in the Internet of Things,* EUR 26459, Brussels: European Commission (http://publications.jrc.ec.europa.eu/repository/bitstream/111111111/30547/1/lbna26459enn.pdf) accessed Aug. 2014.
Hardy, Q. 2013. Why big data is not truth, *New York Times,* 1 June (http://bits.blogs.nytimes.com/2013/06/01/why-big-data-is-not-truth) accessed Aug. 2014.

Jakson, T. 2009. *Prosperity without Growth? The Tansition to a Sustainable Economy,* Sustainable Development Commission (http://www.sd-commission.org.uk/publications. php?id=914) accessed Aug. 2014.

Latour, B. 2005. From Realpolitik to Dingpolitik or how to make things public, in *How to Make Things Public: Atmospheres of Democracy,* Cambridge, MA: MIT Press, pp. 4–31.

Mannermaa, M. 2007. Living in the European ubiquitous society, *Journal of Future Studies,* 11(4): 105–20.

Palmisano, S. 2008. A smarter planet: The next leadership agenda, Remarks to the Council on Foreign Relations, New York City, 8 Nov.

Palmisano, S. 2010. Welcome to the decade of smart, Royal Institute of International Affairs Chatham House, London, 12 Jan.

Palmisano, S. 2013. How to compete in the era of smart (http://www.ibm.com/smarterplanet/ global/files/us__en_us__overview__win_in_the_era_of_smart_op_ad_03_2013.pdf) accessed Aug. 2014.

Rockström, J., *et al.* 2009. A safe operating space for humanity, *Nature,* 461: 472–5.

Rose, D. 2014. *Enchanted Objects: Design, Human Desire, and the Internet of Things.* New York: Scribener.

*The Economist.* 2010. It's a smart world: a special report on smart systems, 6 Nov.

Thompson, C. 2010. What is I.B.M.'s Watson? *New York Times,* 16 June.

Toulmin, S. 1990. *Cosmopolis: The Hidden Agenda of Modernity,* Oxford: Oxford University Press.

Van Kranenburg, R. 2008. *The Internet of Things: A Critique of Ambient Technology and the All-Seeing Network of RFID,* Institute of Network Cultures (http://www. networkcultures.org/_uploads/notebook2_theinternetofthings.pdf) accessed Aug. 2014. Ebook published by http://networkcultures.org.

Verbeek, P. 2006. Materializing morality: Design ethics and technological mediation, *Science, Technology and Human Values,* 31(3): 361–80.

Wildavsky, A. 1979. *Speaking Truth to Power,* Boston, MA: Little Brown & Co.

# 6 From biobanks to genetic digital networks

## Why official preidentified values may not work

*Mariachiara Tallacchini*

### Cartesian normative approaches to regulating technologies?

The Cartesian worldview has been repeatedly evoked as an ideal deterministic simplification of the natural and social world. Indeed, the attempt to reduce the complexity of socio-technological deployment still embodies the ambitions of a consistent and persistent part of modernity. This attempt has been radicalised as technoscience has become a major force in validating and legitimising existing economic and political systems.

The recent developments of emerging technologies and their governing instruments provide an illustration of how, both in the life sciences and ICT domains, technoscience and normativity have been used to sustain and justify each other, and have reciprocated in sharing and taking for granted the assumptions about control and predictability. On the one hand, the presumed physical control and predictability of new technological systems has been extended to control and predictability of the relevant values associated with them; on the other hand, ethics and law have been invested with the task of normalising innovative processes.

The reflections proposed in this chapter look at these seemingly parallel assumptions in the scientific and normative domains as *de facto* reciprocally produced, namely co-produced (Jasanoff 2004). According to the interpretive notion of co-production, the dynamics amongst science, technology, and normativity are intertwined: they proceed through the mutual shaping of scientific and ethical or legal languages that mutually inform and modify each other. Descriptive and prescriptive languages are established through exchange of contents, negotiation of concepts and meanings, a constant shift between facts and norms (Jasanoff 2004).

However, while highlighting the inextricable genealogies of facts and values, co-production *per se* does not provide any guarantee of how this process takes place. Indeed, the facts-and-values co-production happens even in quite opaque and covert ways. A radical example of this seemingly neutral establishment of a discipline that is actually strongly value-laden is synthetic biology: here, the very construction of the scientific identity of the field is at the same time predetermining its normative status. Synthetic biology has been intentionally framed as a branch of engineering with hardware and software components (Andrianantonandro *et al.* 2006, 1), not only to propose a mechanistic understanding of its processes, but also to evoke a predefined normative framework made of professional practices, safety standards and property rights (De Lorenzo and Danchin 2008, 824).

Therefore, for co-production to correspond to a constitutional and democratic perspective, its (often implicit and invisible) dynamics have to be opened up to critical public debate. The preventative identification of the ethical and legal concepts and practices that should be associated with, and govern, the emergence of new technologies can be seen as a reflex of what in this book is called Cartesian approach. Specific ethical and legal mechanisms have been framed as the adequate ways for coping with new realities, for handling unexpected effects, for making their implementation in society smooth and eventless, and therefore for creating a sense of social trust and legitimation.

Indeed, the effort to justify technological innovation through respect for individual rights and fundamental societal values has been at the core of the development of specific ethical and legal instruments. Notwithstanding, when implemented, these instruments have often turned out as somehow too simplistic and deterministic. The assumption that all relevant normative tips can be preidentified and listed in order to neutralise and control the potential unknowns of innovation has often proved inadequate.

The case explored in this chapter concerns the biobanking of biological materials and information, one of the first biomedical technologies where biomedicine and Information and Communication Technologies (ICT) have merged and produced deep influences on each other. The institutionally preidentified values and rights that should have oriented the intended development of biobanks have been widely dismissed and are currently going through a redesigning phase where public reactions as well as proactive initiatives convey radically different normative perspectives.

The reflections around this case aim to contribute to some of the questions posed in this book: for instance, by highlighting how normalising innovation does not necessarily require the establishment of an exhaustive normative framework, but instead the opening up of multiple spaces for problems to rapidly emerge and be debated (von Schomberg and Davies 2010); and by suggesting how the genuine appreciation of the plurality of knowledge can be relevant to public policies (Funtowicz and Strand 2007).

A broader issue that can be only impressionistically suggested and depicted here concerns the normative resemblances between the bio- and ICT fields. Indeed, even though the governance strategies of emerging bio- and IC technologies have followed different normative paths and strategies, some common features can be identified.

A major similarity between the life sciences and ICT domains consists in the common identification of a privileged interpretive instrument to normalise the field. The selection and crystallisation of what has to count as relevant human values and their construction as 'institutional ethics' have played a prominent role in the attempt to normalise biotechnology both in the US and in the European Communities/European Union. First established as a tool for governing the (then) emerging field of biotechnology, the ambitious role framed for ethics has been that of supporting and speeding up biotechnological development while linking democratic legitimacy to innovation.

In ICT, the soft and hard normative framework built around the concept of privacy has been critical. Indeed, the right to privacy has been and still is a major area of concern and increasing intervention, as well as an incredibly fruitful notion in the attempt to protect several aspects of the human life. However, because of its flexibility and adaptability in covering and making sense of a variety of human expressions, in ICT privacy it has become a symbolic icon charged with the role of summarising, and responding to, most social issues (US Presidential Commission 2012; EGE 2012).

Preidentifying and listing 'the' ethical 'implications' in the field of life sciences, on the one hand, and conveying most ICT normative implications through privacy (and data protection) appear as two different ways in which normative simplification and, to some extent, determinism have taken place. Both strategies have often turned out not to be fully capable of capturing all relevant aspects of new technologies, even when not mismatched with the actual issues raised by them.

As said, this topic cannot be explored here. The complex and different histories of bio-ethics and ICT ethics and law require a dedicated analysis and comparison in order to bring to light if and how similar or even identical concepts have travelled from one domain to the other, and through which adjustments (for instance, privacy and informed consent have been discussed in both biotechnology and ICT, but in quite different ways), while other issues and notions have remained separated and unrelated for a long time – for instance, concerns about dignity and identity have been introduced in ICT ethics quite recently; while requirements of openness, free access and transparency do not originally belong to the ethics of biotechnology).

The challenges that, in the last few decades, life sciences and ICT have been posing to humanity have shaken most conceptions of human nature and raised the issue of how to make normative continuity compatible with individual and societal constant change. Technological artefacts and bio-artefacts are reshaping the dynamics of social order at many levels, from ideas of identity to the boundaries between subjects and objects, to conceptions of liberty, autonomy and agency (Jasanoff 2003, 6).

However, the twentieth century's politics of normativity have mostly addressed these changes through quite paternalistic measures and expert forms of decision-making: complex questions and unstable, fluctuating conditions have been stabilised and solidified by focusing only on a few aspects and through simplified means to establish which values should count.

As more distributed forms of knowledge and technology production have increasingly taken place in both life sciences and ICT (and their hybridisations), the scientific and normative landscape has become more complex and debated. As the case for biobanking suggests, all these new trends are showing the limits of the still lasting idea(l)s of control and simplicity in knowledge and in normative processes.

## Normalising emerging technologies by predefining values

The contemporary emergence of ethics as a public discourse integrating the law dates back to the end of the Second World War and to the tragic effects of disregard towards human subjects in scientific research. Ethics has since become a way to reflect on new issues at the interface between science and society.

The vision of ethics as 'the determination, so far as that is possible, of what is right and wrong, good and bad, about the scientific developments and technological deployments of biomedicine' (Callahan 1999, 276) has accompanied and justified the rise and role of ethics as a means to improve the rationality and the rationale of public decisions in the domain of life sciences and technology. In this narrative, ethics has been regarded as a 'neutral' normative tool, endowed with the potential to speak for rationality.

Such reflections have progressively led to the shaping of ethics as an institutional practice within the field of health and life sciences to identify and define relevant values. Establishing ethics at the institutional level has provided moral thought with unprecedented features, provoking a radical departure from the fundamental need for a public ethical discourse in modern democracies, namely a more intense and open dialogue between science and society (Stevens 2000).

Historical reconstructions of the establishment of institutional practices of ethics and official bodies have shown how, starting in the US in the 1970s and in Europe in the late 1980s, the notion of ethics was isolated and purified from other social values and concerns in order to achieve control of the public debate, and of the framing of relevant issues; however, this has been done at the price of reducing ethical inquiries and discussions to an expression of the intellectual-bureaucratic establishment (Jecker *et al.* 1997; Stevens 2000; Kelly 2003).

The need to foresee and assess the potential impacts of new technologies in the regulation and governance of biosciences led, initially in the US, to experiments in the early 1970s with a variety of consultative/deliberative committees set up primarily to deal with biomedical research issues (OTA 1987).[1] The first broad attempt to explore the social, legal and political environment for technologies (both bio and emerging ICT) was related to the (controversial) establishment, by the US Congress in 1972, of the Office of Technology Assessment (Bimber 1996).[2] However, in the OTA mandate ethics was not a separate issue isolated from the other social values. Only in the 1990s did ethics attract major institutional attention as a separate requirement. When asked to give their opinion about the establishment of a new ethics governmental body, two prominent advisory institutions – OTA and the Institute of Medicine, an independent arm of the National Academy of Sciences (NAS) (OTA 1993; IOM 1995) – similarly highlighted the ambiguities of the proposed initiative, namely that the body would be 'inherently political' (OTA 1993, 38) and that it would imply the identification of what makes 'an issue an ethical issue and the circumstances under which it is determined that an ethical issue should be publicly deliberated' (IOM 1995, 1).

Institutional ethics was 'invented' and framed as expert, specialised knowledge, associated with appointed bodies that produce and approve policy opinions on the ethical, legal and social aspects of new technologies (Jasanoff 2005). Despite this focus on values underlying policy-making, ethical advice has been mostly constructed as expert advice, *de facto* allowing the framing of a well-defined and more controllable decision-making mechanism and the passage from an explorative perspective of value-laden options to the normative identification of 'the' ethical aspects.

The powerful 'simplicity' of ethics as an instrument to normalise innovation depended on its simultaneous referring to, and merging, rationality in the moral domain, and democracy in evoking citizens' values. Despite the connection with renewed forms of technocracy (Jasanoff 2005; Evans 2006; Elliott 2007), ethics has been instrumentally justified both through academic philosophical norms and the democratic debate.

Within the European institutions, ethics was created as a form of policy advice to make biotechnological developments more legitimate and socially accepted in the delicate passage from the economic to the politically integrated vision of the European Communities through the Maastricht Treaty of 1993. In 1991 ethical issues were institutionally established – through the creation of an expert body for policy advice (the GAEIB, then EGE)[3] – within the context of promoting a competitive environment for the biotech industry (CEC 1991). In the European Commission's view, public discussion would have triggered confusion and diversion of investment as the public was deemed unable to clearly articulate the diverse social issues at stake; instead, an advisory structure on ethics determining (and reassuring about) the relevant values at stake in the emerging field of biotechnology was to identify and clarify what ethics was (CEC 1991, 8). The Commission further established that 'ethical considerations relating to human life' (and to some extent animal welfare issues) should be properly defined as ethics, as distinct from 'other value-laden issues', such as environmental issues, health and safety related issues, transparency and socio-economic impacts. The proposed ethics structure was framed as an expert one, as it 'would enable recognised experts to participate in guiding the legislative process' (CEC 1991, 11).

Besides contributing to rationalising the discussion about values, the ethics commission was also charged with the task of evoking/representing citizens. As the Commission pointed out, without giving a human and social dimension to technoscientific development, science and technology, European citizenship would not have been established. The biotechnological and biomedical origins and expertise of institutional ethics have definitely influenced the more limited institutional[4] development of ICT ethics. In the US, the bioethics commissions (including the current Presidential Commission for the study of bioethical issues)[5] only deal with medical and life sciences issues – although, due to the hybridisation of bio and IC technologies, in its 2012 opinion on whole genome sequencing, the Presidential Commission had to deal with privacy as the main value at stake in ICT-related genomics (US Presidential Commission 2012).[6]

The general background of the relevant European 'ICT ethics resources'[7] still encompasses the legal and soft law documents on privacy (Art. 29 of the Working Party's and European Data Protection Supervisor's opinions); and a sign of the still emerging role of ethics in the field is that research ethics in ICT has been mostly framed by borrowing principles from traditional biomedical ethics.

Only quite recently, and primarily in relation to ICT's fast developments and pervasive implications for people's lives (e.g. social networks and the Internet of Things), other ethical aspects (e.g. identity and agency) have become relevant. In 2012, for the first time,[8] the European Group on Ethics in Science and New Technologies (EGE) was asked to address the ethical issues raised by ICT, essentially identified (again) in privacy and the (more traditionally bioethical) protection of individual identity (EGE 2012).

However, in the passage from one emerging technology to another, a learning process is taking place as to the role of ethics (to some extent, and with their structural political differences, both in the US and the EU), now providing institutions with hints for anticipatory governance of still unknown technologies.[9] Indeed, institutional ethics is increasingly framed to embody a public form of non-binding and autonomous normativity that can be directly endorsed by citizens and private stakeholders, to reconstruct moral codes for diverse and scattered scientific communities, and to enable complex, recursive and networked relationships amongst all institutional, corporate, societal and individual actors.

## Opening up normative spaces? From biobanks to genetic digital networks

The case for biobanks, namely the storage and use for research purposes of human biological materials and information, and their scientific and normative evolution, not only represents an example of the complex interactions between the biological and the digital domain, and of how they have mutually redefined each other, but also illustrates how their current developments are moving away from the simplified official normative framework offering narratives of prediction and control as well as narrow visions of autonomy, privacy and property.

During the past 30 years human biological materials associated with personal, medical and genetic information have become crucial for research and therapeutic uses, and their related commercial exploitation. In the normative puzzle that has taken place around their ethical and legal framing, the concepts of autonomy, privacy and property have been used not only as protecting measures and rights for citizens, but also as defensive tools to prevent requests from the public to participate in decisions concerning research and its potential benefits (Tallacchini 2013).

The normative frameworks that have been shaped through time in the US and in Europe have mixed legislative and judicial norms with the official opinions of ethics bodies (OTA 1987; EGE 1998). In the US the issue has been primarily debated, mostly through court decisions, as a contrast between privacy and property. The European normative framework has avoided dealing with the property of the body – framed as a *res extra commercium* (non-marketable) that as such cannot give rise to financial gain – and has mostly referred to the concepts of individual dignity, autonomy and privacy (EGE 1998; Gottweis *et al.* 2012).[10]

However, in both cases, the wide application of the concept of privacy depended on its adaptability to cover, as an extendable blanket, most aspects of human personality, and on its capability to separate, isolate and therefore exclude the private dimensions of life from what is relevant in public life.

The beginnings of the storing of biological samples and information oscillated between ethical unawareness in both scientists and patients, and attempts to regulate the new practices through regulatory categories aimed at excluding individual donors from participation in research. Indeed, in the 1950s case of Henrietta Lacks and the HeLa cell-line derived from her tissue, the lack of precedents and the general unpreparedness towards the new situation largely explains why the subject–patient–donor could not enter the normative picture (Skloot 2010).

However, the solution envisaged by the California Supreme Court in 1990 in the John Moore case revealed how an emerging technology could be controlled through a normative design. In *Moore v. Regents of University of California* (Cal. App. 2 Dist. 1988; *Regents of University of California v. Moore* 51 Cal. 3d 1990), dealing with the personal and economic aspects of human biological materials, the dichotomy between privacy and property was used to establish that bodily materials and information belong to the sphere of 'private autonomy' as far as they remain in the body, but, once detached, they become abandoned things (*res derelictae*) that some legally entitled subject or entity (research institutions and corporations) may acquire and creatively make eligible for intellectual property rights. Privacy and property had been already framed as the mutually exclusive, single relevant values in the field of research. As an OTA opinion helped confirm (OTA 1987), John Moore was entitled to his privacy, expressed through informed consent to medical treatment and to the economic exploitation of his cells; doctors and industry were entitled to the intellectual property of bodily materials and information. Even more, despite belonging to the US legal system, the case strongly inspired and influenced the European normative arrangements on the use of bodily materials and its related knowledge (Tallacchini 2013).

Towards the end of the millennium several biobanking initiatives, especially in Europe, were started as totally top–down, state-driven initiatives led by scientists and experts, where citizens were only recognised as legitimately concerned about informed consent and privacy (through anonymisation) of their biological materials and information. Citizens' interests were thus normatively predefined and constrained within the limited scope of their private 'autonomous' lives, encompassing consenting to scientific procedures and not being identified in the public space; all other potential concerns, such as participation in public decisions, research interests and contributions to defining the common good had been heteronomously decided and inadvertently dismissed.

In the late 1990s some state initiatives were challenged by citizens, disappointed that all their genealogical, medical and genetic information could be used with their presumed consent in the name of a human progress defined by experts. A most infamous situation, in 1998, concerned Iceland, where the Parliament authorised by law the private company DeCODE Genetics to build a National

Health Database, where all Icelanders' personal and genetic information should be stored through an opt-out system for consent – namely inclusion by default and the right to withdraw. The case triggered a number of criticisms of the existence of an all-encompassing genetic social contract between the state and its citizens that escalated to courts (Winickoff 2006).

Most arrangements excluding citizens turned out to be mostly unsuccessful and to generate public distrust. After the Icelandic experience, several technical and legal fixes have been used to tame citizens and convince them that personal data and biomaterials were irrelevant to them once privacy was granted (through anonymisation) and autonomy respected (through informed consent). Still, people have remained quite sceptical towards top–down managed biobanking, and reluctant to accept it.

Issues about trust and citizens/patients involvement have continued to be debated since *Moore* in several major US courts' decisions. In 2003, in *Greenberg v. Miami Children's Hospital* (264 F. Supp. 2d 1064 S.D. Fla. 2003), where the samples donated for the study of Canavan disease were patented by Dr Reuben Matalon, a researcher at Miami Children's Hospital, the relationship between researcher and donor was framed as more disenchanted than the doctor–patient one. While doctors are obliged to make full disclosure, researchers are allowed to be more entrepreneurial. Having acquired a patent on Canavan disease, Dr Matalon was the only owner of materials and information involved in the invention.

In 2006, *Washington University v. Catalona* (437 F. Supp. 2d 985 E.D. Missouri 2006) added a further piece to this normative picture. The prostate samples received by Dr William Catalona from his patients while he was working at Washington University, and that he and his patients wanted to transfer to Northwestern University in Chicago, were declared by the Court of Appeals of Missouri to belong to Washington University. Washington University, according to the court, received the biological materials through an 'unconditional donation'; and the US Supreme Court declined to accept the case in 2007.

Starting in the mid-2000s, some experimentation has taken place together with the connectivity made possible by the internet and the social dynamics triggered by it. These experiments, coming from both the for-profit and not for-profit spheres, have moved towards forms of genetic social networks and called for direct citizen involvement and engagement (with different degrees of real or rhetoric empowerment). What is emerging from them is that rather than being mostly concerned about privacy and/or abstract concepts of autonomy, patients and consumers and citizens seem more focused on contributing to knowledge production, on having access to information and its reuse, and on sharing decisions and potential health benefits.

The turn towards more participatory and participant-driven initiatives in genomic research has dramatically changed the picture. Several personal genomics initiatives have seemingly started treating consumers/participants as *partners* in scientific research, and granting them some powers and access to knowledge. Certainly some corporate activities such as 23andMe have both pushed for change and benefited from it, thus becoming commercially very successful. Their success, however – despite the fights and defeats with the US health agencies trying to restrict the sales of genetic tests – is strongly dependent on their campaigning to support genetic freedom and knowledge as an autonomous educated citizen choice (Saha and Hurlbut 2011; Hernandez 2012).

Other personal genomic digital initiatives seem to be even more seriously committed to raising patients' awareness about holding the power in research – such as PatientslikeMe (Wicks *et al.* 2014) – and some extreme experiments, such as the Personal Genome Project – where scientists and citizens equally contribute to research as subjects of research and peer-producers of knowledge, and publish on the web all their personal and genetic information – are exploring the potential for broad anthropological changes (Lunshof *et al.* 2008; Church *et al.* 2009; Kaye 2012).

A range of new activities, from genetic social networks, to online collection of self-reported data, to participatory epidemiology are radically modifying the quantitative impact, timing and working methods of research (Lee and Crawley 2009; Gibson and Copenhaver 2010; Eriksson *et al.* 2010). Public involvement in genetic research has been increasingly perceived and promoted as implementing the idea of scientific citizenship, respecting individuals' dignity, reconciling individual and public health (Gottweis and Lauss 2010; Saha and Hurlbut 2012; Tallacchini 2013), and showing that issues of privacy and autonomy need to be reconceived and redefined in the light of new forms of agency.

Indeed, these ongoing phenomena are not free from criticisms: scientific perplexities related to the new roles of lay-scientists providing samples and manipulating data (Janssen and Kraft 2012, 2), and normative concerns connected to the dominant role of the private sector in genetic social networks (Gutmann 2012) are well-founded concerns. Institutional reactions to these movements have been quite strong both in the US and in Europe, ranging from the prohibition by FDA of unauthorised direct-to-consumer tests to the European depiction of scary psychological scenarios for users/citizens.[11]

Though reflecting a deep anthropological and social change towards bottom–up processes of collaboration and cooperation (Benkler and Nissenbaum 2006), the shift towards 'occupying science' (Saha and Hurbut 2012) still has to reveal its potential. While individuals are increasingly willing to set aside some of their concerns about privacy when their biological samples and personal information become part of a peer-production of knowledge of both scientists and citizens, and when participants can control and make decision about research and its benefits (Lunshof *et al.* 2014); the wide-range effects and impacts of this openness and disclosure are still unknowns.

With all these question marks about the future development of biobanking, the distance and the difference between the pre-cooked forms of normalisation and the current experiential and experimental normative trends are huge. The imagined ways of controlling biobanking activities and directions, as well as the imagined relevant values for citizens, have quite remarkably failed to match the reality.

## Experimenting with normativity

A complement to the scientific vision referred to as the 'Cartesian world' in this volume, regulatory activities of emerging technologies have tried to propose a similar 'illusion' (rather than dream) of control and predictability. There are signs suggesting that similar forms of normalisation have been used to address the challenges triggered by life sciences and ICT. Some values and rights, though relevant and meaningful when properly implemented, have become *normative fixes* played as *technical fixes* to avoid deep questioning of the new dimensions involved by science and technology.

Though in different ways, Jasanoff and Lessig have endorsed, respectively in the biological and the digital domain, the metaphors of the technoscientific and normative codes to argue in favour of their being opened up, shifting from black boxes to new spaces for deliberation (Jasanoff 2011; Lessig 2006). Neither Jasanoff nor Lessig think of the bio and digital architectures as being 'entitled' to deterministically impose their own structures, ontologies, mechanisms, explanations over social normativity; instead they think of a complex evolution of the relationships between technoscience and normativity, and of opening up choices to make them available to citizens.

In both views, the descriptive–prescriptive blurred boundaries or black boxes should be disentangled to make the protection of certain values a matter of awareness and choice. Indeed, the question about whose subjects are legitimately entitled to propose and provoke normative changes has been increasingly framed as a matter of democracy and participation.

Both authors understand the relations between scientific and normative codes as relevant at a 'constitutional' level, and requiring a rethinking of the fundamental characters of the principles, values and rights we live by. In fact, at the same time, the deep, entrenched, pervasive ways technoscience is restructuring all aspects of our lives, our ways of knowing and using knowledge, as well as our experiences of relations and values, are affecting normative principles, concepts, understanding; and, in turn, normativity structures and stabilises technologies themselves.

Constitutions – widely referred to as the foundational agreements for social life – are increasingly appearing as the most significant and symbolic 'normative spaces' where democratic societies can deal with technoscientific changes (Jasanoff 2011). They look today to be the deliberative environments that citizens can factually and symbolically reinterpret as the dynamic epistemic and normative repositories of meaning for human and societal developments.

The most common tendencies and experimentations are now mostly focusing on citizens' participation 'in both the epistemic and the normative evaluation of competing options' (Jasanoff 2011, 295). These tendencies are increasingly taking the shape of dispersed activities of reordering knowledge and society: a reconstitution of the social fabric by citizens for citizens with far-reaching democratic implications (Jasanoff 2011, 295). What Jasanoff argues primarily about citizens' self-reinterpretation of life and rights has *de facto* merged with similar and even more extended practices through information and communication spaces and devices.

Rethinking the constitutional dimensions of our lives implies more than just *listing* the *ethical implications* of new technologies or protecting individuals' privacy and data, but also requires looking inside the intricacies of knowledge and normativity. This means opening up the epistemic and legal imagination entrenched in new technologies and their architectural structures. Rather than prescribing moral codes, a *redesign* of our normative practices in technoscientific innovation is needed (Benkler and Nissenbaum 2006). This means, for instance, favouring human integrity and agency, preserving it from impoverished human relations, and from unlearning humanness and all knowledge related to it; and it implies going beyond an atomistic vision of society and supporting a variety of forms of collaboration and cooperation, learning processes, empowerment and usability of knowledge.

### Notes

1  For a short history of the bioethics commissions in the US see http://bioethics.gov/ history (accessed May 2014).
2  Office of Technology Assessment Act, Public Law 92–484, 92d Congress, H.R. 10243, 13 Oct. 1972.
3  In 1991 the GAEIB (Group of Advisers on the Ethical Implications of Biotechnology) was established; in 1997 the EGE (European Group on Ethics in Science and New Technologies) replaced it and has been constantly renewed since. The GAEIB had 'to identify and define the ethical issues raised by biotechnology; to assess, from the ethical viewpoint, the impact of the community's activities in the field of biotechnology; to advise the commission, in the exercise of its powers, on the ethical aspects of biotechnology; and to ensure that the general public is kept properly informed.' http:// ec.europa.eu/bepa/european-group-ethics/archive-mandates/mandate-1991-1997/ index_en.htm (accessed May 2014).
4  Certainly not the scholarly work on computer and information ethics that has been widely developed.
5  See http://www.bioethics.gov (accessed Aug. 2014).
6  In common law countries – primarily based on the 'judge made law' approach – and especially in the US, courts' decisions provided the general framework for defining and refining extended meanings of privacy in order to cover very different issues. Privacy is not a right stated by the US Constitution – even though several US states mention it in their constitutions. However, its elaboration has been framed through courts' decisions, where a variety of privacy interests have been designed since the late 1960s. The Supreme Court found sources for a right to privacy in several amendments, namely: (1) freedom of speech, freedom of religious, political and personal association, and related forms of anonymity (First Amendment); (2) freedom from government appropriation of one's home (Third Amendment); (3) freedom from unreasonable search and seizure of one's body and property (Fourth Amendment); (4) freedom from compulsory self-incrimination (Fifth Amendment); (5) freedom from cruel and unusual punishment, including unnecessarily extreme deprivations of privacy (Eight Amendment); and (6) other personal freedoms (Ninth Amendment). In addition to the Bill of Rights, the Supreme Court and state courts have marshalled the due process clause and language of 'liberty' of the Fourteenth Amendment to strike down laws interfering with autonomous medical, marital, sexual and family decision-making.

Moreover, since the late 1960s, in *Katz v. United States* (389, US 347-350 (1967)), the Supreme Court recognised the privacy interest protecting an individual against electronic surveillance, while cautioning that 'the Fourth Amendment cannot be translated into a general constitutional "right to privacy"' (*Katz v. United States* 389, US 347–50 (1967)). Congress enacted the Privacy Act of 1974 (5 U.S.C. § 552a (2012)) to provide legal protection for and safeguards on the use of personally identifiable information maintained in federal government record systems. The E-Government Act of 2002 (44 U.S.C. § 3501 note (2012)) updated the previous law for taking into account technological changes in computers, digitised networks, internet access, and the creation of new information products. In Europe, where privacy is a fundamental right, the civil law approach based on legislation has taken care of the concerns raised by innovations in the information and communication sector by trying to summarise and convey them within the extended boundaries of privacy and data protection. A comprehensive legal framework, composed of both hard and soft laws – namely the Council of Europe Convention for the Protection of Individuals with regard to Automatic Processing of Personal Data (1981), the European Directive 46/95/EC, as well as the Opinions of the Art.29 Working Party and the European Data Protection Supervisor – was meant to homogenise and cover all ICT normative issues.

7   See: http://cordis.europa.eu/fp7/ethics-ict_en.html (accessed May 2014).
8   With the exception of Opinion 20 on *Ethical Aspects of ICT Implants in the Human Body* (2005).
9   See, for instance, the documents on synthetic biology drafted by EGE and the US Presidential Commission for the Study of Bioethical Issues.
10  At the same time, it has to be said, the denial of the marketability of biological materials has gone hand in hand with the construction of a European market for tissue.
11  See, for instance, Nuffield Council on Bioethics, *Medical Profiling and Online Medicine: The Ethics of 'Personalised Healthcare' in a Consumer Age*, Abingdon: Nuffield Press, 2010; European Science Foundation, ESF Forward Look, *Personalised Medicine for the European Citizen: Towards More Precise Medicine for the Diagnosis, Treatment and Prevention of Disease (iPM)*, Sept. 2012; EASAC (European Academies Science Advisory Council) and FEAM (Federation of European Academies of Medicine), *Direct-to-Consumer Genetic Testing for Health-Related Purposes in the European Union*, EASAC policy report 18, July 2012.

# References

Andrianantoandro, E., Basu, S., Karig, D.K., and Weiss, R. 2006. Synthetic biology: New engineering rules for an emerging discipline, *Molecular Systems Biology*, 2: 1–14.
Benkler, Y., and Nissenbaum, H. 2006. Commons-based peer production and virtue, *Journal of Political Philosophy*, 14(4): 394–419.
Bimber, B. 1996. *The Politics of Expertise in Congress: The Rise and Fall of the Office of Technology Assessment*, Albany NY: SUNY Press.
Callahan, D. 1999. The social sciences and the task of bioethics, *Daedalus*, 128: 275–94.
CEC (Commission of the European Communities). 1983. *Biotechnology in the Community*, Communication from the Commission to the Council, COM (83) 672 final/2, 4 Oct., E11.
CEC. 1991. *Promoting the Competitive Environment for the Industrial Activities Based on Biotechnology within the Community*, Commission Communication to Parliament and the Council, Brussels, SEC, 629 final.
Church, G., *et al.* 2009. Public access to genome-wide data: Five views on balancing research with privacy and protection, *PLoS Genetics*, 5(10): 1–4 (http://www.ncbi.nlm.nih.gov/pmc/articles/PMC2749921) accessed Aug. 2014.

Coates, J.F. 1975. Why public participation is essential in technology assessment, *Public Administration Review*, 35(1): 67–9.

De Lorenzo, V., and Danchin, A. 2008. Synthetic biology: Discovering new worlds and new words, *EMBO Reports*, 9(9): 822–7.

Descartes, R. 1983. *Œuvres de Descartes*, 11 vols, ed. Charles Adam and Paul Tannery, Paris: Librairie Philosophique J. Vrin, vol. 5, 86–7.

EGE (European Group on Ethics in Science and New Technologies). 1998. *Ethical Aspects of Human Tissue Banking*, Opinion 11, 21 July.

EGE. 2012 *Ethics of Information and Communication Technologies*, Opinion 26, 22 Feb.

EGE. 2014. *Ethics of Security and Surveillance Technologies*, Opinion 28, May

Elliott, C. 2007. The tyranny of expertise, in L.A. Eckenwiler and F. Cohn (eds), *The Ethics of Bioethics: Mapping the Moral Landscape*, Baltimore, MD: Johns Hopkins University Press, pp. 43–6.

Eriksson, N., Macpherson, J.M., Tung, J.Y., Hon, L.S., Naughton, B., Saxonov, S., Avey, L., Wojcicki, A., Pe'er, I., and Mountain, J. 2010. Web-based, participant-driven studies yield novel genetic associations for common traits, *PLoS Genetics* 6(6), 1 June (http://www.plosgenetics.org/article/info%3Adoi%2F10.1371%2Fjournal.pgen.1000993#pgen-1000993-g011) accessed 19 October 2014.

Evans, J.H. 2006. Between technocracy and democratic legitimation: A proposed compromise position for common morality public ethics, *Journal of Medicine and Philosophy*, 31: 213–34.

Floridi, L., and Sanders, J.W. 2002. Mapping the foundationalist debate in computer ethics, *Ethics and Information Technology*, 4: 1–9.

Funtowicz, S., and Strand, R. 2007. Models of science and policy, in T. Traavik and L.C. Lim (eds), *Biosafety First: Holistic Approaches to Risk and Uncertainty in Genetic Engineering and Genetically Modified Organisms*, Trondheim: Tapir, pp. 263–78.

Gibson, G., and Copenhaver, G.P. 2010. Consent and internet-enabled human genomics, *PLoS Genetics*, 6(6), 1 June (http://www.ncbi.nlm.nih.gov/pmc/articles/PMC2891701/pdf/pgen.1000965.pdf) accessed Aug. 2014.

Gottweis H., and Lauss, G. 2010. Biobank governance in the post-genomic age, *Personalized Medicine*, 7(2): 187–95.

Gottweis, H., Bignami, F., Rial-Sebbag, E., Lattanzi, R. and Macek, M. 2012. *Biobanks for Europe: A Challenge for Governance*, Report of the Expert Group on Dealing with Ethical and Regulatory Challenges of International Biobank Research, Luxembourg: Publications Office of the European Union.

Gutmann, K.V. 2012. PGTandMe: Social networking-based genetic testing and the evolving research model, *Health Matrix*, 22: 33–74.

Hernandez, G. 2012. Social codes: Sharing your genes online, *Wired*, 11 (http://www.wired.com/wiredscience/2012/11/social-codes/#more-132544) accessed Aug. 2014.

IOM (Institute of Medicine) 1995. *Society's Choices: Social and Ethical Decision Making in Biomedicine*, Washington DC: National Academy Press.

Janssens, A.C.J.W., and Kraft, P. 2012. Research conducted using data obtained through online communities: ethical implications of methodological limitations, *PLoS Medicine* 9(10): 1–4.

Jasanoff, S. 2003. In a constitutional moment: Science and social order at the millennium, *Sociology of the Sciences*, 23: 155–80.

Jasanoff, S., ed. 2004. *States of Knowledge: The Co-Production of Science and Social Order*, London: Routledge.

Jasanoff, S. 2005. *Designs on Nature. Science and Democracy in Europe and the United States*, Princeton, NJ: Princeton University Press.

Jasanoff, S., ed. 2011. *Reframing Rights: Bioconstitutionalism in the Genetic Age*, Cambridge, MA: MIT Press.

Jecker, N.S., Jonsen, A.R., and Pearlman, R.A. 1997. *Bioethics: An Introduction to the History, Methods, and Practice*, Sudbury, MA: Jones & Bartlett Publishers.

Kaye, J. 2012. From patients to partners: Participant-centric initiatives in biomedical research, *Nature Reviews Genetics*, 13 (May): 371–6.

Kelly, S. 2003. Public bioethics and publics: Consensus, boundaries, and participation in biomedical science policy, *Science Technology and Human Values*, 28: 339–64.

Lee, S.S., and Crawley, L. 2009. Research 2.0: Social networking and direct-to-consumer (DTC) genomics, *American Journal of Bioethics*, 9(6–7): 35–44.

Lessig, L. 2006. *Code – Version 2.0*, New York: Basic Books.

Lunshof, J.E., Chadwick, R., Daniel, B., Vorhaus, D.B., George, M., and Church, G.M. 2008. From genetic privacy to open consent, *Nature Reviews Genetics*, 5 (9 May): 406–11.

Lunshof, J.E., Church, G.M., and Prainsack, B. 2014. Raw personal data: Providing access, *Science*, 343 (24 Jan.): 373–4.

OTA (US Congress, Office of Technology Assessment). 1987. New developments in biotechnology: ownership of human tissues and cells—special report, OTA-BA-337, Washington DC: Government Printing Office.

OTA (US Congress, Office of Technology Assessment). 1993 Biomedical ethics in U.S. public policy—background paper, OTA-BP-BBS-1O5, Washington DC: Government Printing Office.

OTA (US Congress, Office of Technology Assessment). 1994. *Information Security and Privacy in Network Environments*, OTA-TCT-606, Washington, DC: US Government Printing Office.

Saha, K., and Hurlbut, J.B. 2012. Opinion: Occupy science? *The Scientist*, 24 Jan. (http://www.the-scientist.com/?articles.view/articleNo/31624/title/Opinion--Occupy-Science-) accessed May 2014.

Skloot, R.L. 2010. *The Immortal Life of Henrietta Lacks*, New York: Broadway Books.

Stevens, Tina M.L. 2000. *Bioethics in America: Origins and Cultural Politics*, Baltimore, MD: Johns Hopkins University Press.

Tallacchini, M. 2009. Governing by values: EU ethics: Soft tools, hard effects, *Minerva*, 47: 281–306.

Tallacchini, M. 2013. Human tissues in the 'public space': Beyond the property/privacy dichotomy, in G. Pascuzzi, U. Izzo, and M. Macilotti (eds), *Comparative Issues in the Governance of Research Biobanks*, Dordrecht: Springer, pp. 87–104.

US Presidential Commission for the Study of Bioethical Issues. 2012. *Privacy and Progress in Whole Genome Sequencing*, Washington, DC: US Presidential Commission.

Von Schomberg, R., and Davies, S., eds. 2010. *Understanding Public Debate on Nanotechnologies: Options for Framing Public Policy*, Luxembourg: Publication Office of the European Union.

Wicks, P., Vaughan, T., and Heywood, J. 2014. Subjects no more: What happens when trial participants realise they hold the power? *BMJ*, 348 (http://www.bmj.com/content/348/bmj.g368) accessed Aug. 2014.

Winickoff, D.E. 2006. Genome and nation: Iceland's health sector database and its legacy, *Innovations* (Spring): 80–105.

# 7 Geoengineering dreams

*Paula Curvelo*

## On Cartesian dreams

More than half a century ago, in his book *Landmarks of Tomorrow*, Peter Drucker described his 'tangible present' – a period of fundamental shift in worldview – as an age of transition and overlap (Drucker 1957). According to Drucker, that was an age where the Cartesian worldview of the past three hundred years was still providing the means of expression, standards of expectations and tools of ordering, but was no longer acting effectively, and where 'the new post-Cartesian, post-modern world', though controlling human action and its impact on the world, was still lacking definition, vocabulary, methods and tools.

While discussing the philosophical shift from the Cartesian universe of mechanical cause to the new universe of pattern, purpose and processes, Drucker identifies the twofold contribution of Descartes to the modern world:

- first, his basic axiom about the nature of the universe and its order, a lawlike, mathematically determinate universe whose intelligibility became clearly expressed in the definition of science proposed by the Académie Française:[1] 'the certain and evident knowledge of things by their causes';
- second, inspired by the 'long chains of utterly simple and easy reasonings that geometers commonly use to arrive at their most difficult demonstrations' Descartes provided the method to make his axiom effective, that is: a 'method that contains everything that gives certainty to the rules of arithmetic and that teaches one to follow the true order and to enumerate exactly all the circumstances of what one is seeking' (Descartes 1988, 11–12).

Although recognising that few philosophers since Descartes have accepted his substantive claims or have followed him in his answers to the major problems of systematic philosophy, Drucker still considered that the dominant worldview of the modern West was the Cartesian worldview: 'More than Galileo or Calvin, Hobbes, Locke or Rousseau, far more even than Newton, he determined, for three hundred years, what problems would appear important or even relevant, the scope of modern man's vision, his basic assumptions about himself and his universe, and above all, his concept of what is rational and plausible' (Drucker 1957, 2).

But if this is so, it is because Descartes's legacy to the modern world cannot be reduced to his basic axiom about the nature of the universe and its intelligibility, nor to the method upon which one would be able 'to establish anything firm and lasting in the sciences'. In fact, the epistemological ideals of clarity, detachment and objectivity that Descartes bequeathed to modern science can only be understood if we consider the underlying 'Cartesian anxiety' that hovers in the background, and which has spread to all areas of human inquiry and activity (Bernstein 1983). As Hannah Arendt reminds us, the two nightmares that haunt Cartesian philosophy –the possibility that all we take for reality is only a dream, and that humans may be nothing more than a plaything at the hands of an all-powerful malicious demon – became the nightmares of the whole modern age (Arendt 1958, 277, 279). The dark side of the Cartesian dream thus forces us to look at Descartes's legacy from a perspective that tends to expose the obsessive concern with the loss of certainty that became decisive for the whole development of modern thought, and which is inseparable from the all-pervasive radical doubt that forms the crux of Descartes's method.

Descartes's doubt concerning the reality of everything (*de omnibus dubitandum est*), and his attempt to conceptualise this modern doubt – the search for an Archimedean point that could serve as a foundation upon which we could ground our knowledge – has profoundly influenced our modern worldview, transforming the way we think about the universe, ourselves, Nature, God and knowledge, and determined the problems, metaphors and questions that have since then been at the centre of philosophy (Bernstein 1983; Tlumak 2007; Capra 1983). As Hannah Arendt noted, modern philosophy and thought began with the rise of the Cartesian doubt. In its radical and universal significance, the Cartesian doubt became the invisible axis around which all thinking has been centred, occupying much the same vital position as that occupied by the ancient Greek *thaumazein* (Arendt 1958) – the attitude of wondering that inaugurated the ascending development of philosophy, and which, according to Brentano, made it vigorous (Brentano 1998).[2]

From this perspective, questioning the end of the Cartesian dream is not only an attempt to articulate the reconstruction of an alternative understanding of scientific knowledge without the foundational metaphor that lies at the very basis of Cartesian philosophy, but it is also an attempt to understand how far we have come from the worldview that derived from it and from the problems, metaphors and questions that Descartes bequeathed to the modern age.

It is against this background that we propose to look at current proposals for the deliberate manipulation of the Earth's climate in order to alleviate the impacts of climate change. The assumption that geoengineering proposals can provide a privileged perspective from which to address the aforementioned questions follows from three lines of reasoning:

- First, because geoengineering seems to translate into reality the Cartesian dream of a practical philosophy by means of which we could 'render ourselves as masters and possessors of Nature', it can help us gain insight into current narratives of science and technology that propose scientific and technological innovation as the solution to our current environmental problems, and give meaning to human action within Nature.

- Second, inasmuch as climate engineering can arguably be considered as a typical scientific field that 'not only generates knowledge but also increases ignorance concerning the possible side effects of scientific innovation and their technological application' (Böschen *et al.* 2006, 294),[3] it constitutes a pertinent locus from which to investigate the far-reaching epistemic consequences of moving from the Holocene to the Anthropocene,[4] i.e. to a 'new geologic epoch' where the epistemic ideal of the certainty of scientific knowledge seems to coexist with – or have increasingly been replaced by – a new sort of *science-based ignorance*[5] (Ravetz 1990) that not only threatens our faith in sciences, but also threatens our new man-made world.

- Lastly, the efforts that have been made to address the array of ethical concerns associated with geoengineering (and which are far from being restricted to its unintended side effects[6]) offer some useful insights into the attempts that have been made to overcome the illusory dichotomies between mind and matter, facts and values, and subject and object, which lay at the very heart of Cartesian philosophy and of the worldview derived from it.

The main focus of our analysis is the Fifth Assessment Report (AR5) of the United Nations Intergovernmental Panel on Climate Change (IPCC),[7] which includes, for the first time in this report series, an assessment of geoengineering technologies. After a brief description of how geoengineering technologies are assessed in the three Working Group (WG) contributions to the AR5, we will critically examine the scientific and technical ideas underlying geoengineering proposals in order to address the three main questions of this chapter, which are:

- To what extent have we moved away from the Cartesian belief in scientific truth and the worldview derived from it?
- How have we reconstructed an alternative understanding of scientific knowledge without the foundational metaphor that lies at the very basis of Cartesian philosophy?
- Is geoengineering bringing into reality the Cartesian dream of rendering humankind the master and possessor of Nature?

## The Science of Geoengineering: Geoengineering in the Fifth Assessment Report of the United Nations Intergovernmental Panel on Climate Change

In its Fourth Assessment Report (AR4), released in 2007, the IPCC stated that 'Geo-engineering options, such as ocean fertilisation to remove $CO_2$ directly from the atmosphere, or blocking sunlight by bringing material into the upper atmosphere, remain largely speculative and unproven, and with the risk of unknown side-effects' (IPCC 2007, 15). However, since the publication of the AR4, geoengineering has attracted increasing attention as a means to address climate change, having been 'transformed from a topic discussed largely in science fiction and esoteric scientific papers into mainstream scientific and policy debate' (Macnaghten and Szerszynski 2013, 465). The 'grossly unsuccessful' efforts to lower carbon dioxide emissions (Crutzen 2006) – a symptom of what has been described as a 'problem of political inertia' (Gardiner 2010, 286–7) – the call for greater planetary management and Earth-system control (Global Environmental Change Programmes 2001) and the tendency to favour transformational rather than incremental responses to climate change (New *et al.* 2010) are all factors that may help explain why the scepticism and suspicion with which geoengineering was greeted is now giving way to a more pragmatic and serious consideration of its latest scientific and technological breakthroughs and the challenges ahead.

## *The IPCC Expert Meeting on Geoengineering: The definitional issues*

Against this background, in June 2011 the IPCC convened a joint Expert Meeting of WGI, WGII, and WGIII to discuss the latest scientific basis of geoengineering, its impacts and response options, and to identify key knowledge gaps for consideration by the author teams of the IPCC's Fifth Assessment Report (IPCC 2010, 2012).

The expert meeting proposed the use of a coherent framework for assessing geoengineering technologies across the three IPCC AR5 Working Groups, having identified the following preliminary set of criteria: effectiveness, feasibility, scalability, sustainability, environmental risks, cost and affordability, detection and attribution, governance challenges, ethical issues, social acceptability, and uncertainty related to all these criteria. It could then be expected that the consistent treatment of geoengineering options across the three contributions to the Fifth Assessment Report would add to a better understanding of: (i) the physical science basis of geoengineering (WGI), (ii) the impacts of geoengineering proposals on human and natural systems (WGII), and (iii) the role of geoengineering within the portfolio of response options to anthropogenic climate change (WGIII).

As stated in the meeting report, a substantial amount of time was spent discussing terminology in and around geoengineering (Boucher *et al.* 2011). Accordingly, the summary of the synthesis session not only provided the set of common definitions for the terms *Geoengineering* (Box 7.1), *Solar Radiation Management* (SRM) and *Carbon Dioxide Removal* (CDR) to be used in the Fifth Assessment Report, but also presented an illustration of the conceptual relationship between these terms and those of mitigation and adaptation[8], as used by the IPCC in its Fourth Assessment Report (see Figure 7.1).

The definition of geoengineering proposed by the Expert Meeting participants seems to take into account previous attempts to identify the key 'markers of geoengineering', which are: (i) the scale (global or continental); (ii) the intent (the deliberate nature of the action rather than a side effect of it) (Schelling 1996), and (iii) the degree to which the action is a countervailing measure (Keith 2000). However, special attention should be paid to the inclusion in this list of a new key characteristic of geoengineering methods – that is, that they 'could have substantive unintended effects that cross national boundaries'.

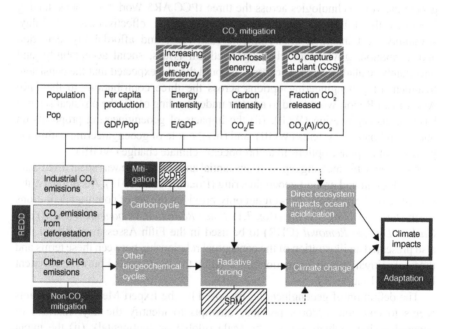

*Figure 7.1* Illustration of mitigation, adaptation, solar radiation management (SRM) and carbon dioxide removal (CDR) methods in relation to the interconnected human, socio-economic and climatic systems and with respect to mitigation and adaptation. The top part of the figure represents the Kaya identity. REDD stands for Reduced Emissions from Deforestation and forest Degradation. (Source: Boucher *et al.* 2011)

In fact, as we will see next, the attempt to untangle the ambiguities associated with the term through the identification of this key characteristic of geoengineering actions generates even more obscurity in an already clouded field. This becomes particularly evident when we take into account how uncertainty surrounding geoengineering is addressed across the IPCC AR5 and how the confidence scale[9] is used to synthesise author team's judgements about the validity of findings in the field. In fact, on the rare occasions where a high or very high level of confidence is assigned to a finding concerning geoengineering, either it refers to the uncertainties about the potential of these technologies to counteract climate change or it refers to their almost certain side effects that are 'difficult if not impossible to forecast' (IPCC 2014b). The quotations in Box 7.2 are illustrative of this.

*Box 7.2* What is known and unknown about the potential of geoengineering technologies to counteract climate change and about their unintended side effects.

There is robust agreement among models and *high confidence* that the compensation between GHG warming and SRM cooling is imprecise.

(IPCC 2013b, 635)

There is only limited evidence on the potential of geoengineering by CDR or solar radiation management (SRM) to counteract climate change, and all techniques carry risks and uncertainties (*high confidence*).

(IPCC 2014c, 7)

If SRM were terminated for any reason, a rapid increase in surface temperatures (within a decade or two) to values consistent with the high GHG forcing would result (*high confidence*).

(IPCC 2013b, 635)

The knowledge base on the implementation of SRM and CDR techniques and associated risks is presently insufficient. Comparative assessments suggest that the main ocean-related geoengineering approaches are very costly and have large environmental footprints (*high confidence*, Boyd 2008; Vaughan and Lenton 2011; Russell *et al.* 2012).

(Pörtner *et al.* 2014, 43)

Depending on the level of the overshoot, overshoot scenarios typically rely on the availability and widespread deployment of BECCS and afforestation in the second half of the century. The availability and scale of these and other Carbon Dioxide Removal (CDR) technologies and methods are uncertain and CDR technologies and methods are, to varying degrees, associated with challenges and risks (*high confidence*).

(IPCC 2014d, 13)

Thus, there seems to be a clear inconsistency between the definition of geoengineering presented in the IPCC AR5 and the main findings presented by the three WG. Would it make sense to review the definition of geoengineering accordingly? What level of scientific credibility could be attached to geoengineering were it to be defined as *a set of technologies and methods that intend to manipulate the climate system to counteract climate change, but whose potential to achieve this goal is still imprecise and whose unintended side effects of large scale are difficult if not impossible to forecast?*

Moreover, the option to use in this same definition two words with the very opposite meaning ('deliberately' and 'unintended') translates much of what has been said about the ignorance generated by science and reflects the growing awareness of the new unresolved problems that arise in the context of scientific and technological applications. But bringing these issues into the very definition of geoengineering is nevertheless surprising, particularly if we consider the scale to which those intended and unintended effects refer. What account of science and technology can be grasped from a field that defines itself as the intentional intervention in the global climate system to counteract the unintended effects of greenhouse emissions, and which may carry unintended (and unknown) large-scale side effects? And given this definition, what can be said about the research object of geoengineering? As M. Carrier and A. Nordmann have pointed out, 'on the technoscientific account, it is no longer possible even to construe objects like the hole in the ozone-layer or the cancer-mouse as natural. They have been created by humans but they constitute objects of scientific research all the same' (Carrier and Nordmann 2011, 4).

### Geoengineering is here to stay: meanings across the three Working Groups contributions to the IPCC Fifth Assessment Report

As suggested by the participants of the IPCC Expert Meeting on Geoengineering, the assessment of geoengineering technologies across the three WG contributions to the IPCC AR5 is presented 'within the context of the risks and impacts of climate change and other responses to climate change, rather than in isolation' (IPCC 2012, 4). Accordingly, the physical science basis of CDR and SRM is assessed in chapters 6 (Carbon and Other Biogeochemical Cycles) and 7 (Clouds and Aerosols) of AR5 WGI report, while additional impacts of geoengineering proposals on human and natural systems are assessed in chapters 6 (Ocean Systems) and 19 (Emergent Risks and Key Vulnerabilities) of WGII contribution to AR5. The social, economic and ethical implications of geoengineering are assessed in section 3.7.7 of AR5 WGIII report. Further, section 6.9 of AR5 WGIII report discusses how the use of geoengineering methods can change the relationships between GHG emissions and radiative forcing and their potential role in the context of transformation pathways. Lastly, chapter 13 (International Cooperation: Agreements and Instruments) assesses the special case of geoengineering governance.

One of the aspects that drew special attention to the WGI contribution to the Fifth Assessment Report of the IPCC was the inclusion of the topic of geoengineering in the final paragraph of the 'Summary for Policymakers' (SPM) – perhaps one of the most-read sections of this report series.[10]

Although this paragraph seems intended to convey the alleged policy neutrality[11] of the IPCC, its very presence at the end of the Summary for Policymakers raised several concerns as to the new scientific status that geoengineering appears to have acquired, the way it was prematurely placed on the climate change agenda as a legitimate topic of debate and, thereby, the political leverage that can be exercised over geoengineering research and deployment (ETC Group 2014; Stilgoe 2014). The following quotation clearly illustrates this:

> In the scientific world, a final paragraph is often the place to put caveats and suggestions for further research. In the political world, a final paragraph is a coda, a big finish, the place for a triumphant, standing-ovation-inducing summary. The IPCC tries to straddle both worlds. The addition of the word 'geoengineering' to the most important report on climate change for six years counts as a big surprise ... There is an argument that the taboo has already been broken and that, like sex education, it therefore has to be discussed. Those of us interested in geoengineering were expecting it to appear in one or two of the main reports when they are published in the coming months. To bring it up front is to give it premature legitimacy.
>
> (Stilgoe 2014)[12]

But perhaps the most interesting aspect of this paragraph is that it reflects much of the approach followed by the AR5 authors to present the key findings of the assessment of geoengineering techniques and their judgements about the validity of those findings. In fact, the (almost) absence of quantified measures of uncertainty to communicate the degree of certainty in the assessment of CDR and SRM methods and the option to assign a confidence level to speculative conditional sentences are two aspects of the geoengineering assessment in the AR5 that deserve closer attention. The emphasis on the side effects of CDR and SRM methods is also a key feature of all three WG contributions to the IPCC AR5 that deserves equal consideration. In the remaining part of this section we will focus our attention on these three aspects in order to address the key questions presented at the beginning of this chapter.

When assessing geoengineering technologies, the option to use a *quantitative likelihood scale* to describe a probabilistic estimate of the occurrence of a specific outcome is confined to CDR methods, particularly when referring to their side effects on carbon and other biogeochemical cycles, or to biogeochemical and technological limitations to their potential. An example of this can be seen in Chapter 6 of AR5 WGI report:

> The 'rebound effect' in the natural carbon cycle *is likely* to diminish the effectiveness of all the CDR methods.

Uncertainties make it difficult to quantify how much $CO_2$ emissions could be offset by CDR on a human time scale, although it is *likely* that CDR would have to be deployed at large-scale for at least one century to be able to significantly reduce atmospheric $CO_2$. In addition, it is *virtually certain* that the removal of $CO_2$ by CDR will be partially offset by outgassing of CO2 from the ocean and land ecosystems.[13]

Despite the (i) low level of confidence on the effectiveness of these methods, (ii) the limited evidence on the potential for large-scale deployment of these technologies and (iii) their unpredictable (but almost certain) side effects and long-term consequences on a global scale, the Representative Concentration Pathway (RCP) scenarios,[14] used as a basis for future projections in the AR5, already include some CDR methods. In fact, long-term mitigation scenarios typically rely on the availability and widespread use of bioenergy with carbon capture and storage (BECCS) and large-scale afforestation in the second half of the century. As recognised in the WGII contribution to the AR5, the political implication of this is clear: 'increasing dependence of pathways on CDR options reduces the ability of policymakers to hedge risks freely across the mitigation technology portfolio'. But what does this tell us about the assumptions behind the different RCPs? What are the imaginaries of science and technology underlying the long-term mitigation scenarios?

Perhaps one of the most intriguing aspects of the assessment of geoengineering conducted by WGI refers to the level of confidence assigned to conditional sentences in order to communicate the degree of certainty in key findings. The following quotations are examples of this:

> Theory, model studies and observations suggest that some Solar Radiation Management (SRM) methods, if practicable, could substantially offset a global temperature rise and partially offset some other impacts of global warming, but the compensation for the climate change caused by GHGs would be imprecise (*high confidence*).
>
> (IPCC 2013b, 574)

> If SRM were terminated for any reason, a rapid increase in surface temperatures (within a decade or two) to values consistent with the high GHG forcing would result (*high confidence*).
>
> (IPCC 2013b, 635)

What can we infer from these statements? Can they be considered policy-relevant? If so, what scientific basis do they provide for policy-makers?

If we now return to our initial questions we have to conclude that, although we have long since recognised the severe limitations of the mechanistic paradigm informed by the Cartesian belief in scientific truth, our worldview is still entrenched in it. And this is so because the *alternative* understanding of scientific knowledge – the systemic paradigm that recognises that all scientific concepts and theories are limited and approximate, that science can never provide any complete and definitive understanding and that we always deal with limited and approximate knowledge (Capra and Luisi 2014) – has yet to recognise that there is no point in post-normal science problems in trying to emulate the mechanistic and reductionist views of classical physics in its control of uncertainty (Funtowicz and Ravetz 1990). This is one of the paradoxes of our time. The attempt to communicate uncertainties with the traditional language of science seems to run into a profound contradiction: how can one address what is not fully known in a scientific problem with the same (and expected?) quantitative scientific tools and concepts that are used to communicate what is known? In this attempt to understand system uncertainties and to explain the inexactness of scientific knowledge, as well as to communicate the limits of what can be known, science has primarily been using numerical language (see Sarewitz in this volume), the language of *objectivity*, namely what we have been educated to think of as the language of precision. The risk is clear: we may have been led to overestimate what we know about uncertainty and to underestimate the inexactness, unreliability and – most of all – our ignorance of it.

Moreover, the pressure of practice under which science operates today is giving rise to the emergence of new objects of research through which we gain a new understanding and control of Nature (Carrier and Nordmann 2011; Carrier 2011). As the assessment of geoengineering technologies in the IPCC AR5 demonstrates, the techno-scientific framing of climate change, although involving different ways of perceiving human's attempts to 'act into Nature', is giving meaning to human action within Nature and provides guidance for humans' domination of Nature.

## The geoengineering worldview: Halfway between the Cartesian dream and the Cartesian nightmare?

In the mid-1980s, when the Earth System Sciences Committee of the NASA Advisory Council put forward a more complete and unified approach to Earth studies – Earth System Science – a new way of understanding and analysing the Earth system began to gain ground among scientific institutions around the world. Fundamental to this approach is a view of the Earth system as a related set of interacting processes operating on a wide range of spatial and temporal scales, rather than as a collection of individual components. Several factors have combined to stimulate this new approach to Earth studies and global change: the maturity of the traditional Earth science disciplines, developments in remote sensing systems and related earth observation activities, advances in conceptual and numerical models of Earth system processes, and the recognition of the growing role of human activity in global change (ESSC 1988, 1986).

A few years after NASA acknowledged the need to strengthen international cooperation for a truly worldwide study of the Earth, the 1992 Rio Declaration on Environment and Development and Agenda 21 (a comprehensive plan of action to facilitate the transition towards the goal of truly sustainable development), unanimously adopted by 178 Governments at the United Nations Conference on Environment and Development (UNCED), gave a major boost to the development of an integrated approach to sustainable development and the interdisciplinary focus of Earth system science and global change (Johnson *et al.* 1997).

The next important step towards a holistic perception of the Earth system as a whole and, on this cognitive basis, developing concepts for global environmental management was taken in 2001 with the establishment of the Earth System Science Partnership (ESSP), which brought together the four international global change research programmes: DIVERSITAS, the International Geosphere-Biosphere Programme (IGBP), the International Human Dimensions Programme (IHDP), and the World Climate Research Programme (WCRP).[15]

The orchestrated effort to integrate disciplinary knowledge, insights and understanding of parts of the Earth system within Earth system science gave rise to the idea of a 'global system of global systems science'. Seen as a 'substantive science of integration', this new system of global environmental science is today presented as the key to implementing any approach towards global sustainability (Steffen *et al.* 2004).

> The challenge of understanding a changing Earth demands not only systems science but also a *new system of science* ... Human-driven changes are pushing the Earth System beyond its natural operating domain into planetary *terra incognita.* Management strategies for global sustainability are urgently required. *Earth System science is the key to implementing any approach towards good planetary management,* as it can provide critical insights into the feasibility, risks, trade-offs and timeliness of any proposed strategy.
>
> (Global Environmental Change Programmes 2011, 23–7, emphasis added)

This new way of understanding and studying the Earth system, the recognition that humanity itself has become a global geophysical force, allied with new approaches and a growing commitment to achieving successful and effective planetary stewardship, are leading to a profound reorientation of the global environmental change research agenda, thereby opening up a wide range of new practices, techniques and mechanisms for global governance (Lövbrand *et al.* 2009).

> The advent of the Anthropocene, the time interval in which human activities now rival global geophysical processes, suggests that we need to fundamentally alter our relationship with the planet we inhabit. Many approaches could be adopted, ranging from geoengineering solutions that purposefully manipulate parts of the Earth System to becoming active stewards of our own life support system.
>
> (Steffen *et al.* 2011, 739)

It is against this background that the idea of geoengineering, as a potential new tool for addressing climate change, is gaining ground. In fact, each new step in the direction of an integrated Earth System Science seems to have reinforced the plausibility of geoengineering proposals within the wide range of options 'towards good planetary management' (Steffen and Tyson 2001). As the results of our analysis suggest, the Cartesian mechanistic worldview, with its emphasis on the instrumental mastery of nature, is deeply embedded in the dominant techno-scientific framing of climate change and in the range of practices that have produced the 'coupled human and ecological system' as a 'thinkable' and and governable domain. Accordingly, the first step towards understanding why geoengineering 'migrated from marginal to mainstream science and policy making' (Scott 2012) should consist of a critical examination of the salient narratives that captured the shift in the relationship between humans and the global environment, in order to suggest the beginning of a potentially new geological epoch in which human beings appear to have become a driving force in the evolution of the planet and geoengineering starts to look acceptable in preventing the worst effects of climate change.

## Final remarks

In this chapter we questioned the 'end of the Cartesian Dream' by taking into account the assessment of geoengineering solutions included in the Fifth Assessment Report of the IPCC. As the results of our analysis suggest, the Cartesian mechanistic worldview, with its emphasis on the instrumental mastery of Nature, is deeply embedded in the dominant techno-scientific framing of climate change and in the range of practices that have produced the 'coupled human and ecological system' as a 'thinkable' and governable domain. Although recent proposals to 'geoengineer' the climate can be seen as an early-twenty-first-century embodiment of the Cartesian dream of human mastery over Nature, they entail a particular way of thinking about the world, leading to different assumptions about stability, different processes that affect that stability, and different policies that are considered appropriate to achieving successful and effective planetary stewardship. This reinforces the need to unbind the geoengineering debate from the deeply embedded narratives of science, technology, and society which present technoscientific innovation as the solution to our most critical problems and as a substitute for social change. Similarly, the fundamental beliefs, both about Nature and about human beings, underlying geoengineering proposals need to be questioned if the social and ethical implications of these proposals are to be taken seriously. In fact, the fundamental issues of fairness, justice and responsibility that are deemed important in the ethical debate about geoengineering can only be considered if we move beyond the rhetoric of risk, fear, and control, which is providing the justification to embrace geoengineering proposals within a 'risk management strategy for climate change'.

## Notes

1   In this respect, it is worth mentioning that this definition of science is still included in the 1762 4th edn of the *Dictionnaire de l'Académie Française* and only in the 6th edn of 1832 does science become defined by its subject matter, rather than by its method (Lee 2010).

2   With this in mind it is worth recalling what Descartes wrote about the first of the six major passions of the human soul (Descartes 1989, articles 70 and 76): 'Wonder is a sudden surprise of the soul which makes it tend to consider attentively those objects which seem to it rare and extraordinary … But it happens much more often that one wonders too much and is astonished, in perceiving things worth considering only a little or not at all, than that one wonders too little. This can entirely eradicate or pervert the use of reason. That is why, although it is good to be born with some inclination to this passion, since it disposes us to the acquisition of the sciences, we should still try afterwards to emancipate ourselves from it as much as possible …'

3   For an illuminating discussion of this topic see for instance Winter 2012; Hulme 2014; Rayner 2014..

4   Paul Crutzen and Eugene Stoermer coined the term Anthropocene to describe a new geological epoch 'in which humankind has emerged as a globally significant – and potentially intelligent – force capable of reshaping the face of the planet' (Clark *et al.* 2004, 1).

5   J. Ravetz has coined the term 'science-based ignorance' to designate 'an absence of necessary knowledge concerning systems and cycles that exist out there in the natural world, but which exist only because of human activities' (Ravetz 1990, 287).

6   Some significant contributions to the discussion of the ethical issues posed by geoengineering include: Hamilton 2011, 2013; Gardiner 2011; Betz and Cacean 2012; Hourdequin 2012; Preston 2012; Jamieson 2009, 1996; Schneider 1996.

7   As defined in the *Principles Governing IPCC Work:* 'the role of the IPCC is to assess on a comprehensive, objective, open and transparent basis the scientific, technical and socio-economic information relevant to understanding the scientific basis of risk of human-induced climate change, its potential impacts and options for adaptation and mitigation' (IPCC 2008, 1). To this end the IPCC produces periodic assessment reports that use a calibrated language to characterise the scientific understanding and associated uncertainties underlying assessment findings. For more information about the treatment of uncertainties in the IPCC Assessment Reports see: Mastrandrea *et al.* 2010, 2011.

8   In this regard it is worth mentioning that in the IPCC AR5 the definition of 'adaptation' differs in breadth and focus from that used in earlier IPCC reports (IPCC 2013a, 2014a, 2014b). In spite of the fact that the Expert Meeting 'did not address the question of whether these definitions should be updated to differentiate them better from geoengineering' (Boucher *et al.* 2011, 2), the new term of 'adaptation', as defined in the WGII AR5 Glossary, is supposed 'to reflect scientific progress'. However, the question of whether it resulted from an attempt to better differentiate conventional adaptation approaches from geoengineering proposals is not clear.

9   The AR5 relies on two metrics for communicating the degree of certainty in key findings (Mastrandrea *et al.* 2010): (i) Confidence in the validity of a finding, based on the type, amount, quality and consistency of evidence (e.g. mechanistic understanding, theory, data, models, expert judgment) and the degree of agreement. Confidence is expressed qualitatively; (ii) Quantified measures of uncertainty in a finding expressed probabilistically (based on statistical analysis of observations or model results, or expert judgement).

10   Reference to geoengineering in the last paragraph of the Summary for Policymakers (SPM) of the Working Group I contribution to the IPCC Fifth Assessment Report (WGI AR5): 'Methods that aim to deliberately alter the climate

system to counter climate change, termed geoengineering, have been proposed. Limited evidence precludes a comprehensive quantitative assessment of both Solar Radiation Management (SRM) and Carbon Dioxide Removal (CDR) and their impact on the climate system. CDR methods have biogeochemical and technological limitations to their potential on a global scale. There is insufficient knowledge to quantify how much $CO_2$ emissions could be partially offset by CDR on a century timescale. Modelling indicates that SRM methods, if realisable, have the potential to substantially offset a global temperature rise, but they would also modify the global water cycle, and would not reduce ocean acidification. If SRM were terminated for any reason, there is *high confidence* that global surface temperatures would rise very rapidly to values consistent with the greenhouse gas forcing. CDR and SRM methods carry side effects and long-term consequences on a global scale' (IPCC 2013c, 29).

11  The term 'policy neutrality' is used here to refer to the *Principles Governing IPCC Work*, which states that 'IPCC reports should be neutral with respect to policy' (IPCC 2008, 1).

12  Excerpt of the post 'Why has geoengineering been legitimised by the IPCC?' published on the Political Science blog hosted by the *Guardian*.

13  In the AR5, the following terms have been used to indicate the assessed likelihood of an outcome or a result: virtually certain 99–100% probability, very likely 90–100%, likely 66–100%, about as likely as not 33–66%, unlikely 0–33%, very unlikely 0–10%, exceptionally unlikely 0–1%.

14  Four Representative Concentration Pathway (RCP) scenarios produced from Integrated Assessment Models (IAMs) were used in the Fifth Assessment Report of IPCC as a basis for the climate predictions and projections presented by WG1 (AR5 WG1, chapters 11 to 14). These four RCPs are identified by their approximate total radiative forcing in year 2100 relative to 1750: 2.6 W m$^{-2}$ for RCP2.6, 4.5 W m$^{-2}$ for RCP4.5, 6.0 W m$^{-2}$ for RCP6.0, and 8.5 W m$^{-2}$ for RCP8.5. The RCPs with lower radiative forcing levels already include some CDR methods: the RCP2.6 scenario achieves the negative emission rate through the use of large-scale bioenergy with carbon capture and storage (BECCS) and the RCP4.5 also assumes some use of BECCS to stabilise $CO_2$ concentration by 2100 and, to a lesser extent, afforestation.

15  The ESSP was launched in 2001 as a response to the Amsterdam Declaration on Global Change, which called for closer cooperation between global environmental research programmes and for greater integration across disciplines, environment and development issues, and the natural and social sciences.

# References

Arendt, H. 1958. *The Human Condition*, 2nd edn, Chicago, IL: University of Chicago Press.

Bernstein, R. 1983. *Beyond Objectivism and Relativism: Science Hermeneutics and Praxis*, Philadelphia: University of Pennsylvania Press.

Betz, G., and Cacean, S. 2012. *Ethical Aspects of Climate Engineering*, Karlsruhe: KIT Scientific Publishing.

Böschen, S., Kastenhofer, K., Marschall, L., Rust, I., Soentgen, J., and Wehling, P. 2006. Scientific cultures of non-knowledge in the controversy over genetically modified organisms (GMO): The cases of molecular biology and ecology, *GAIA*, 15(4): 294–301.

Boucher, O., Gruber, N., and Blackstock, J. 2011. Summary of the synthesis session, in O. Edenhofer *et al.* (eds), *IPCC Expert Meeting Report on Geoengineering*, Potsdam, Germany: IPCC Working Group III Technical Support Unit Potsdam Institute for Climate Impact Research.

Boyd, P.W. 2008. Ranking geo-engineering schemes, *Nature Geoscience*, 1(11): 722–4.

Brentano, F.C. 1998. The four phases of philosophy and its current state, in B.M. Mezei and B. Smith (eds) *The Four Phases of Philosophy*, Amsterdam: Rodopi, pp. 81–112.

Capra, F. 1983. *The Turning Point: Science Society and the Rising Culture*, New York: Bantam Books.

Capra, F. and Luisi, P.L. 2014. *The Systems View of Life: a Unifying Vision*, Cambridge: Cambridge University Press.

Carrier, M. 2011. Knowledge, politics, and commerce: Science under the pressure of practice, in M. Carrier and A. Nordmann (eds), *Science in the Context of Application*, Dordrecht: Springer, pp. 11–30.

Carrier, M., and Nordmann, A. 2011. Science in the context of application: Methodological change conceptual transformation cultural reorientation, in M. Carrier and A. Nordmann (eds), *Science in the Context of Application*, Dordrecht: Springer, pp. 1–7.

Clark, W., Hans, C., Schellnhuber, J., and Crutzen, P.J. 2004. Science for global sustainability: Toward a new paradigm, in H.J. Schellnhuber, P.J. Crutzen, W.C. Clark, M. Claussen, and H. Held (eds), *Earth System Analysis for Sustainability: Dahlem Workshop Reports*, Cambridge, MA: MIT Press, pp. 1–28.

Crutzen, P.J. 2006. Albedo enhancement by stratospheric sulfur injections: A contribution to resolve a policy dilemma? *Climatic Change*, 77: 211–19.

Descartes, R. 1988. *Discourse on Method (1637) and Meditations on First Philosophy (1641)*, tr. A. C. Donal, 4th edn, Indianopolis, IN: Hackett Publishing Co.

Descartes, R. 1989. *The Passions of the Soul*, tr. Stephen H. Voss, Indianapolis, IN: Hackett Publishing Co. (Original edn 1649.)

Drucker, P.F. 1957. *Landmarks of Tomorrow: A Report on the New Post-Modern World*, New York: Harper & Row.

ESSC. 1986. *Earth System Science: A Program for Global Change Report of the Earth System Sciences Committee to the NASA Advisory Council*, Washington, DC: National Aeronautic and Space Administration Advisory Committee.

ESSC. 1988. *Earth System Science: A Closer View, Report of the Earth System Sciences Committee to the NASA Advisory Council*, Washington, DC: National Aeronautics and Space Administration.

ETC Group. 2014. *The IPCC's AR5 and Geoengineering* (http://wwwetcgrouporg/content/ipcc-ar5-geoengineering-march2014) accessed June 2014.

Funtowicz, S.O., and Ravetz, J.R. 1990. *Uncertainty and Quality in Science for Policy, Futures*, Dordrecht, The Netherlands: Kluwer Academic Publishers.

Gardiner, S.M. 2011. *A Perfect Moral Storm: The Ethical Tragedy of Climate Change*, Oxford: Oxford University Press.

Gardiner, Stephen M. 2010. Is 'arming the future' with geoengineering really the lesser evil? Some doubts about the ethics of intentionally manipulating the climate system, in S.M. Gardiner, S. Caney, D. Jamieson, and H. Shue (eds), *Climate Ethics: Essential Readings*, New York: Oxford University Press, pp. 284–312.

Global Environmental Change Programmes. 2011. Global change and the Earth system: A planet under pressure, in W. Steffen and P. Tyson (eds), *IGBP Science*, 4th edn, Stockholm: UNT Digital Library, (http://digitallibraryuntedu/ark:/67531/metadc12041) accessed Aug. 2012.

Hamilton, C. 2011. *The Ethical Foundations of Climate Engineering* (http://clivehamilton.com/the-ethical-foundations-of-climate-engineering) accessed Aug. 2014.

Hamilton, C. 2013. *Earthmasters: The Dawn of the Age of Climate Engineering*, New Haven, CT: Yale University Press.

Hourdequin, M. 2012. Geoengineering solidarity and moral risk, in C.J. Preston (ed.), *Engineering the Climate: The Ethics of Solar Radiation Management*, Lanham, MD: Lexington Books, pp. 15–32.

Hulme, M. 2014. *Can Science Fix Climate Change? A Case Against Climate Engineering*, Cambridge: Polity Press.

IPCC. 2007. Climate change 2007, in B. Metz, O.R. Davidson, P.R. Bosch, R. Dave and L.A. Meyer (eds), *Mitigation Contribution of Working Group III to the Fourth Assessment Report of the Intergovernmental Panel on Climate Change*, Cambridge and New York: Cambridge University Press.

IPCC. 2008. *Principles Governing IPCC Work: Approved at the Fourteenth Session (Vienna 1–3 October 1998) on 1 October 1998 Amended at the Twenty-First Session (Vienna 3 and 6–7 November 2003) the Twenty-Fifth Session (Mauritius 26–28 April 2006) the Thirty-Fifth Session (Geneva 6–9 June 2012) and the Thirty-Seventh Session (Batumi 14–18 October 2013)* (http://wwwipccch/pdf/ipcc-principles/ipcc-principlespdf) accessed June 2014.

IPCC. 2010. *The Intergovernmental Panel on Climate Change Fifth Assessment Report: Proposal for an IPCC Expert Meeting on Geoengineering* (http://wwwipccch/meetings/session32/doc05_p32_proposal_EM_on_geoengineeringpdf) accessed Sept. 2010.

IPCC. 2012. Meeting report, in O. Edenhofer *et al.* (eds), *Intergovernmental Panel on Climate Change Expert Meeting on Geoengineering*, Potsdam: IPCC Working Group III Technical Support Unit, Potsdam Institute for Climate Impact Research.

IPCC. 2013a. Annex III: Glossary, in T.F. Stocker *et al.* (eds), *Climate Change 2013: The Physical Science Basis Contribution of Working Group I to the Fifth Assessment Report of the Intergovernmental Panel on Climate Change*, Cambridge and New York: Cambridge University Press, 1447–66.

IPCC. 2013b. *Climate Change 2013: The Physical Science Basis Contribution of Working Group I to the Fifth Assessment Report of the Intergovernmental Panel on Climate Change*, Cambridge and New York: Cambridge University Press.

IPCC. 2013c. Summary for policymakers, in T.F. Stocker *et al.* (eds), *Climate Change 2013: The Physical Science Basis Contribution of Working Group I to the Fifth Assessment Report of the Intergovernmental Panel on Climate Change*, Cambridge and New York: Cambridge University Press, 1–29.

IPCC. 2014a. Annex I: Glossary, in J.M. Allwood, V. Bosetti, N.K. Dubash, L. Gómez-Echeverri, and C. von Stechow (eds), *Climate Change 2014: Mitigation of Climate Change Working Group III Contribution to the IPCC 5th Assessment Report of the Intergovernmental Panel on Climate Change*, Cambridge and New York: Cambridge University Press.

IPCC. 2014b. Annex XX: Glossary, in J. Agard *et al.* (eds), *Climate Change Impacts Adaptation and Vulnerability Part B: Regional Aspects Contribution of Working Group II to the Fifth Assessment Report of the Intergovernmental Panel on Climate Change*, Cambridge and New York: Cambridge University Press.

IPCC. 2014c. Introductory chapter (final draft: a report accepted by Working Group III of the IPCC but not approved in detail), in A. Grübler and A. Muvundika (eds), *Climate Change 2014: Mitigation of Climate Change Contribution of Working Group III to the Fifth Assessment Report of the Intergovernmental Panel on Climate Change*, Cambridge and New York: Cambridge University Press, ch. 1.

IPCC. 2014d. Assessing transformation pathways (A report accepted by Working Group III of the IPCC but not approved in detail), in C. Wenying and J. Weyant (eds), *Climate Change 2014: Mitigation of Climate Change Contribution of Working Group III to* the *Fifth Assessment Report of the Intergovernmental Panel on Climate Change*, Cambridge and New York: Cambridge University Press, ch. 6.

IPCC. 2014e. Summary for policymakers, in O. Edenhofer *et al.* (eds), *Climate Change 2014 Mitigation of Climate Change Contribution of Working Group III to the Fifth Assessment Report of the Intergovernmental Panel on Climate Change*, Cambridge and New York: Cambridge University Press.

Jamieson, D. 1996. Ethics and intentional climate change, *Climatic Change*, 33: 323–36.

Jamieson, D. 2009. The ethics of geoengineering, *People and Place*, 1(2) (http://www. peopleandplace.net/perspectives/2009/5/13/the_ethics_of_geoengineering) accessed Sept. 2010.

Johnson, D.R., Ruzek, M., and Kalb, M. 1997. What is Earth system science? Geoscience and remote sensing in IGARSS '97 Remote Sensing – A Scientific Vision for Sustainable Development, *Proceedings of the 1997 International Geoscience and Remote Sensing Symposium Singapore*, August 4–8, pp. 688–91.

Keith, D.W. 2000. Geoengineering the climate: History and prospect, *Annual Review of Energy and the Environment*, 25: 245–84.

Lee, N. 2010. Planetary perspectives in enlightenment fiction and science, in C. McDonald and S. Rubin Suleiman (eds), *French Global: A New Approach to Literary History*, New York: Columbia University Press, pp. 94–109.

Lövbrand, E., Stripple, J., and Wiman, B. 2009. Earth System governmentality: Reflections on science in the Anthropocene, *Global Environmental Change*, 19: 7–13.

Macnaghten, P., and Szerszynski, B. 2013. Living the global social experiment: An analysis of public discourse on solar radiation management and its implications for governance, *Global Environmental Change*, 23(2): 465–74.

Mastrandrea, M.D., *et al.* 2010. *Guidance Note for Lead Authors of the IPCC Fifth Assessment Report on Consistent Treatment of Uncertainties*, Intergovernmental Panel on Climate Change (IPCC) (http://www.ipcc.ch/pdf/supporting-material/uncertainty-guidance-note.pdf) accessed May 2014.

Mastrandrea, M.D., *et al.* 2011. The IPCC AR5 guidance note on consistent treatment of uncertainties: a common approach across the working groups, *Climatic Change* 108(4): 675–91.

New, M., Liverman, D., Schroder, H., and Anderson, K. 2010. Four degrees and beyond: The potential for a global temperature increase of four degrees and its implications, *Philosophical Transactions of the Royal Society A: Mathematical Physical and Engineering Sciences*, 369(1934): 6–19.

Pörtner, H.O.D., *et al.* 2014. Ocean systems, in C. B. Field *et al.* (eds), *Climate Change 2014: Impacts Adaptation and Vulnerability Part A: Global and Sectoral Aspects Contribution of Working Group II to the Fifth Assessment Report of the Intergovernmental Panel on Climate Change*, Cambridge and New York: Cambridge University Press.

Preston, C.J. 2012. Re-thinking the unthinkable: Environmental ethics and the presumptive argument against geoengineering, *Environmental Values*, 20(4): 457–79.

Ravetz, J.R. 1990. *The Merger of Knowledge with Power: Essays in Critical Science*, London: Mansell.

Rayner, S. 2014. *To Know or Not to Know? A Note on Ignorance as a Rhetorical Resource in Geoengineering Debates Climate*, Geoengineering Governance Working Paper Series, 010 (http://geoengineering-governance-research.org/perch/resources/ workingpaper10raynertoknowornottoknow-1.pdf) accessed Apr. 2014.

Russell, L.M., *et al.* 2012. Ecosystem impacts of geoengineering: a review for developing a science plan, *Ambio*, 41(4): 350–69.

Schelling, T.C. 1996. The economic diplomacy of geoengineering, *Climatic Change,* 33(3): 303–7.

Schneider, S.H. 1996. Geoengineering: Could – or should – we do it? *Climatic Change,* 33(3): 291–302.

Scott, K.N. 2012. Transboundary environmental governance and emerging environmental threats: Geo-engineering in the marine environment, in R. Warner and S. Marsden (eds), *Transboundary Environmental Governance: Inland Coastal and Marine Perspectives,* London: Ashgate Publishing, pp. 223–45.

Steffen, W., and Tyson, P., eds. 2001. *IGBP Science,* 4th edn, Stockholm: UNT Digital Library (http://digitallibraryuntedu/ark:/67531/metadc12041) accessed Aug. 2012.

Steffen, W., *et al.* 2004. *Global Change and the Earth System: A Planet under Pressure,* Berlin: Springer.

Steffen, W., *et al.* 2011. The Anthropocene: From global change to planetary stewardship, *Ambio,* 40(7): 739–61.

Stilgoe, J. 2014. Why has geoengineering been legitimised by the IPCC? Political Science (Guardian science blogs) (http://wwwtheguardiancom/science/political-science/2013/sep/27/science-policy1) accessed Feb. 2014.

Tlumak, J. 2007. *Classical Modern Philosophy: A Contemporary Introduction,* London: Routledge.

Vaughan, N.E., and Lenton, T.M. 2011. A review of climate geoengineering proposals. *Climatic Change,* 109(3–4): 745–90.

Winter, G. 2012. Climate engineering and international law: Last resort or the end of humanity? *Review of European Community and International Environmental Law,* 20(3): 277–89.

# Part III
# Quality in an interconnected world

# 8 Animals and beggars
## Imaginative numbers in the real world

*Daniel Sarewitz*

In the Cartesian world, things are made understandable and controllable through the identification and investigation of their component parts. The attributes and behaviour of those parts are most precisely and accurately conveyed with numbers. A drawing or a verbal description of an electron, for example, provides a weaker claim of correspondence to the actual electron than a numerical measure of its mass, its charge, its velocity. Indeed, to describe something with a number is to make a claim about a direct correspondence between the thing being represented by the number, and the real world out there. The number is reality's most faithful translator.

Here I want to take a different stance. I will not be referring to technical disagreements about the scientific correctness of numbers, for example the several-decades-long dispute about the flux of neutrinos emitted by the sun (Pinch 1981; McDonald *et al.* 2003). Rather, it seems sometimes that it is simply not possible to say much at all about the correspondence between the numbers given to us by science, and the real world out there, despite the assumptions of, and our belief in, such a correspondence. In such cases, the numbers must mean something entirely different than they are supposed to mean, perhaps they are signifiers, or consequences, of things complex and inchoate inside, rather than outside, of us; perhaps they are mystical or artistic symbols upon which we project our own meanings.

I will begin to develop this stance by considering efforts to assign a number to something that most people agree must be a real quantity, much as the number of grains of sand on a beach is a real quantity, even if most would also acknowledge that coming up with an accurate number would be impossible, as with counting all the grains of sand. But unlike sand-grain-counting, what I have in mind here is a very real and specific scientific activity – the effort to quantify the amount of natural gas in the Earth's crust. Estimating how much natural gas is contained in rocks in various parts of the world is thought to be a useful exercise for many reasons. And scientists try to come up with reasonable numbers to characterise these volumes of gas. For example, in 1975, geologists in the United States estimated that a total of about 960 trillion cubic feet of natural gas, likely to be accessible by known technological means, were housed in rocks beneath the surface of the US (Miller *et al.* 1975, 725). 960 trillion cubic feet, that is a good, solid number. Is it a lot or a little? Well, US natural gas consumption in 1975 was about 20 trillion cubic feet per year – a rate that hasn't changed all that much since then (US Energy Information Administration 2014), so one way of thinking about the number is to say it was the equivalent of about 50 years of 1975-level natural gas consumption. This is one indirect but intuitively appealing way of expressing what the number was supposed to correspond to.

Fast forward about 40 years, to the present. How much gas is left? In those four intervening decades, Americans have burned or otherwise consumed about 860 trillion cubic feet of natural gas (US Energy Information Administration 2014) – approximately 90 per cent of the 960 trillion-cubic-foot reserve estimated in 1975. If 960 trillion cubic feet were an accurate estimate, then the US should be nearing the end of its gas supply right about now.

Instead, according to 2013 assessments, there is more natural gas today than there was in 1975 – almost 25 five per cent more, or 1440 trillion cubic feet (US Geological Survey 2013). If today's number is right, then the total reserve in 1975 should have been at least 2300 trillion cubic feet (860 + 1440), so the estimate was low by a factor of about 2.4. What a great thing, the more gas you use, the more you seem to have.

There are, of course, very good reasons for these changing numbers. Knowledge improves, technologies improve, things that were barely imagined, like the horizontal drilling and fracking techniques that allow extraction of shale gas from regions that before weren't even considered potential gas sources, completely change the assumptions for making the calculations, and so on. We can be sure that the scientists who made the 1975 estimates mustered all the available expertise and knowledge at the time, and were doing the best they could. Indeed, the growth of the natural gas resource over time is pretty much what economists say we should expect – that humans figure out how to overcome scarcity of a resource through innovation that allows the resource to be expanded, or a substitute to be developed.

But the question remains: what did that number, then, actually mean? What were the scientists who produce the number actually doing? The number is meant to correspond to the amount of gas that is accessible at the time the assessment is made. It is meant to reflect, as well as possible, the state of something real. The verisimilitude of the number at the time it is created, however, can never be tested. We could treat the number as a prediction of what can be extracted – a prediction that can be tested by seeing whether the amount of gas that's removed corresponds to the amount that was said to exist. And that test shows that the number didn't correspond at all to the real thing in the world that it was supposed to represent. What it actually corresponded to was a set of quantified beliefs of a group of scientists that turned out to be wrong.

Perhaps it would be better to treat the number as the product of a thought experiment, where we hold economics and technology constant in time, and then extract all the available gas at that price, using those technologies. But such a world can never exist, for example as supply went down, price would go up, consumption would go down, alternatives would be sought, and so forth. The number can never be tested against real things, and the value of the thought experiment seems at best completely abstract. The beliefs about the world which create the number trigger the very activities that will ensure that the beliefs must be false. We have confidence in those beliefs because they are held by experts in the field. But it is not possible to confirm them.

There's no dishonour in being wrong. Now, again, in the standard accounting of science, science is always being wrong, and then getting better with time. So does that mean that we should expect that the resource estimates should improve with later assessments? We have no way to test whether such improvement occurs, for the same reasons we couldn't test the first number. Indeed, the newer numbers, generated in later assessments, do not seem to correspond any better to something real under the Earth than do the old ones; there is nothing that looks like a convergence of reserve estimates towards some stable set of numbers over the decades, and the exogenous uncertainties that falsified the past numbers – changes in extraction technologies, in competing energy technologies, in price and demand, and so on – are not likely to get any less vexing in the future.

Which is not to say these numbers are not important, or that they lack meaning, it's just that they do not mean what they are said to mean, and what most people would reasonably assume them to mean. The numbers are important not because they are true, but because we believe them. Because they send a signal to energy markets, they influence decisions made by corporations, governments and investors, they inform our understanding of geopolitical relations and expectations about future environmental changes. They create a shared sense of a reality, even if that sense does not correspond to any scientifically confirmable or testable measure of reality. The numbers are taken seriously because they are generated through the work of scientific experts, using scientific knowledge and principles that are applied through rigorous analytical and statistical methods. They have, as William James (1907) would say, 'cash value'. But unlike our conventional understanding of what scientifically generated numbers mean, these numbers do not really seem to be about the thing that is being quantified, they are about something else.

A perhaps surprising point here, and the reason I'm starting with this particular example, is that no one really seems to care very much that the numbers are always turning out to be wrong – which is very different than saying that no one cares what the numbers *are*. In a superb recounting of the politics behind hydrocarbon resource assessments, Donald Gautier (2000), who has led these activities for the US Geological Survey, explains how, in 1988, the hydrocarbon industry strongly protested the assumptions and criteria used by Geological Survey scientists to make natural gas estimates, because the assumptions led to very low numbers. Industry leaders felt that these low numbers would make it difficult for them to convince the government to deregulate the gas market. This problem was solved during the subsequent resource assessment in 1995, by including industry and academic experts in the scientific assessment process. Assumptions and criteria were duly changed, the numbers went up – by 270 per cent over the eight-year period. Everyone was satisfied.

This process of greater inclusion in the scientific endeavour approximates what sociologists of science have termed a transition from reliable knowledge – the product of a closed group of experts working with their own set of scientific norms – to socially robust knowledge, where participation of diverse interests leads to results that satisfy everyone (Gibbons 1999). Gautier (2000, 247) writes, with considerable analytical subtlety: 'The predictions of the quantity … of essentially unknown entities such as oil and gas accumulations is, by definition, an attempt to narrow uncertainty surrounding decisions. *The value of an assessment must be in its usefulness*' (emphasis added) – usefulness to garner political support for regulatory policy, to maintain public confidence about energy security, to justify investments in infrastructure like pipelines and the innovation that leads to ever-improved technologies for gas extraction. The value of the assessment is not in its accuracy – not in its correspondence to anything real under the ground, which is unknowable. It is in the creation of a number that people can believe in.

Numbers of this sort are common in the world. Consider a number called 'climate sensitivity', the temperature increase that the Earth's atmosphere would experience with a doubling of carbon dioxide content. What does this number correspond to in the real world? In its most common definition, climate sensitivity assumes both an instantaneous doubling of carbon dioxide and the achievement of an equilibrium (steady) state, neither of which are possible. Obviously the concept of climate sensitivity has heuristic value, and assigning a number to the concept helps to convey a sense of the scale of the global warming phenomenon, as well as to provide a test of how well mathematical models of climate change conform to theoretical expectations. Indeed, understanding and quantifying this value has occupied climate scientists for more than a century. In particular, scientists have long sought to quantify and narrow the uncertainties around climate sensitivity. But what does it mean to assign an uncertainty to a number that does not represent anything real in Nature, that cannot exist? Van der Sluijs *et al.* (1998, 304) showed how negotiations among scientists over two decades served to keep this uncertainty range stable – at 1.5° to 4.5° Celsius – despite changing science, in part because no one really understood what the range meant, and thus no one could formulate a compelling reason for changing it. In an article by Andronova *et al.* (2007, 15), the importance of climate sensitivity is explained in terms very much like those used by Gautier for natural gas resource estimates:

> The concept of climate sensitivity has served well during the past hundred years … Vast progress has been made, particularly with the process of science integration when climatology, mathematics, economics and policy come together to formulate demands for the empirical and model data to understand anthropogenic influences on climate and environment. This science integration taught climate scientists to present the uncertainties in estimates of climate sensitivity, and it taught policy-makers not to ignore the climate-change problem.

The value of the number, that is, is *in its usefulness*, not in its accuracy in corresponding to something real *out there*, which it does not, because there is no such real thing. What, then, does the number correspond to?

Issues of environment and public health are replete with numbers whose very existence seems to provoke the creation of a different, often highly contradictory number. The result is not a gradual approach to a more rigorous scientific portrayal of reality, but an increasing sense of incoherence, contradiction and dismay. In a paper on deforestation in the Himalayas, Michael Thompson *et al.* (2007, 11–29) examined well-publicised scientific claims that forest cover in Nepal was being depleted at an alarming rate (e.g. Eckholm 1975). They discovered that, on close scrutiny, one could find estimates of deforestation varying by a factor of more than 25, depending on one's assumptions about rates of firewood use, forest growth, the distance that people will travel to collect wood and so on, and that one could use those numbers to show that the mountain forests were in imminent danger of disappearing, or that they were actually being sustainably managed and perhaps even expanding.

The brilliant and mischievous philosopher Mark Sagoff has examined efforts in the field of ecological economics to assign numbers – monetary value – to ecosystem services. These numbers are supposed to correspond to something real if intangible – the utility provided by particular natural functions – and thus guide economic decisions about resource use. But Sagoff (2010) shows that such numbers are inherently contradictory and incoherent. One published case, for example (of the many he examines in this paper and others), estimates the ecosystem value of a wetland at $34,700 per acre based on the market value of waste treatment that the wetland provides for an adjacent potato chip factory (which gets this treatment for free from the wetland; the economic valuation reflects what it would cost to pay for the waste treatment, assuming a 9 per cent discount rate over 15 years). Sagoff notes, however, that the potato chip waste products actually add beneficial nutrients to the wetland. Perhaps it is the factory that provides the ecosystem service? And what happens to the value of those services when, as actually happened, the potato chip factory expands and moves and buys a waste treatment plant? Does the value of the wetland go to zero? Or perhaps it goes negative given the disappearance of factory-derived nutrients? What Sagoff shows is that the calculated value for the services delivered by the wetland not only cannot be applied to any other wetland, but that it changes over time based on factors that have nothing to do with the function of the wetland. What is that valuation of ecosystem services actually calculating, then?

If one is brave enough to wade into the dispiriting literature surrounding public-health-related debates, such as the one on dietary salt and hypertension, or on the benefits of different dietary mixes, or on the impacts of yearly mammograms for women in their forties and fifties, one immediately discovers an utterly bewildering array of mutually contradictory numbers that are advanced with confident spirit in peer-reviewed journals and newspapers alike. For example, Bayer *et al.* (2012), in their excellent summary of the state of scientific understanding about the health effects of salt intake, note that some reputable scientists believe that reduced salt intake could lengthen the lives of hundreds of thousands of people, whereas others believe that not only is there no compelling evidence of such a positive benefit, but that 'to assume that no deleterious effects would follow from salt reduction at the population is simply wrong' (Bayer *et al.* 2012, 2743). In these sorts of cases, it's not just that one has no idea what to make of the numbers, it's that even their very sign seems indeterminate.

That a number derived from the scientific study of something real in the world must correspond in some direct if perhaps imprecise way to that real thing, and must tell us something more precise and accurate than could otherwise be rendered, sometimes appears to be just a comforting belief, a necessary superstition, deeply held by us moderns. In saying this, my point is certainly not that such numbers are not important or even essential. They are the nucleus of much productive economic, social and political activity, in many ways helping to promote both civic stability and vibrant democratic debate through the creation of symbols that are understood in more or less similar ways across diverse ways of life.

What is important about these sorts of numbers is that they really are the creation of true science, carried out by the best experts, using the latest knowledge and methods, often involving enormous amounts of carefully measured data, vetted through the appropriate review processes and so on. All this scientific effort to create an obvious fiction – a fiction that helps to structure behaviour and expectations, a fiction that is useful. The scientific efforts that I describe here, and many others of similar ilk, cannot be understood as progressing towards ever-better correspondence to *the real number*. Perhaps they are best understood, then, as ritual, as the activity that a modern, rational society is supposed to undertake in order to help structure and focus action in the world. And the number itself is the sacred product of the ritual, a totemic symbol whose value is ensured and protected by the shared scientific norms that govern the conduct of the ritual, norms which in turn imbue the number with the legitimacy that allows so much activity to be organised around it.

Numbers that get bigger the more you subtract from them; uncertainty estimates for numbers that do not actually exist; numbers whose creation calls into existence directly contradictory numbers; numbers whose sign is unknowable. This sounds less like Galileo, who told us that mathematics was the language of Nature, and more like the magical fictions of Borges or Lewis Carroll. Indeed, Borges (1998) has a one-paragraph story 'On Exactitude in Science' (the idea for which, it turns out, he stole from Carroll's last novel, *Sylvie and Bruno Concluded*) that posits an ancient empire whose dedication to accuracy was such that the map of that domain 'coincided point for point' with the empire itself. Such a map was useless, of course, so it was 'delivered ... up to the Inclemencies of Sun and Winters'. Borges tells us that there is nothing left of the map now except 'Tattered Ruins ... inhabited by Animals and Beggars' (1998, 325).

In 1972, Alvin Weinberg coined the term 'trans-science' to describe 'questions which can be asked of science and yet *which cannot be answered by science*' (p. 209; emphasis in original). Given this impossibility, Weinberg (1972, 220) asked: 'What are the responsibilities of the scientist in the trans-scientific debate?' And his answer was that the scientist's responsibility was 'to make clear where the science ends and trans-science begins. Now this is not at all easy since experts will often disagree as to the extent and reliability of their expertise.'

The numbers I have been talking about are the products of trans-science – of science devoted to questions that cannot be answered by science. No wonder they are so very strange. Of course one response to this whole stance would simply be to insist that science, as an enterprise, cannot possibly know what is answerable and what is not, and if scientists did not try to answer questions that cannot be answered today, science would quickly become useless. Progress is hard; given enough time, we should expect questions that sound like trans-science now to be gradually domesticated by the brick-by-brick pursuit of scientific progress.

Perhaps, but one can hardly doubt that enormous amounts of what we actually call science today is really trans-science – the attempt to answer the unanswerable. Between 1976 and 2014, the *New York Times* has printed more than 1,400 articles on mammograms. I have only sampled perhaps 5 per cent of those articles for this chapter, but each of them reports on scientific results, and their implications for medical practice and the health of women. Numbers are central to the work: changes in mortality rates; changes in life expectancies. Here are some headlines spanning nearly four decades:

- 'Mammography Test for Cancer in Women Under 50 Defended' (Brody 1976).
- 'Cancer Institute Proposes Limits on Breast X-Rays' (*New York Times* 1976).
- 'Mammograms: Safer and More Accurate' (Kolata 1987).
- 'Study Finds Women in 40's Benefit from Mammograms' (Brody 1988).
- 'New Data Revive the Debate Over Mammography Before 50' (Kolata 1992).
- 'Mammograms Urged Yearly at 40 and Older' (*New York Times* 1997).
- 'Experts Take up Divisive Issue: Mammograms for Women in 40's' (Kolata 1997).
- 'Mammograms Validated as Key In Cancer Fight' (Kolata 2005).
- 'Vast Study Casts Doubts on Value of Mammograms' (Kolata 2014).

Just to compare the numbers reported at the beginning of the most recent two stories, in 2005 we learn that '28 to 65 per cent of the sharp decrease in breast cancer deaths from 1990 to 2000 was due to mammograms' (Kolata 2005), while a decade later we learn 'that the death rates from breast cancer from all causes were the same in women who got mammograms and those who did not' (Kolata 2014). This transition seems very much to be going in the other direction, from science to trans-science.

On a related matter, more than 90 per cent of potential new cancer drugs do not make it through clinical trials. There are likely many reasons for this, but the core of the problem is that the evidentiary basis for designing new drugs must not be very good. One biotechnology company has reported that over a 10-year period it was only able to replicate 10 per cent of the peer-reviewed, pre-clinical research studies that it investigated. A study by another company put the number somewhat higher, at around 25 per cent, still amazingly low (Begley and Ellis 2012). A commentary in *Nature* (Poste 2011) reported that there are more than 150,000 publications that document biomarkers – early molecular indicators of disease – but less than 100 have been validated for clinical research. Such revelations are giving rise to concerns that unreliability, non-replicability and positive bias are endemic in biomedical research and perhaps other fields as well

(*The Economist* 2013; Ioannidis 2005). What does any scientific claim mean amidst such numbers? The din of scientific noise threatens to drown out any potential for recognising a signal from reality. Prescriptions for managing this growing chaos are being offered – mostly having to do with the need for better statistics and data management, for changing the culture and incentives of science, for tightening the peer-review process and so on (*Nature* 2013; *The Economist* 2013). None of these things is very easy to accomplish, and no one knows what might really work or how we could even tell if it did. But what really seems to be happening is exactly the opposite of what is supposed to happen: what everyone thought was normal science is turning out to be trans-science. Chaos is supplanting order, not the other way around.

Optimists insist that the chaos is really the excitement and opportunity of the revolution in theory- and data-based molecular medicine. In this vein, a May 2013 *New England Journal of Medicine* editorial proclaimed 'The beginning of the end of the beginning in cancer genomics', and argued that 'as terabytes of observational data yield new insights into disease biology ... the usefulness of such approaches is becoming undeniable' (Steensma 2013, 2138). A different view was recently offered in *Cell*, where a leading cancer researcher didn't see a new beginning, but an old one, in an essay titled 'Coming full circle: From endless complexity to simplicity and back again.' Was this progress? 'I wouldn't pretend to know,' the author writes (Weinberg 2014, 271).

I suspect that these issues are most conspicuously emerging in the biomedical sciences because that is where they cannot be evaded. If 90 per cent of published claims about the correspondence between a scientific result and reality turn out to be wrong, the consequences for translating science into reliable medical therapies cannot long remain hidden. But in fields where technological applications cannot provide a test of correspondence between a scientific result and reality, imaginative numbers may often exist and persist with impunity, even if – and sometimes particularly because – they are usefully deployed in various endeavours.

Forty years ago, when Alvin Weinberg first articulated the idea of trans-science, he was quite aware of the dangers that it created for normal science, and as I have said, he warned not only that scientists had a responsibility to try to enforce the boundary between them, but as well that they would have a hard time doing so. Indeed, on the whole they have failed in this task, for a variety of reasons that are very difficult to combat, including the political allure of asking science to take care of political problems, the simple political economics of science funding with its embedded constituencies – comprising the scientific community – who want to keep doing more of what they have been doing, and the power of expertise and bureaucracy in protecting such constituencies. Then there are the deeper seductions of our identities as moderns and our conviction that our problems must be amenable to solution along certain pathways of rational inquiry, and that progress in understanding always follows from more inquiry, and shortly on its heels, then, must come progress in action. Meanwhile, the exponential expansion of data gathering and analytic capabilities provided by the information technology revolution provides the scientific aphrodisiac for these seductions.

Nonetheless, the numbers that trans-science produces would seem to command some critical attention. They are not simply numbers that need improvement or correction; errors to be reduced through Bayesian statistics or made more accurate with better experimental tools and more precise observations. The mammography example is particularly illustrative here. Every category that seemed to have some stable meaning in the science related to assessing the value of mammograms turns out to be unstable and heterogeneous: genes, mutations, tumours, malignancy, survival rates, randomised trial, and above all, breast cancer itself, which is now recognised as many different diseases. Not only is there no possibility of developing any decent causal theory linking a mammogram result to a physiological state, but there is little prospect of a theoretical convergence among competing fields of scientific expertise, each of which is touching a different part of an elephant – an elephant that does not even exist because all of the component parts are continually being understood in new ways. For the same reason, then, incremental statistical improvement through self-correction – Bayesian inference – will often not lead to more accurate probabilities (of, say, a mammogram predicting dangerous cancer) but simply to different ones.

In some cases, of course, *more science* may help, and where we get new and better correspondences between our numbers and the world out there, good things can happen. But as an empirical matter, and as science is seduced through politics, technological tools and the continued power of the Cartesian dream into the world of trans-science, we ought to expect to see many more animals and beggars as well. Just as past worlds were fuelled by phlogiston and measured by phrenology, today the numbers of trans-science seem to call into existence imaginary and sometimes ephemeral worlds of their own.

There is nothing necessarily bad about this; as I have tried to emphasise, in cases like hydrocarbon reserve estimates, animals and beggars may do us little harm, and act as useful boundary objects around which social activities may organise. But since these sorts of numbers borrow social and epistemological status from our more conventional notions of what numbers are supposed to tell us about real worlds, they make a claim to privilege that is, in many cases, undeserved. Since, as Weinberg anticipated, the (trans-)scientists aren't likely to be restrained in making such claims, democratic societies can improve their effectiveness by cultivating responsible and legitimate competition.

The opportunity here, perhaps, is to begin to move toward what Richard Rorty (2004) has called a 'literary culture'. What he means by this, I take it, is a society which tolerates and welcomes multiple competing imaginations about what the purposes of our lives ought to be and how they ought to be led. From this perspective, the problem with trans-scientific numbers is not with their imaginariness, but with their borrowed status, which imbues the products of one general type of imagination with more legitimacy, influence, and power than others. In a literary culture, the animals and beggars flowing from trans-science would still be there, but they would coexist on a pretty much equal level with the products of other imaginations as well.

Thus, in the biomedical world, we see not only a rising awareness that much of what was assumed to be science is really trans-science, but also a rising insistence by patients that they have something to say about how they should be studied and treated as well (e.g. Jain 2013; Epstein 1995). This is not a coincidence; the two trends are related.

We should expect and cultivate similar tensions in other areas of trans-science, for two reasons. First is simply that trans-science is on the march. As sensing and information technologies allow everything to be measured, modelled and assessed, everything will be subject to description by numbers, real and imaginative, with little way to tell them apart. Infinite possible (trans-)scientific meanings and causal hypotheses will be extractable from equally infinite bodies of data. This will complete the melding of science and politics. As a brief example, consider an imaginative number such as the World Health Organisation's estimate that global climate change causes 150,000 deaths a year (World Health Organisation 2014). What could such a number possibly correspond to in the real world? Let us say that some percentage of that number is attributed to heat waves that are in turn attributed in some part to anthropogenic greenhouse gas warming of the atmosphere. But at the other end of the problem we also know that deaths from heat waves (which, after all, are nothing new) are strongly linked to lack of social and physical infrastructure for the poor and elderly, especially those living alone in urban areas with low social cohesion (Klinenberg 2003). We need to start having arguments between the scientists and technocrats who have never been in a blighted urban neighbourhood and are demanding higher fuel prices and less energy consumption to slow greenhouse warming, and the community activists who are demanding air conditioners and more energy for poor communities so they can have the same indoor climates as the scientists and technocrats, global warming or not.

The second reason we should expect a growing tension between the trans-scientific imagination and other sources of meaning is that the scientific endeavour itself is increasingly seeking to take intellectual ownership of all meaning, including the personal. Big data analytics and cognitive neuroscience are converging to provide mechanistic explanations of all subjective experiences, from moral and religious beliefs to love, rage, artistic creation and even, presumably, scientific insight. Whatever you think you're feeling can be reduced to a neurochemical environment subject to various stimuli that add up to the subjective experience of being you. In one sense we've know this for a long time, but only now do we have the sensing, data processing and molecular manipulation capacities to begin to do something about it. So the question becomes: who will decide what is to be done? We let the trans-scientists try something like this once; it was called eugenics.

The problem with imaginative numbers thus is not their capacity to mobilise, focus and inspire human aspiration in the absence of correspondence to what is real, but that the aspirations are narrow because they reflect and emerge from narrow interests and narrow views of human purpose. If, as Rorty argues and seems apparent, conventional science has eliminated any possibility of ultimate purpose in our lives (because, after all, it's just neurochemistry that has evolved in response to Darwinian selection), then we must find purpose through a never-ending process of expanding the limits of our imagination about the kinds of worlds that we could, and should, aspire to. If we can openly acknowledge that much of what we call science is actually trans-science, and that many of our numbers correspond to our imaginations of the world not to the world itself, then we may well find, and rather unexpectedly, that the animals and beggars are beginning to show us the way to an expanded democratic imagination as well.

# References

Andronova, N., Schlesinger, M., Dessai, S., Hulme, M., and Li, B. 2007. The concept of climate sensitivity: History and development, in M.E. Schlesinger *et al.* (eds), *Human Induced Climate Change: An Interdisciplinary Assessment*, Cambridge: Cambridge University Press, pp. 5–17.

Bayer, R., Johns, D.M., and Galea, S. 2012. Salt and public health: Contested science and the challenge of evidence-based decision making, *Health Affairs*, 31(12): 2738–46.

Begley, C.G., and Ellis, L. 2012. Raise standards for pre-clinical cancer research, *Nature,* 483 (29 March): 531–3.

Borges, J.L. 1998. On exactitude in science, in *Collected Fictions*, New York: Penguin, 325.

Brody, J. 1976. Mammography test for cancer in women under 50 defended, *New York Times,* 20 July, 10.

Brody, J. 1988. Study finds women in 40's benefit from mammograms, *New York Times,* 21 Sept. (http://wwwnytimescom/1988/09/21/us/study-finds-women-in-40-s-benefit-from-mammogramshtml) accessed Aug. 2014.

Eckholm, E.P. 1975. The deterioration of mountain environments, *Science,* 189 (5 Sept.): 764–70.

Epstein, S. 1995. The construction of lay expertise: AIDS activism and the forging of credibility in the reform of clinical trials, *Science Technology and Human Values,* 240(4): 408–37.

Gautier, D. 2000. Oil and gas resource appraisal: Diminishing reserves increasing supplies, in D. Sarewitz, R.A. Pielke, Jr and R.A. Byerly, Jr (eds), *Prediction: Science Decision Making and the Future of Nature,* Covelo, CA: Island Press, pp. 231–49.

Gibbons, M. 1999. Science's new social contract with society, *Nature,* 402 (2 Dec. suppl.): c81–c84.

Ioannidis, J.P.A. 2005. Why most published research findings are false, *PloS Medicine,* 2(8): 101–6.

Jain, S.L. 2013. *Malignant: How Cancer Becomes Us,* Berkeley, CA: University of California Press.

James, W. 1907. Pragmatism's Conception of Truth (Lecture 6), in James, W. *Pragmatism: A New Name for Some Old Ways of Thinking.* New York: Longman Green and Co, pp. 76–91.

Klinenberg, E. 2003. *Heat Wave: A Social Autopsy of Disaster in Chicago,* Chicago: University of Chicago Press.

Kolata, G. 1987. Mammograms: Safer and more accurate, *New York Times,* 17 Oct. (http://wwwnytimescom/1987/10/17/us/mammograms-safer-and-more-accuratehtml?module=Search&mabReward=relbias%3Ar%2C%7B%221%22%3A%22RI%3A11%22%7D) accessed Aug. 2014.

Kolata, G. 1992. New data revive the debate over mammography before 50, *New York Times,* 16 Dec. (http://wwwnytimescom/1992/12/16/health/new-data-revive-the-debate-over-mammography-before-50html?module=Search&mabReward=relbias:r{%221=%22:=%22RI:11=%22}=&pagewanted=2&pagewanted=all) accessed Aug. 2014.

146    *Daniel Sarewitz*

Kolata, G. 1997. Experts take up divisive issue: Mammograms for women in 40's, *New York Times*, 22 Jan. (http://wwwnytimescom/1997/01/22/us/experts-take-up-divisive-issue-mammograms-for-women-in-40-shtml?module=Search&mabReward=relbias%3Ar%2C%7B%221%22%3A%22RI%3A11%22%7D) accessed Aug. 2014.

Kolata, G. 2005. Mammograms validated as key in cancer fight, *New York Times*, 27 Oct., A24.

Kolata, G. 2014. Vast study casts doubts on value of mammograms, *New York Times*, 11 Feb., A1.

McDonald, A.B., Klein, J.R., and Wark, D.L. 2003. Solving the solar neutrino problem, *Scientific American*, 288(4): 40–9.

Miller, B.M., *et al.* 1975. *Geological Estimates of Undiscovered Recoverable Oil and Gas Resources in the United States*, Washington, DC: US Geological Survey Circular.

*Nature.* 2013. Reducing our irreproducibility, 496 (24 April): 398.

*New York Times.* 1976. Cancer institute proposes limits on breast x-rays, 23 Aug., 12.

*New York Times.* 1997. Mammograms urged yearly at 40 and older, 24 March (http://wwwnytimescom/1997/03/24/us/mammograms-urged-yearly-at-40-and-olderhtml?module=Search&mabReward=relbias%3Ar%2C%7B%221%22%3A%22RI%3A11%22%7D) accessed Aug. 2014.

Pinch, T.J. 1981. The sun-set: The presentation of certainty in scientific life, *Social Studies of Science*, 11(1): 131–58.

Poste, G. 2011. Bring on the biomarkers, *Nature*, 469 (13 Jan.): 156–7.

Rorty, R. 2004. Philosophy as a transitional genre, in R. Bernstein, S. Benhabib and N. Fraser (eds), *Pragmatism Critique Judgment: Essays for Richard J. Bernstein*, Cambridge, MA: MIT Press, pp. 3–28.

Sagoff, M. 2010. The quantification and valuation of ecosystem services, *Ecological Economics*, 70: 497–502.

Steensma, D.P. 2013. The beginning of the end of the beginning in cancer genomics, *New England Journal of Medicine*, 368(22): 2138–40.

*The Economist.* 2013. Trouble at the lab, 19–25 Oct.: 26–30.

Thompson, M., Warburton, M., and Hatley, T. 2007. *Uncertainty on a Himalayan Scale: An Institutional Theory of Environmental Perception and a Strategic Framework for the Sustainable Development of the Himalaya*, Patan Dhoka, Nepal: Himal Books. (Originally published 1987.)

US Energy Information Administration. 2014. *Natural Gas* (http://wwweiagov/dnav/ng/hist/n9140us2ahtm) accessed Aug. 2014.

US Geological Survey. 2013. *National Oil and Gas Assessment 2013 Assessment Updates* (http://energyusgsgov/OilGas/AssessmentsData/NationalOilGasAssessment/AssessmentUpdatesaspx) accessed Aug. 2014.

Van der Sluijs, J., van Eijndhoven, J., Shackley, S., and Wynne, B. 1998. Anchoring devices in science for policy: The case of the consensus around climate sensitivity, *Social Studies of Science*, 28(2): 291–323.

Weinberg, A. 1972. Science and trans-science, *Minerva*, 10: 209–22.

Weinberg, R. 2014. Coming full circle: From endless complexity to simplicity and back again, *Cell*, 157 (27 March): 267–71.

William, J. 1948. The will to believe, in *Essays in Pragmatism*, New York: Hafner Press, 88–109.

World Health Organization. 2014. *Health and Environment Linkages Initiative* (http://wwwwhoint/heli/risks/climate/climatechange/en) accessed Aug. 2014.

# 9 Evidence-based policy at the end of the Cartesian dream
## The case of mathematical modelling

*Andrea Saltelli and Silvio Funtowicz*

## The end of the dream

Other authors in this volume have already discussed at length their interpretation of the end of the Cartesian dream. New reflections of their analyses were provoked by an article in *The Economist*, a weekly business magazine of largely neoclassical and positivistic views on economics. Commenting on the poor state of current scientific practices, the magazine proclaims 'How Science goes wrong' on its cover, and its first editorial reads (*The Economist* 2013a, 11):

> Science still commands enormous – if sometimes bemused – respect. But its privileged status is founded on the capacity to be right most of the time and to correct its mistakes when it gets things wrong. ... The false trails laid down by shoddy research are an unforgivable barrier to understanding.

This attack on science's privilege reminded us of another quote, coming from Paul Feyerabend (2010, p. xviii), *enfant terrible* of modern epistemology and *bête noire* of all positivisms:

> Science must be protected by ideologies; and societies, especially democratic societies, must be protected from science. ... The theoretical authority of science is much smaller than it is supposed to be. Its social authority, on the other hand, has now become so overpowering that political interference is necessary to restore a balanced development.

When *The Economist* and Feyerabend speak with one voice, a dream must be at its end.

What prompted *The Economist* to devote its cover page to an issue of science's governance? One of several reasons was the troubling wave of retractions affecting applied science. Laboratory experiments cannot be trusted without further, independent verification (Sanderson 2013) and 'bloggers put chemical reactions through the replication mill'. In another article, rules are proposed to spot 'suspected work [ ... in] the majority of preclinical cancer papers in top tier journals' (Begley 2013).

*The Economist* (2013b, 21–4) argues that technical shortcomings are among the main causes of trouble with scientific practice, including scientists' incapacity to balance false positives and false negatives[1] and poor refereeing. The truth is perhaps even more worrisome, as revealed by one of the sources quoted by the same magazine, J.P.A. Ioannides (2005), according to whom:

> In this framework, a research finding is less likely to be true when [ … *a list of statistical limitations*]; when there is greater financial and other interest and prejudice; and when more teams are involved in a scientific field in chase of statistical significance.

In other words Ioannides hints at normative issues associated with scientific practice. The ethos of science is normally associated with the Mertonian principles known by the acronym of CUDOS (Merton 1942); one of which, under the name of Organized Scepticism, prescribes that 'All ideas must be tested and are subject to rigorous, structured community scrutiny'. These norms[2] must have had a powerful appeal to previous generations of scientists; so Richard Feynman (1974, 341):

> there is one feature … that we all hope you have learned in studying science in school … It's a kind of scientific integrity, a principle of scientific thought that corresponds to a kind of utter honesty – a kind of leaning over backwards. … Details that could throw doubt on your interpretation must be given, if you know them. … give all of the information to help others to judge the value of your contribution.

If this is not enough to appreciate the anti-climax of lost innocence, here is Danish writer Peter Høeg (1993, 19):

> That is what we meant by science. That both question and answer are tied up with uncertainty, and that they are painful. But that there is no way around them. And that you hide nothing; instead, everything is brought out into the open.

What separates Feynman and Høeg from the sloppy practitioners harshly criticised by *The Economist*? Could it be that a set of counter-norms, as described by Mitroff (1974, 592):

- solitariness (secrecy, miserism) often used to keep findings secret in order to be able to claim patent rights;
- dogmatism, because careers are built around the purported truth of a particular theory or hypothesis

are becoming the new norms, replacing the Mertonian principles?

It may appear that there is today a greater incentive to operate in the context of *pseudo-science*, here defined as 'where uncertainties in inputs must be suppressed lest outputs become indeterminate' (Funtowicz and Ravetz 1990). Not only is the concealment of uncertainty widespread, as suggested by *The Economist*, but also its opposite, its amplification, e.g. the fabrication of uncertainty, driven by policy agendas or industrial interests (Michaels 2005; Oreskes and Conway 2010).

A useful discussion on present-day practices in science and how these must appear to scientists faithful to the old traditions is Philip Mirowski's *Science-Mart: Privatizing American Science* (2011a). Mirowski argues that there is a crisis in the self-governance practices of science, and that the decline in the quality and character of science is linked to its commoditisation, driven by a combination of neoliberal credo and a close adherence to a neoclassic economics paradigm. Accordingly after the 1980s, neoliberal ideologies succeeded in decreasing state intervention in the funding of science, which became increasingly privatised.

Mirowski describes how in-house science laboratories of major corporations were closed, and research outsourced to universities which became more and more committed to the commercialisation of research findings. He then goes on to illustrate how research was further outsourced, this time to contract-based private organisations. As a result, knowledge as a monetised commodity has replaced knowledge as public good, 'when there is greater financial and other interest and prejudice' as expressed by Ioannides. In other words, there is a positive incentive to engage in pseudo-science.

A similarity can be detected between Mirowski's account of the neoclassic economic agenda as applied to research, recent critiques of Ricardian economics as applied to innovation (Reinert 2008; Mazzucato 2013) and the postmodern account of knowledge's legitimisation as formulated by Jean-François Lyotard in *La condition postmoderne* (1979).

Increased controversy is another visible characteristic of present scientific practices, particularly in innovation research or technoscience. From GMOs to climate, from bees and pesticides to shale gas fracking, from endocrine disruptors to refrigerant in Mercedes cars: an ever larger number of issues appear to become *wicked*, meaning that they are deeply entangled in a web of hardly separable facts, interests and values (Horst *et al.* 1973).

The media play an increasingly ambiguous role, opening an advertising channel to entrepreneurial scientists on one hand, and on the other, openly challenging trust in science with a language previously reserved to more mundane types of controversies. The manner for settling scientific disputes has evolved or degenerated, according to different perspectives. The media offer, for instance, headings such as 'Beware the rise of the government scientists turned lobbyists' (Monbiot 2013), and in the journal *Nature* an article proclaims that 'European bans on MON810 maize is the clear evidence of government interference with science' (Kuntz *et al.* 2013).

Stringent standards for policy-relevant science and for the quality of the evidence are now insistently called for, even from the columns of *Nature*, where Ian Boyd (2013), speaking in his capacity of science adviser to DEFRA, the UK government department for environment, food and rural affairs, laments 'concern about unreliability in scientific literature' and 'systematic bias in research'.

Norms associated with scientific enterprise and scientific advice are under concerned scrutiny (see e.g. Pielke 2007; Jasanoff 2013; Gluckman 2014), and the media show a keen interest in the topics of Science's governance and science–policy interaction. See, for instance, *The Economist* (2014a) taking good note of the creation of the Meta-Research Innovation Centre launched at Stanford (METRICS), involving the already cited I. Ioannidis, to combat *bad science*. According to Jasanoff (2013) 'a prime casualty in the age of information and informatics appears to be public confidence in the power of reason'. Perhaps the public is simply learning that science should not be trusted as faith, and that emerging scientific practices, so closely related to economics, policy and politics, should be democratically scrutinised.

## Battling 'bad modelling'

How should we interpret the Cartesian dream in the context of mathematical modelling? A particularly explicit formulation of the dream was made by the French philosopher, mathematician and political scientist Marie Jean Antoine Nicolas de Caritat (1743–94), known as Marquis de Condorcet. 'Condorcet elaborated the utopia of a science-based society as one of welfare, equality, justice and happiness' (Rommetveit *et al.* 2013). Central to this vision was the ability of humans to calculate, to master mathematics, seen after Galileo as the language used by God to code the universe.

Fast forward to the present time and we read in the *Washington Post* that 'Based on mountains of data from 39 models and accurate within five years in either direction for any of the locations they studied ... Washington DC climate will shift in 2047' (Bernstein 2013). *Prima facie* the dream of Condorcet has come true. We can predict nature and make the necessary arrangements to prevent problems ahead. Or can we? Some journalistic exaggeration needs to be taken into consideration. In the more sober scientific article at the source of the *Washington Post*'s piece (Mora 2013) the uncertainty is assessed at 14 years rather than five. Still it is legitimate to suspect that this is one of the many instances where the Knightian concept of uncertainty has been reduced to quantitative risk.[3] Should one be reassured by the fact that 39 models were used (or were deemed necessary) to arrive at the 2047 forecast? Or should we reflect on the forbiddingly complex nature of these inferences?

Another telling example is in Saltelli and d'Hombres (2010), discussing the so-called Stern Review, a cost benefit analysis of the merits of early intervention to mitigate climate change.[4] In this particular case the analysis extended two centuries beyond the present time and was equipped with a sensitivity analysis which was particularly unconvincing. A rich literature is by now available to criticise mathematical hubris, from Taleb's *Black Swan* (2007) to Pilkey and Pilkey-Jarvis's *Useless Arithmetic* (2007). Mathematical modelling paradox is best described by Naomi Oreskes (2000, 35), according to whom:

In many cases, these [model-based] temporal predictions are treated with the same respect that the hypothetic-deductive model of science accords to logical predictions. But this respect is largely misplaced. ... to be of value in theory testing, the predictions involved must be capable of refuting the theory that generated them ... This is where predictions ... become particularly sticky. ... models are complex amalgam of theoretical and phenomenological laws (and the governing equations and algorithms that represent them), empirical input parameters, and a model conceptualisation. When a model generates a prediction, of what precisely is the prediction a test? The laws? The input data? The conceptualisation? Any part (or several parts) of the model might be in error, and there is no simple way to determine which one it is.

A different perspective from which to look at mathematical modelling is through the *ceteris paribus* assumption. According to Joseph Stiglitz (2011, 594): 'Models by their nature are like blinders. In leaving out certain things, they focus our attention on other things. They provide a frame through which we see the world.' The problem is when those things we leave out come back to haunt us. Said otherwise: *ceteris* are never *paribus*.

The issue is not new, and it is endemic in the parameters-rich models used in natural sciences, as well as the parsimonious models wanted in econometrics. Keynes alluded to it with his usual style in a dispute with Tinbergen, asking the rhetorical question (1940):

It will be remembered that the seventy translators of the Septuagint were shut up in seventy separate rooms with the Hebrew text and brought out with them, when they emerged, seventy identical translations. Would the same miracle be vouchsafed if seventy multiple correlators were shut up with the same statistical material?

In recent papers (Saltelli *et al.* 2013; Saltelli and Funtowicz 2014) a new set of specific criteria has been proposed for proper use of model-based inference in the policy process (sensitivity auditing). The rules, aimed at ensuring transparency and balance in the use of models, are:

1   Check against rhetoric use of mathematical modelling.
2   Adopt an 'assumption hunting' attitude.
3   Detect pseudo-science.
4   Find sensitive assumptions before these find you.
5   Aim for transparency.
6   Do the right sums.
7   Focus the analysis on the key question answered by the model, exploring holistically the entire space of the assumptions.

It may be interesting to compare these rules with a suggestion from Ian Boyd (2013, in the *Nature* article already cited):

We need an international audited standard that grades studies, or perhaps journals. It would evaluate how research was commissioned, designed, conducted and reported. This audit procedure would assess many of the fundamental components of scientific studies, such as appropriate statistical power; precision and accuracy of measurements; and validation data for assays and models. It would also consider conflicts of interest, actual or implied, and more challenging issues about the extent to which the conclusions follow from the data. Any research paper or journal that does not present all the information needed for audit would automatically attract a low grade. Such a system would provide policy officials and others with a reliable way of assessing evidence quality, and it would drive up standards in scientific research to reverse the worrying trends that suggest underlying bias.

Though Boyd's proposed international standards are independent from our rules, the similarity of context and intents is evident.

An important caveat is in order before introducing the rules in detail. The purpose of the rules is not to discourage the use of mathematical modelling in policy-related science. On the contrary, we do believe that modelling has a role to play, provided it is not used rhetorically or inappropriately. We distinguish between policy simulations, when, for example, macro-economic models are used to explore the effects of different shocks on economic variables, from policy justification, when the same models are used to justify policy interventions.

In 2010, the Hearing Charter of the House Committee on Science and Technology received sworn testimony by economists Sidney Winter, Scott Page, Robert Solow, David Colander and V.V. Chari on why the financial and economic crisis was not foreseen by existing modelling tools, and in particular, from the dynamic stochastic general equilibrium models (DSGE; Mirowski 2011b). The chairman of the committee made precisely this point in remarking:

> DSGE and similar macroeconomic models were first conceived as theorists' tools. But why, then, are they being relied on as the platform upon which so much practical policy advice is formulated? And what has caused them to become, and to stay, so firmly entrenched? And, finally, the most important question of all: What do we get when we apply the various tools at our disposal to the urgent economic problems we're facing today?

The last question sounds rhetorical, though we appreciate the distinction between a *theorist tool*, what we would call a policy simulation tool, and a platform for policy advice, which we would call a policy justification tool. It is somewhat implicit in this formulation that policy simulation and policy justification perform quite different functions, though it must be extremely tempting, not to say an automatic reflex of the analysts, to assume that the former can be deployed for the latter.

# The seven rules

The point of departure for the development of the rules is the consideration that good practices for sensitivity analysis, enshrined in existing guidelines for mathematical modelling, are insufficient to ensure quality in the treatment of uncertainty in the contested arena of science for policy. In an adversarial context, not only the nature of the evidence, but also the degree of certainty and uncertainty associated with the evidence will be the subject of heated debate by all the relevant parties.

The problem is succinctly illustrated in the following coastal zone oil drilling example in the Norwegian islands of Lofoten:

> When there is low uncertainty, it is often because a topic is not interesting. But as soon as the stakes rise, uncertainty becomes important. ... uncertainty is the result of three things: incomplete science, bad science and corrupted science. In this latter case, corrupted science is produced purposefully to create debate or even confusion. ... Uncertainty can be seen as a tool that is used to prevent or support action. In the case of Lofoten, uncertainty is part of the political game, and is used by decision-makers, industry actors, the local population, environmentalists and NGOs. (Blanchard 2013)

It is in this type of context, that of post-normal science, where *facts are uncertain, values in dispute, stakes high and decisions urgent* (Funtowicz and Ravetz 1993), that the rules find their justification. The rules presuppose a participatory style of decision-making, one where knowledge is co-produced, where a hybridisation of science and politics takes place and where a new public, capable of bringing fresh insight in the solution of a problem, is created (Lane *et al.* 2011; Feyerabend 1975, 262[5]). In such a situation, the rules facilitate the work of mediation between the abstract rules of mathematical modelling and the policy issues at stake.

In the case of the deployment of mathematical models for impact assessments, the rules of the checklist could be introduced as a set of potentially adversarial questions to be *anticipated* by practitioners, including the following:

- X was treated as a constant when we know it is uncertain by at least 30 per cent.
- A 5 per cent error in X would be sufficient to make your statement about Z fragile.
- The model is but one of the plausible models – model uncertainty has been neglected.
- The level of confidence in a desired result has been artificially inflated by minimizing the inputs' uncertainty.
- Uncertainty in the input has been inflated in order to invalidate an undesired inference.
- The model is a black box – why should we trust your results?
- The framing of the analysis is not socially robust (a class of stakeholders has been neglected).
- The question which was answered is a question nobody asked.

Sensitivity auditing can also be related to NUSAP (Funtowicz and Ravetz 1990; van der Sluijs *et al.* 2005), a system for the quality assessment of quantitative information. NUSAP also belongs to the tradition of post-normal science, and has been used, for example, in the field of climate science (Kloprogge and Van der Sluijs 2006). When using NUSAP, a relevant number (N) comes with its units (U), its standard error (S), as well as with an assessment (A) of the process leading to the formulation of the number. Finally, relevant numbers (e.g. those which may feed into a policy decision) must have a pedigree (P), which may describe the track record of the team proposing the number, or the available history of related or similar number predictions. Both assessment and pedigree can be in the form of checklists (see also www.nusap.net).

As mentioned above we can relate the checklist to the NUSAP tradition. In this case the sensitivity auditing checklist could be seen as part of a model-assessment or pedigree, answering questions such as:

1   Is the model redundant?
2   Are there important implicit assumptions?
3   Is uncertainty instrumentally amplified or compressed?
4   Was a sensitivity analysis performed prior to publication of the inference?
5   Is the model transparent?
6   Does the model address the right question?
7   Was sensitivity analysis performed holistically?

We'll now introduce the checklist, illustrating the rules in detail.

### Rule 1. Check against rhetorical use of mathematical modelling

This rule should be rather evident to the reader at this point of our discussion. We term rhetorical, a model use which aims to confirm (at times with a disproportionate use of mathematics and computer time) an already taken decision, based on considerations of power or interest. The larger the model, the easier it is to fiddle with its parameters to obtain whatever result one might wish (Hornberger and Spear 1981). As noted by Stiglitz (2010, 161) – discussing the case of the mathematical tools used to price collateralised debt obligations leading to the financial crisis – perverse incentives generate flawed models.

The issue was popularised by Douglas Adams in his book series *Dirk Gently, The Holistic Detective*:

> Well, Gordon's great insight was to design a program which allowed you to specify in advance what decision you wished it to reach, and only then to give it all the facts. The program's task, ... was to construct a plausible series of logical-sounding steps to connect the premises with the conclusion.
>
> (Adams 1987, 69)

### *Rule 2. Adopt an 'assumption hunting' attitude*

We refer here to our discussion on the *ceteris paribus* assumption. The rule could thus be read as: which *ceteris* were assumed to be *paribus*? What was assumed out (which effect or process was not included)? What was assumed in (which parameters were fixed by the developers and on which basis). It is frequently easy to deconstruct the model by reconstructing the series of assumptions which went into its construction.

### *Rule 3. Detect pseudo-science*

Pseudo-science or Garbage In Garbage Out (GIGO) was defined by Funtowicz and Ravetz (1990) as a situation in which 'uncertainties in inputs must be suppressed lest outputs become indeterminate'. The modeller in violation of this rule fiddles with the uncertainty present in the input, in order to ensure that the output, the inference, is not so vague as to be practically useless (e.g. a policy's payoff bracketed between a big loss and a large gain). Similar prescriptions in econometrics recommend a thorough exploration of the space of the input assumptions (Kennedy 2007). As noted above, this rule can be played in reverse, with a party inflating uncertainty instead of minimising it, with the objective, for instance, of resisting a regulation by overestimating the uncertainty in a class of health effects (see examples in Saltelli *et al.* 2013).

### *Rule 4. Find sensitive assumptions before they find you*

This rule reminds model developers, and *a fortiori* those building the case for a policy, to be clear about the limits of their analysis before going public with the findings. In an adversarial context an opposing party could otherwise apply rule 2 to invalidate the case. Doing such an analysis *a posteriori*, to fend off a received criticism, usually results in protracted and costly arguments. In the case of the Stern Review mentioned above, sensitivity analysis was performed by the team led by Nicholas Stern after its main findings had been criticised by an expert in cost benefit analysis. As discussed in Saltelli and d'Hombres (2010), Stern's position would have been stronger if he had performed the analysis before going public with his results.

### *Rule 5. Aim for transparency*

This rule recommends that proponents of a policy present their evidence in a way that the relevant audiences, including the opponents, can understand. In other words, black box models, or proprietary models, owned by a third party, which cannot be consequently explored, are generally interpreted as an attempt to hide more than to show. At the time of writing the present chapter, a piece of legislation is under discussion in the US. The bill,[6] named the Secret Science Reform Act, 'would force the EPA to publicly release its research on a topic before issuing a policy recommendation, and require that the research be 'reproducible.' Supporters claim the bill will increase transparency in public policy, while opponents have accused the bill's authors of trying to 'keep the EPA from doing its job' (Wilkey 2014). The consequences of this draft bill are clearly ambiguous; a positive outcome might entail making a mathematical model fully available to all parties so it can be used as a policy simulation tool, with its assumptions made transparent.

### Rule 6. Do the right sums

As the saying goes, doing the right sums is more important than doing the sums right, in line with Keynes's famous remark that it is better to be roughly right than precisely wrong. In the context of a policy study this would imply asking the relevant questions in order to resolve the problem that is salient and pertinent to the relevant stakeholders. As an example we can take a current and popular wicked issue: the case of genetically modified organisms (GMOs) used for crops and foods. Proponents of GMOs observe that citizens' hostility to these products is at odds with the evidence that GMOs do not have negative health effects. According to the results of an EU-funded study (Marris *et al.* 2001), food safety is not prominent in the list of citizens' concerns on GMOs. A list of concerns registered by Marris *et al.* includes:

1   Why do we need GMOs? What are the benefits?
2   Who will benefit from their use?
3   Who decided that they should be developed and how?
4   Why were we not better informed about their use in our food, before their arrival on the market?
5   Why are we not given an effective choice about whether or not to buy and consume these products?
6   Do regulatory authorities have sufficient powers and resources to effectively counter-balance large companies who wish to develop these products?

For a recent illustration of this case, if we believe in the findings from the report cited above, we would consider this rule as violated by articles lambasting the US state of Vermont for its recently introduced GMO labelling law on the basis that scientific evidence proves GMO food safe for consumption.

> Montpelier is America's only McDonald's-free state capital. A fitting place, then, for a law designed to satisfy the unfounded fears of foodies.
>
> (*The Economist*, 10 May 2014)

> Just ask about genetically modified crops, declared safe by the scientific establishment, but reviled as Frankenfoods by the Subarus-and-sandals set.
>
> (*The Economist*, 10 May 2014)

While the GMO example does not refer to a particular mathematical model, there is an entire class of models which may fall under the watch of rule 1. These are all the cost benefit analysis or risk analysis performed to demonstrate the safety of a new technology after the technology has been introduced. As cogently noted by Langdon Winner (1986, 138–63), ecologists should not be led into the trap of arguing about the 'safety' of a technology after the technology has been introduced. They should instead question the broader power, policy and profit implications of that introduction.[7]

### Rule 7. Focus the analysis on the key question answered by the model, exploring holistically the entire space of the assumptions

This rule, more technical, is a summary of good practices belonging to the discipline of sensitivity analysis (Saltelli *et al.* 2012). In a model-based study for impact assessment it is important that the sensitivity of the input assumption is directly related to what is being assessed, and not to some intermediate model result. At the same time, the space of the input assumptions should be explored thoroughly. The most popular sensitivity analysis practice found in the literature is that of *one-factor-at-a-time* (OFAT; Saltelli and Annoni 2010). This consists of analysing the effect of varying one model input factor at a time while keeping all others fixed. The shortcomings of OFAT are known from the statistical literature, but its use among modellers is still widespread.

## Where do we go from here?

There is still a strong movement of scientists in favour of performing analyses of the cost of climate change. So, for instance, Revesz *et al.* (2014), writing in *Nature*:

> Costs of carbon emissions are being underestimated, but current estimates are still valuable for setting mitigation policy.
> ... These [Those from climate change] are real risks that need to be accounted for in planning for adaptation and mitigation. Pricing the risks with integrated models of physics and economics lets their costs be compared to those of limiting climate change or investing in greater resilience.
> Yet the social-cost benchmark is under fire. Industry groups, politicians – including leaders of the energy and commerce committee of the US House of Representatives – and some academics say that uncertainties render the estimate useless.
> As legal, climate-science and economics experts, we believe that the current estimate for the social cost of carbon is useful for policy-making, notwithstanding the significant uncertainties.

Here we find all the ingredients of a science–policy mix: the normative stance of the embattled authors, together with the acknowledgment of the pervasive uncertainties, and the belief that costs of damage and costs of remedial actions can be compared. It is evident that even a weak application of the rules of the checklist would put these analyses into serious methodological difficulties, as the case of the Stern Review discussed above has shown. Ultimately we agree with Brian Wynne that 'science can be led to overreach itself in arbitrating public facts, meanings and norms' (Wynne 2010), and with Pilkey and Pilkey-Jarvis (2007, 86) that progress would be achieved if

> ... the global change modelling community would firmly and publicly recognise that its efforts to truly quantify the future are an academic exercise and that existing field data on atmospheric temperatures, melting glaciers, ... and other evidence should be relied on to a much greater degree to convince politicians that we have a problem.

In conclusion we believe that current modelling practices, in their development and use, are a significant threat to the legitimacy and the utility of science in contested policy settings, and that organised forms of quality control are needed. Transparency and parsimony seem to be important elements of quality control, which will encourage modellers to focus on the truly relevant assumptions and mechanisms.

The conditionality of model predictions must be a constant concern for those operating models in support of policy. This will result in greater credibility for models and greater clarity about what can be adjudicated by quantitative model-based quantification, and what should be deferred instead to democratic political institutions.

## Acknowledgements

Helpful suggestions and corrections were offered by Bruna De Marchi, University of Bergen (NO), Centre for the Study of the Sciences and the Humanities (SVT). The views expressed in the present chapter are those of the authors and do not represent the views of the European Commission.

## Notes

1  'In medical testing, and more generally in binary classification, a false positive is when a test result indicates that a condition – such as a disease – is present (the result is positive), but it is not in fact present (the result is false), while a false negative is when a test result indicates that a condition is not present (the result is negative), but it is in fact present (the result is false)' (Wikipedia). According to Ioannidis (2005) false positives and false negatives are poorly accounted for in the appraisal of the results of ongoing medical research.
2  The CUDOS set of norms runs as follows: Communalism – the common ownership of scientific discoveries, according to which scientists give up intellectual property rights in exchange for recognition and esteem ... Universalism – according to which claims to truth are evaluated in terms of universal or impersonal criteria, and not on the basis of race, class, gender, religion, or nationality; Disinterestedness – according

to which scientists are rewarded for acting in ways that outwardly appear to be selfless; Organised Scepticism – all ideas must be tested and are subject to rigorous, structured community scrutiny.

3  In *Risk, Uncertainty, and Profit*, F.H. Knight distinguishes between risk that can be computed and uncertainty which cannot. Knight's prescriptions are largely ignored in the modelling community. According to John Kay, a British economist, the issue was felt as crucial by Maynard Keynes: 'For Keynes, probability was about believability, not frequency. He denied that our thinking could be described by a probability distribution over all possible future events, ... In the 1920s he became engaged in an intellectual battle on this issue, in which the leading protagonists on one side were Keynes and the Chicago economist Frank Knight, opposed by a Cambridge philosopher, Frank Ramsey, and later by Jimmie Savage, another Chicagoan. Keynes and Knight lost that debate, and Ramsey and Savage won, and the probabilistic approach has maintained academic primacy ever since. A principal reason was Ramsey's demonstration that anyone who did not follow his precepts – anyone who did not act on the basis of a subjective assessment of probabilities of future events – would be "Dutch booked". I used to tell students who queried the premise of "rational" behaviour in financial markets – where rational means are based on Bayesian subjective probabilities – that people had to behave in this way because if they did not, people would devise schemes that made money at their expense. I now believe that observation is correct but does not have the implication I sought. People do not behave in line with this theory, with the result that others in financial markets do devise schemes that make money at their expense.'

4  A cost benefit analysis extending till 2200 of a socio-economic-ecological system at the planetary scale seems to us an illustration of George Soros's Postulate of 'radical fallibility': 'Whenever we acquire some useful knowledge, we tend to extend it to areas where it is no longer applicable' (2009).

5  '... in a democracy local populations not only will, but also should, use the sciences in ways most suitable to them. The objections that citizens do not have the expertise to judge scientific matters overlooks that important problems often lie across the boundaries of various sciences so that scientists within these sciences don't have the needed expertise either. Moreover doubtful cases always produce experts from one side, experts for the other side, and experts in between. But the competence of the general public could be vastly improved by an education that exposes expert fallibility instead of acting as if it did not exist' (Feyerabend, 1975, 262).

6  See  http://science.house.gov/sites/republicans.science.house.gov/files/documents/HR4012%20.pdf (last accessed April 2014). The peremptory wording of the bill is interesting: 'To prohibit the Environmental Protection Agency from proposing, finalizing, or disseminating regulations or assessments based upon science that is not transparent or reproducible.'

7  '... the risk debate is one that certain kinds of social interests can expect to lose by the very act of entering. In our times, under most circumstances in which the matter is likely to come up, deliberations about risk are bound to have a strongly conservative drift. The conservatism to which I refer is one that upholds the status quo of production and consumption in our industrial, market oriented society, a status quo supported by a long history of economic development in which countless new technological applications were introduced with scant regard to the possibility that they might cause harm' (Winner 1986).

# References

Adams, D. 1987. *Dirk Gently's Holistic Detective Agency*, New York: Pocket Books.

Begley, C.G. 2013. Reproducibility: Six red flags for suspect work, *Nature*, 497: 433–4.

Bernstein, L. 2013. DC climate will shift in 2047 researchers say; tropics will feel unprecedented change first, *Washington Post*, 9 Oct.

Blanchard, A. 2013. Interview in Sverre Ole Drønen, *Oil and Uncertainty*, 11 Nov. (http://wwwuibno/en/news/45772/oil-and-uncertainty-watch-new-video-messages-lofoten) accessed April 2014.

Boyd, I. 2013. A standard for policy-relevant science: Ian Boyd calls for an auditing process to help policy-makers to navigate research bias, *Nature Comment*, 501 (12 Sept.): 160.

Feyerabend, P. 1975/2010. *Against Method*, London: Verso.

Feynman, R. 1974. Cargo cult science, Caltech commencement address; also in *Surely You're Joking Mr Feynman!*, New York: W.W. Norton & Co., 1997.

Funtowicz, S.O., and Ravetz, J.R. 1986. Policy-related research: A notational scheme for the expression of quantitative technical information, *Journal of the Operational Research Society*, 37: 1–5.

Funtowicz, S., and Ravetz, J. 1990. *Uncertainty and Quality in Science for Policy*, Dordrecht: Kluwer Academic.

Funtowicz, S.O., and Ravetz, J.R. 1993. Science for the post-normal age, *Futures*, 25(7): 739–55.

Gluckman, P. 2014. The art of science advice to government, *Nature*, 507: 163–5.

Høeg, P. 1993. *Borderliners*, Toronto: Delta Publishing.

Hornberger, G.M., and Spear, R.C. 1981. An approach to the preliminary analysis of environmental systems, *Journal of Environmental Management*, 12(1): 7–18.

Horst, W.J., Rittel, M., and Webber, M. 1973. Dilemmas in a general theory of planning, *Policy Sciences*, 4: 155–69.

Ioannidis, J.P.A. 2005. Why most published research findings are false, *PLoS Medicine*, 2(8): 696–701.

Jasanoff, S. 2013. The science of science advice, in Robert Doubleday and James Wilsdon (eds), *Future Directions for Scientific Advice in Whitehall* (http://www.csap.cam.ac.uk/events/future-directions-scientific-advice-whitehall) accessed Aug. 2014.

Kennedy, P. 2007. *A Guide to Econometrics*, 5th edn, Oxford: Blackwell Publishing.

Keynes, J.M. 1940. On a method of statistical business-cycle research: A comment, *Economic Journal*, 50(197): 154–6.

Kloprogge, P., and van der Sluijs, J. 2006. The inclusion of stakeholder knowledge and perspectives in integrated assessment of climate change, *Climatic Change*, 75(3): 359–89.

Knight, F.H. 1921. *Risk, Uncertainty, and Profit*, Ithaca, NY: Cornell University Library.

Kuntz, M., Davison, J., and Ricroch, A.E. 2013. What the French ban of Bt MON810 maize means for science-based risk assessment, Correspondence, *Nature Biotechnology*, 31(6): 498–9.

Lane, S.N., Odoni, N., Landström, C., Whatmore, S.J., Ward, N., and Bradley, S. 2011. Doing flood risk science differently: An experiment in radical scientific method, *Transactions of the Institute of British Geographers*, 36: 15–36.

Lyotard, J.-F. (1979) *La Condition postmoderne*, Paris: Les Éditions de Minuit.

Marris, C., Wynne, B., Simmons, P., and Weldon, S. 2001. *Final Report of the PABE Research Project Funded by the Commission of European Communities*, Contract number: FAIR CT98-3844 (DG12-SSMI) Dec, Lancaster: Lancaster University.

Mazzucato, M. 2013. *The Entrepreneurial State: Debunking Public vs Private Sector Myths,* London: Anthem Press.

Merton, R.K. 1942. The normative structure of science, in R.K. Merton (ed.), *The Sociology of Science: Theoretical and Empirical Investigations,* Chicago, IL: University of Chicago Press.

Michaels, D. 2005. Doubt is their product, *Scientific American,* 292(6): 96–101.

Mirowski, P. 2011a. *Science-Mart: Privatizing American Science,* Cambridge, MA: Harvard University Press.

Mirowski, P. 2011b. The seekers, or how mainstream economists have defended their discipline since 2008, Part IV (http://wwwnakedcapitalismcom/2011/12/philip-mirowski-the-seekers-or-how-mainstream-economists-have-defended-their-discipline-since-2008-%E2%80%93%C2%A0part-ivhtml) accessed April 2014.

Mitroff, I.I. 1974. Norms and counter-norms in a select group of the Apollo moon scientists: A case study of the ambivalence of scientists, *American Sociological Review,* 39: 579–95.

Monbiot, G. 2013. Beware the rise of the government scientists turned lobbyists, *Guardian,* 29 April.

Mora. C., *et al.* 2013. The projected timing of climate departure from recent variability, *Nature,* 502: 183–7.

Oreskes, N. 2000. Why predict? Historical perspectives on prediction in Earth science, in D. Sarewitz, R.A. Pielke, Jr and R. Byerly, Jr (eds), *Prediction: Science Decision Making and the Future of Nature,* Washington, DC: Island Press.

Oreskes, N., and Conway, E.M. 2010 *Merchants of Doubt: How a Handful of Scientists Obscured the Truth on Issues from Tobacco Smoke to Global Warming,* New York: Bloomsbury Press.

Pielke, R.A., Jr. 2007. *The Honest Broker: Making Sense of Science in Policy and Politics,* Cambridge: Cambridge University Press.

Pilkey, O.H., and Pilkey-Jarvis, L. 2007. *Useless Arithmetic: Why Environmental Scientists Can't Predict the Future,* New York: Columbia University Press.

Reinert, E.S. 2008. *How Rich Countries Got Rich and Why Poor Countries Stay Poor,* New York: Public Affairs.

Revesz, R.L. *et al.* 2014. Global warming: Improve economic models of climate change, *Nature Comment,* 508: 173–5.

Rommetveit, K., Strand, R., Fjelland, R., and Funtowicz, S. 2013. What can history teach us about the prospects of a European Research Area? Study procured by the Joint Research Centre, EUR report 2612 (http://wwwuibno/sites/w3uibno/files/attachments/histera_final_report_25_2pdf) accessed April 2014.

Saltelli, A., and Annoni, P. 2010. How to avoid a perfunctory sensitivity analysis, *Environmental Modeling and Software,* 25: 1508–17.

Saltelli, A., and d'Hombres, B. 2010. Sensitivity analysis didn't help: A practitioner's critique of the Stern review, *Global Environmental Change,* 20: 298–302.

Saltelli, A., and Funtowicz, S. 2014. When all models are wrong: More stringent quality criteria are needed for models used at the science–policy interface, *Issues in Science and Technology* (Winter): 79–85.

Saltelli, A., Ratto, M., Tarantola, S., and Campolongo, F. 2012. Sensitivity analysis for chemical models, *Chemical Reviews,* 112(5): PR1–PR21 (Perennial Review of the 2005 version).

Saltelli, A., Guimarães Pereira, A., van der Sluijs, J.P., and Funtowicz, S. 2013. What do I make of your Latinorum? Sensitivity auditing of mathematical modelling, *International Journal of Foresight and Innovation Policy,* 9(2–4): 213–34.

Sanderson, K. 2013. Bloggers put chemical reactions through the replication mill, *Nature*, 21 Jan.

Soros, G. 2009. *The Crash of 2008 and What it Means: The New Paradigm for Financial Markets,* New York: PublicAffairs.

Stiglitz, J. 2010. *Freefall: Free Markets and the Sinking of the Global Economy*, London: Penguin.

Stiglitz, J.E. 2011. Rethinking macroeconomics: What failed and how to repair it, *Journal of the European Economic Association,* 9(4): 591–645.

Taleb, N.N. 2007. *The Black Swan: The Impact of the Highly Improbable*, London: Random House.

*The Economist.* 2013a. How science goes wrong, 19 Oct.

*The Economist.* 2013b. Trouble at the lab, 19 Oct.

*The Economist.* 2014a. Metaphysicians (combating bad science), 15 March.

*The Economist.* 2014b. Genetically modified food: The little state that could kneecap the biotech industry, 10 May.

van der Sluijs, J., *et al.* 2005. Experiences with the NUSAP system for multidimensional uncertainty assessment, *Water Science and Technology,* 52(6): 133–44.

Wilkey, R. 2014. House Republicans aim to limit power of environmental protection agency, *Huffington Post* (http://wwwhuffingtonpostcom/2014/02/07/secret-science-reform-act_n_4748024html) accessed April 2014.

Winner, L. 1986. *The Whale and the Reactor: A Search for Limits in an Age of High Technology,* Chicago, IL: University of Chicago Press.

Wynne, B. 2010. When doubt becomes a weapon, *Nature*, 466: 441–2.

# Index

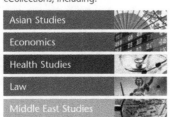